Thomas Sully, Pinx.   J.A.J.Wilcox, Sc.

THOMAS JEFFERSON'S VIEWS

ON

PUBLIC EDUCATION

BY

JOHN C. HENDERSON

———

AMS PRESS
NEW YORK

Reprinted from the edition of 1890, New York
First AMS EDITION published 1970
Manufactured in the United States of America

International Standard Book Number: 0-404-03236-2

Library of Congress Catalog Number: 76-137239

AMS PRESS INC.
NEW YORK, N.Y. 10003

CONTENTS.

PREFACE.

ON one of the dark days of 1778, when the people
of the United States were engaged in a portentous
struggle with the British Crown, Thomas Jefferson arose
in the Assembly of Virginia, and presented to his colleagues a carefully framed bill, designed to establish in
Virginia public schools, and academies or colleges, and a
university. He was a man of fair complexion. His hair
was of a brownish cast. He stood about six feet two and
a half inches in height. He might have been taken for
a highly cultured Scotchman. Indeed not less than
three of his instructors had been Scotchmen. In the
year 1776 he had draughted the Declaration of American
Independence, and had pledged his life, his fortune, and
his honor to the maintenance of the principles which it
contained. But as he stood before the Assembly, he
realized that, however great might be the sacrifices made
by the people of a republic to secure to their posterity the
blessing of civil liberty, they must ultimately fail in doing
so, unless they made suitable provision for the public
education of their youth. The importance of a good
public-school system to a republic he laid before his
colleagues with an earnestness that spoke eloquently of
his devotion to the interests of civil liberty. Years afterwards, when he was the American Minister to France,
alluding to his educational bill in a letter to Washington,
he wrote, under date of January 4th, 1786: " I never saw

one received with more enthusiasm than that was, in the year 1778, by the House of Delegates, who ordered it printed. And it seemed afterwards, that nothing but the extreme distress of our resources prevented its being carried into execution, even during the war."

Jefferson during his long life filled many public positions. He was a member of the Legislature, and, during a critical period in the history of Virginia, the governor of his State. Before the Declaration of Independence, and again at a later period, he was a member of the Continental Congress. He lived at a time when the principles of government were studied to a very remarkable extent in America and in France. For a number of years, during the momentous period which ushered in the great French Revolution which ultimately convulsed the nations of Europe, he was the American Minister to France. For about four years he was Secretary of State, during the formative period of the government of the United States when Washington was President. For four years Jefferson was the Vice-President, and for eight years the President, of the United States. It is found by letters of Jefferson's, which were written to correspondents in different parts of the world, that his belief in the importance of public schools to republics was not a mere inspiration of a moment, but that during a long life he was animated with the same earnest, consistent, and noble desire to serve the cause of civil liberty in all parts of the world by helping in the great work of securing to youth the intelligence which he believed was the only safe basis for republican institutions.

I have been greatly aided, in writing this book, by facilities for study which I have enjoyed in the Astor Library, of New York. Often have I felt deeply grateful to the Astor family as I have thought of the magnificent

treasure-house of books that they have thrown open to
the public. Although I have, while collecting material
for this book, been shown kindly courtesy in the library
of the British Museum, and have visited I hardly know
how many collections of books in State Capitols and
in universities, I have, I think, seldom if ever visited a
better managed library than is the one founded by the
Astors. To its superintendent, Mr. Robbins Little,
I take pleasure in expressing in this public manner my
appreciation of the facilities of research which I have enjoyed within its walls. To the librarian, Mr. Frederick
Saunders, who has given to the world a number of books
—among which is the beautiful volume entitled " Evenings
with the Sacred Poets,"—I desire to express my gratitude
for kindly favors. Indeed, to every one of the gentlemen
connected with that library I feel indebted for kindly
courtesy.

In respect to the source from whence I have obtained
the letters quoted in this volume, I will say that, as a
rule, almost every one of them can be seen in one or the
other of the following volumes:

" Memoir, Correspondence, and Miscellanies, from the
Papers of Thomas Jefferson," edited by his grandson,
T. J. Randolph, in the year 1829. "The Writings of
Thomas Jefferson," " Published by the Order of the Joint
Committee of Congress on the Library, from the Original
Manuscripts Deposited in the Department of State," in
Washington, D. C., in the year 1854. " The Early His-
tory of the University of Virginia, as Contained in the
Letters of Thomas Jefferson and Joseph C. Cabell, Hith-
erto Unpublished; with an Appendix, Consisting of Mr.
Jefferson's Bill for a Complete System of Education, and
Other Illustrative Documents . . . " Published in
Richmond, Virginia, in the year 1856, by J. W. Randolph.

Although Jefferson held some views in respect to the education of youth which are scarcely, if at all, mentioned in this volume,—such as the importance of young people being taught anatomy or physiology, and such as the kind of instruction which American young women should receive,—and although comparatively little is said of his earnest wish to see the United States government found a great university in the city of Washington,—such as Washington and Madison may be said to have advised, in a peculiarly impressive manner, their country to establish,—and in short, although this volume does not claim to do full justice to Jefferson's patriotic labors in behalf of public education, yet it gives an idea of how one of the most distinguished of American statesmen regarded the value of public, unsectarian schools to the people of the United States. It also gives an idea of what, in the best, and in the truest, sense of the term, "Jeffersonian principles" demand that American statesmanship shall do in respect to duly cherishing the interests of learning in all parts of the Republic of the United States.

THOMAS JEFFERSON'S VIEWS

ON

PUBLIC EDUCATION.

_____

I.

AN ADMONITION TO FRIENDS OF CIVIL LIBERTY.

IT is, one may well believe, not too much to say that every land has had at times well-meaning friends of civil liberty. In lands afflicted with a despotic form of government there have sometimes arisen men who by the heroism with which they have made sacrifices to secure to their fellow-citizens a well-ordered form of self-government have given eloquent proof of the sincerity of their patriotism. Their wish to emancipate the land of their birth and of their love from the bondage of a heartless despotism has been most noble—has been indeed worthy of the highest praise ;—but, sadly often, after having taken part in revolutions in which rivers of blood have flowed and in which uncounted treasure has been expended, they have not only failed to secure the priceless blessing of self-government, but they have with anguish seen even their efforts to secure to their country a well-ordered republican form of government result in bringing upon their countrymen a more terrible form of despotism than that from which they had sought deliverance even at the awful cost of revolution. These patriots, from Jefferson's point of view, as will presently be seen, have sadly often made a fatal mistake in the way which they have adopted to secure the inestimably valuable blessing for which they have longed. They have failed to realize the intimate connection that must ever exist between civil liberty and at least a certain degree of intellectual culture. It may well be interesting to a thoughtful student of the science of government to notice the convictions of such a statesman as was Thomas Jefferson respecting the possibility of illiterate nations enjoying the blessing of self-government, and of the way in which friends of civil liberty—especially the way in which the government of a Republic—should look upon public schools.

Among Jefferson's correspondents was the learned and very celebrated Baron Alexander von Humboldt, whose brother Karl Wilhelm Humboldt was the first Minister of Public Instruction of Prussia after the disastrous battle of Jena—a battle which one might have supposed would prove the utter ruin of Germany. Karl Humboldt was called by Frederick William III. to help in regenerating almost ruined Prussia by establishing a good school system. The system which he adopted is still to a large extent in use in Germany. There is reason to infer that he adopted his educational system in part from ideas which he received from Jefferson. Jefferson in a book which he published, entitled " Notes on Virginia," dwelt upon an educational bill which he had himself presented in the Legislature of Virginia in the year 1778. This book was published in France. Karl Wilhelm Humboldt who resided in Paris probably there met with the book. Jefferson, as will presently be seen, presented a copy of the work to Karl Humboldt's celebrated brother who at one time was himself requested by the king of Prussia to act as Minister of Public Instruction. Baron Alexander von Humboldt was Jefferson's guest for three weeks when he visited the United States.

It may readily be supposed that Jefferson's views respecting public education would be highly interesting to the Humboldts. Whoever will read the conclusions of Jefferson on public education as expressed in his " Notes on Virginia," and compare the public-school system which he suggested in his justly celebrated " Bill for the Better Diffusion of Knowledge," and will compare them with the educational system which one of the Humboldts especially helped to give to Prussia, may well feel that American statesmanship has exerted a vastly weightier influence on Germany's history than is generally known.

Two days after retiring from the Presidency of the United States, Jefferson wrote a letter to Alexander von Humboldt,—a part of which reads thus : " You have wisely located yourself in the focus of the science of Europe. I am held by the cords of love to my family and country, or I should certainly join you. Within a few days I shall now bury myself in the groves of Monticello, and become a mere spectator of the passing events. On politics I will say nothing, because I would not implicate you by addressing to you the republican ideas of America, deemed horrible heresies in Europe."

In another letter to Baron Humboldt, under date of April 14th, 1811, Jefferson wrote: " The interruption of our intercourse with France for some time past, has prevented my writing to you. A conveyance now occurs by Mr. Barlow or Mr. Worden, both of them going in a public capacity. It is the first safe opportunity offered of acknowledging your favor of September 23rd, and the receipt at different times of the IIIrd part of your valuable work 2d, 3rd, and 5th, livraisons and the IVth part of 2d, 3d, and 4th, livraisons, with the *Tableaux de la*

Nature, and an interesting map of New Spain. For these magnificent and much esteemed favors, accept my sincere thanks. They give us a knowledge of that country more accurate than I believe we possess of Europe, the seat of a science of a thousand years. It comes out, too, at a moment when those countries are beginning to be interesting to the whole world. They are now becoming the scenes of political revolution, to take their stations as integral members of the great family of nations. All are now in insurrection. In several the Independents are already triumphant, and they will undoubtedly be so in all. What kind of government will they establish? Are their chiefs sufficiently enlightened to form a well guarded government, and their people to watch their chiefs? Have they mind enough to place their domesticated Indians on a footing with the whites? All these questions you can answer better than any other. I imagine they will copy our outlines of confederation and elective government, abolish distinction of ranks, bow the neck to their priests, and persevere in intolerantism. * * * But unless instruction can be spread among them more rapidly than experience promises, despotism may come upon them before they are qualified to save the ground they will have gained. Could Napoleon obtain, at the close of the present war, the independence of all the West India Islands, and their establishment in a separate confederacy, our quarter of the globe would exhibit an enrapturing prospect into futurity. You will live to see much of this. I shall follow, however, cheerfully my fellow laborers, contented with having borne a part in beginning this beatific reformation. * * * In sending you a copy of my 'Notes on Virginia,' I do but obey the desire you have expressed. They must appear chétif enough to the author of the great work on South America. But from the widow her mite was welcome, and you will add this indulgence—the acceptance of my sincere assurances of constant friendship and respect."

It was natural that Jefferson should observe with interest the efforts of the people of South America to free themselves from the withering sway of the monarchs of Spain. One may well doubt whether in the history of the world a people can be named who have suffered at the hands of despots as terribly as had South America from the government of Spain. James Monroe, some time before announcing what is known as the Monroe doctrine, sent a secret Commission of Inquiry to South America to report to the United States Government the condition and political prospects of the Spanish Provinces. Whoever will look over the State papers presented to the United States government by this important Commission will see that the accounts which they give of cruelty and of tyranny on the part of the Crown of Spain are indeed dreadful. It is surprising how little is generally known by citizens of the United States, of the history of the war of Independence in South America—a war in which it has been estimated that a million of lives were lost. * It would not perhaps be too much to say that in Jefferson's day the population south of the United States was four or five times as large as was the population in the English-speaking division of America. Henry Clay, on March 24th, 1818, delivered in Congress a speech in which he urged that the United States should, in addition to what it had already done, recognize the independence of a Spanish State and send to it a Minister. The speech was very eloquent and forcible. It is said to have "burst on Spain herself, and

---

* See account of the struggle for liberty of the Spanish American States in Encyclopedia Britannica, also Memoirs of Gen. Miller in the Service of Peru, by John Miller (London, 1829).

on all Europe, as a clap of thunder from the skies." In his speech Clay sketched the vastness and natural grandeur of the immense territory known as South America, and reviewed the history of the persecution which the people for three hundred years had been made to suffer at the hands of Spain :—how they had had to submit to a debasing course of education,—how useful books had been kept from them ;—and then he characterized the awfulness of the atrocities of the Spanish forces in South America in a deeply impressive manner. This celebrated speech was borne to South America and the governments of the Spanish States voted thanks to Henry Clay. Songs were sung in his honor and monuments were erected to his memory. The South American General Bolivar, who has often been called "The Washington"—"The Liberator" —of South America commanded the speech of Henry Clay to be read to his army.

Let a single instance here suffice to give an idea of the horrors which too often characterized the war for independence in South America. At the capture of the city of Guanaxuato, the Spanish officer, Don Felix Maria Galleja is said to have ordered the prisoners who had been taken in battle,—as well as the defenceless citizens of the town,—men, women and children—to be driven into the great square, and several thousand of them—it has even been said that the number was fourteen thousand— were butchered by having their throats cut. Such a wofully tragic scene is one not to be dwelt upon, nor are the dreadful retaliatory measures adopted by Bolivar a subject which it is fit to here present in all its horrid details. The Spanish officer defended his course,—which however he is said in official communications to the Spanish Crown to have exulted over,—on the ground that he could not afford to spare powder and bullets in putting to death

the enemies of his Catholic Majesty.*   Should it here be
stated that a high Roman Catholic ecclesiastic once
estimated, that under the Spanish rule in South America,
fifteen millions of the wretched people, who had been
reduced to slavery, owing to the hardships incidental to
the cruel bondage to which they were subjected, miserably perished, some idea might be formed of the horrors
of the tyranny under which they had long groaned.   A
well written history of South America would be particularly interesting to the American citizen.   A Motley has
given some faint idea of the acts of the Spanish Monarchy
and of the Inquisition in Holland, but where has there
arisen a writer of equal gracefulness of style, and of
equal research, to give an account of the same awfully
instructive history in South America?   However wretch-
edly poor were the people of South America, yet for a
long period, whenever any of them collected a little
money they were tempted to part with it for indulgences,
—or "Bulls" as they were called by the ignorant people.
Thus their scanty means were made to flow toward Rome
where an Italian Pontiff lived in regal splendor.   The
student of history is apt to be more and more surprised
as he finds how immense was the number of these "Bulls"
which were sent to South America.   It was natural that
such an intelligent lover of civil liberty as was Jefferson,
should view with interest the struggle which was taking
place in South America.

On December 6th, 1813, writing to Humboldt, Jefferson said: "The livraison of your astronomical observations, and the 6th and 7th on the subject of New Spain,

---

* See "Memoirs of the Mexican Revolution : Including a Narrative of
the Expedition of General Xavier Mina," etc., etc. By William Davis
Robinson—a citizen of the United States who was himself in South
America during a part of the war.

with the corresponding atlasses, are duly received, as had been the preceding cahiers. For these treasures of a learning, so interesting to us, accept my sincere thanks. I think it most fortunate that your travels in those countries were so timed as to make them known to the world in the moment they were about to become actors on its stage. That they will throw off their European dependence I have no doubt; but in what kind of government their revolution will end I am not so certain. History, I believe, furnishes no example of a priest-ridden people maintaining a free civil government. This marks the lowest grade of ignorance, of which their civil as well as religious leaders will always avail themselves for their own purposes. The vicinity of New Spain to the United States, and their consequent intercourse, may furnish schools for the higher, and example for the lower classes of their citizens. And Mexico, where we learn from you that men of science are not wanting, may revolutionize itself under better auspices than the Southern provinces. These last, I fear, must end in military despotisms. The different casts of their inhabitants, their mutual hatred and jealousies, their profound ignorance and bigotry, will be played off by cunning leaders, and each made the instrument of enslaving the others."

To Humboldt, on the 13th of June, 1817, Jefferson again wrote, and alluded to Spanish American affairs. " The physical information you have given us," he said, " of a country hitherto so shamefully unknown, has come exactly in time to guide our understandings in the great political revolution now bringing it into prominence on the stage of the world. The issue of its struggles, as they respect Spain, is no longer matter of doubt. As it respects their own liberty, peace and happiness, we cannot be quite so certain. Whether the blinds of bigotry, the shackles of the priesthood, and the fascinating glare of rank and wealth, give fair play to the common sense of the mass of their people, so far as to qualify them for self-government, is what we do not know. Perhaps our wishes may be stronger than our hopes. The first principle of republicanism is, that the *lex majoris partis* is the fundamental law of every society of individuals of equal rights; to consider the will of the society announced by the majority of a single vote, as sacred as if unanimous, is the first of all lessons of importance, yet the last which is thoroughly learnt. This law once disregarded no other remains but that of force, which ends necessarily in military despotism. This has been the history of the French revolution, and I wish the understanding of our Southern brethren may be sufficiently enlarged and firm to see that their fate depends on its sacred observance.

"In our America we are turning to public improvements. Schools, roads, and canals are everywhere either in operation or contemplation. * * * We consider the employment of the contributions which our citizens can spare, after feeding and clothing, and lodging themselves comfortably, as more useful, more moral, and even more splendid, than that preferred by Europe, of destroying human life, labor and happiness."

To Monsieur Dupont de Nemours, Jefferson on April 15th, 1811, wrote saying,

"Another great field of political experiment is opening in our neighborhood, in Spanish America. I fear the degrading ignorance into which their priests and kings have sunk them, has disqualified them from the maintenance or even knowledge of their rights, and that much blood may be shed for little improvement in their condition. Should their new rulers honestly lay their shoulders to remove the great obstacles of ignorance, and press the remedies of education and information, they will still be in jeopardy until another generation comes into place, and what may happen in the interval cannot be predicted, nor shall you or I live to see it."

One of Jefferson's most intimate friends was General Kosciuszko. In a brief sketch of the life of this distinguished Polish friend of America, Jefferson wrote: "The workings of his mind on the subject of civil liberty were early and vigorous; before he was twenty, the vassalage of his serfs filled him with abhorrence, and the first act of his manhood was to break their fetters." As Jefferson hated slavery and longed to see it abolished in the United States, Kosciuszko's abhorrence of slavery endeared him all the more to him. Sympathizing with the Americans in their struggle with the British Government, he obtained in Paris a letter from Benjamin Franklin to Washington. Not long after his arrival in the United States, being an accomplished officer, he was made an engineer with the rank of Colonel in the American army. He planned works on a range of hills called Bemis Heights, in the State of New York. These works Burgoyne's army twice unsuccessfully attacked before surrendering to the Americans. Kosciuszko also planned Fort Putnam at West Point—a fort whose interesting ruins are still sometimes visited by the excursionist or thoughtful traveller. After rendering other services to the United States, and receiving the thanks of Congress, he returned to Poland. In Poland he was made a Major-General. It is not necessary here to dwell upon the causes of the wars which preceded the final partition of Poland. To do so it would be necessary to dwell upon the sad religious history of Poland, upon the evils existing in a nation made up of nobles and serfs; upon the degradation to which an illiterate people sink, and to the dangers to which a people are exposed whose very incompetency for self-government invites foreign interference in their political affairs. Kosciuszko naturally wished to see the Poles as free as were Americans. Whether he took the best method to accomplish his wish need not here be discussed. As a general he became greatly distinguished. On a memorable day in the history of Poland he was wounded and fell bleeding to the earth. Soon afterwards occurred the final partition of Poland. A few years after this last event Kosciuszko, still suffering from his wounds, visited the United States, and received many honors. In Europe he also was treated with high respect. In a conversation with the Emperor of Russia he besought him to give to Poland a constitution, and to establish schools for the education of the peasants. Jefferson in a letter to Mr. Jullien, dated July 23rd, 1818, spoke of Kosciuszko as " The brave auxiliary of my country in its struggle for liberty, and," Jefferson continued, " from the year 1797, when our particular acquaintance began, my most intimate and much beloved friend. On his departure from the United States in 1798, he left in my hands an instrument, appropriating after his death, all the property he had in our public funds, the price of his military services here, to the education and emancipation of as many of the children of bondage in this country, as it would be adequate to." This trust imposed upon him by his Polish friend Jefferson accepted. Kosciuszko greatly admired Jefferson and sometimes called him his " Dear Aristides." When Kosciuszko died the women of Poland went into mourning. The Senate of Poland caused a tomb to be erected which is still a grand monument. In the rotunda of the great Capitol at Washington is a bust of this distinguished friend of liberty.

To Kosciuszko, on April 13th, 1811, Jefferson in a letter said, " Peace then has been our principle, peace is our interest, and peace has saved to the world this only plant of free and rational government now existing in it. If it can still be preserved, we shall soon see the final extinction of our national debt, and liberation of our revenues for the defence and improvement of our country. * * * Our revenues liberated by the discharge of the public debt, and its surplus applied to canals, roads, schools, &c., the farmer will see his government supported, his children educated, and the face of his country made a paradise. * * * And behold! another example of man rising in his might and bursting the chains of his oppressors, and in the same hemisphere, Spanish America is all in revolt. The insurgents are triumphant in many of the States, and will be so in all. But there the danger is that the cruel arts of their oppressors have enchained their minds, have kept them in the ignorance of children, and as incapable of self-government as children. If the obstacles of bigotry and priestcraft can be surmounted, we may hope that common sense will suffice to do everything else. God send them a safe deliverance."

To John Adams on May 17th, 1818, Jefferson wrote: " I enter into all your doubts as to the event of the revolution of South America. They will succeed against Spain. But the dangerous enemy is within their own breasts. Ignorance and superstition will chain their minds and bodies under religious and military despotism. I do believe it would be better for them to obtain freedom by degrees only ; because that would by degrees bring on light and information, and qualify them to take charge of themselves understandingly ; with more certainty, if in the meantime under so much control as may keep them at peace with one another."

When Jefferson was in France he sent a long letter, dated May 4th, 1787, to John Jay. In this letter he alluded to a conversation which he had had with a Mexican, who wished to interest him in a proposed revolution in Mexico. He wrote: " I was still more cautious with him than with the Brazilian, mentioning it as my private opinion (unauthorized to say a word on the subject otherwise) that a successful revolution was still in the distance with them ; that I feared they must begin by enlightening and emancipating the minds of their people."

Jefferson's highly judicious advice to his Spanish brethren to begin their revolution by " emancipating and enlightening the minds of their people " * was worthy of a great statesman. Who can imagine what happy results would to-day be enjoyed in Cuba and in all South America, and in Spain itself, if all friends of civil liberty had exerted themselves to establish schools and libraries, and had cherished the interests of learning ;—and had been friends of religious liberty, without which true civil liberty cannot exist. When Jefferson gave from the fulness of his heart the advice to his Spanish friends to " begin " the great revolution in which they were called to engage, " by enlightening and emancipating the minds of their people," the Inquisition was doing a sad work in Spanish America. It held sessions in Mexico, Lima and Carthagena, and anathematized many books. No books, not even periodicals, not printed in the Spanish language, were permitted to go into circulation until examined by the commissioners of the Inquisition—an institution whose history is so awful that one may well shudder as he lifts for an instant the veil under which its bigotry—its innumerable cruelties

---

* I was once pleased to learn from my bookseller that a book entitled " Our National System of Education," which I had published in 1877, had been bought by some one to send to Cuba.

and murders—is permitted in great measure to rest. Monsieur Dupont, in his work entitled "Voyage dans l'Amérique," * draws attention to the fact that to sell a forbidden book was punished as a crime. For the first offence a bookseller was banished from the place in which his business had been carried on, and was fined one hundred ducats, and he was forbidden to sell or deal in books of any kind for two years. Should he repeat his "crime,"—so-called,—he received a heavier punishment. As the fines were deposited in the coffers of the Inquisition there was a strong temptation on the part of the so-called "Holy Office" to find in books which they examined, heresy, immodesty, or disrespect to the government. If a person received a catalogue of books from abroad, he had to send it to the "Holy Office," which was not bound to restore it. Any man's house could be visited by the commissioners of the Inquisition, to search for prohibited books. Although in some lands even the poor man can feel that "his house is his castle," yet over an immense area in America commissioners of the so-called "Holy Office" could enter any house at any hour of the day or night, and search in every nook and corner to see whether there was a book which the wretched people had been forbidden to read. Monsieur Dupont points out that monks and the Romish clergy were allowed to read some of the books condemned by the "Holy Office," but not all. In 1790 the number of books which the people were forbidden to read, and which were placed upon the Spanish *Index expurgatorius*, numbered at least five thousand four hundred and twenty. The works of at least

---

* See Mr. Charles Lindsey's interesting work entitled "Rome in Canada. The Ultramontane Struggle for Supremacy over the Civil Authority." Sold by Lovell Brothers, Toronto, 1877, Mr. Lindsey quotes from Mr. Dupont's Travels.

that number of authors were on the forbidden list. If a person was merely punished by the public laws of the land—however cruel and tyrannical they were,—he yet escaped much if he was saved from being dragged to the dungeons of the Inquisition !

To a Mr. Coray, who wished to promote the cause of liberty in which the people of Greece were, under very interesting circumstances, engaged, Jefferson wrote a long letter of advice, under date of Oct. 31st, 1823. Alluding to what his correspondent had written respecting the people of Greece, he wrote : "You have certainly begun at the right end towards preparing them for the great object for which they are now contending, by improving their minds and qualifying them for self-government. For this they will owe you lasting honors. Nothing is more likely to forward this object than a study of the fine models of science left by their ancestors, to whom *we* also are all indebted for the lights which originally led ourselves out of Gothic darkness."

Among Jefferson's correspondents was Lafayette. There was much about Lafayette to make Jefferson love him. Believing that titles of nobility made improper distinctions among men who were created equal, this devoted friend of liberty relinquished the proud title of Marquis. When a young man, although possessed of a splendid fortune, he turned away from the luxurious courts of Europe to give his best efforts to the cause of liberty. Great was the sensation produced in Europe when it was known that Lafayette, a member of one of the most illustrious families of France, had enlisted in the cause of freedom. Congress made him a Major-General, dating his commission from July 1st, 1777. He served on the staff of Washington, who "loved him as if he were his own son." He was at times given important commands. It is not necessary to here dwell upon Lafayette's great services in the War of Independence and of the honors which he received from the American nation. Suffice it to say that when John Adams and Franklin were arranging terms of peace with Great Britain, Lafayette with twenty-four thousand troops and sixty vessels of the line, was at Cadiz, ready to sail for America, if peace should not be concluded. Partly through the influence of Lafayette, France gave to the American cause—if the estimate of Calonne, the French minister of finance is to be believed,—about twelve hundred millions of francs. It is but just to say, however, that Jefferson, in his Autobiography, declared that Calonne admitted that the United States ought not to be debited with more than forty-five millions of francs.

When a great man is spoken of, it is sometimes interesting to pause for a moment to contemplate his character. From Lafayette's correspondence, some opinion can be formed of his character. On Feb. 22d, 1786, writing to John Adams he said: "In the cause of my brethren, I feel myself warmly interested, and most decidedly side, so far as respects them, against the white part of mankind. Whatever be the complexion of the enslaved, it does not, in my opinion, alter the complexion of the crime which the enslaver commits; a crime much blacker than any African face. It is to me a matter of great anxiety and concern to find that this trade is sometimes perpetrated under the flag of liberty, our dear and noble stripes, to which virtue and glory have been constant standard bearers." * On the 10th of May, 1786, Washington, who himself wished the abolition of slavery, wrote from Mount Vernon a letter to Lafayette, in which he said : " The benevolence of your heart, my dear Marquis, is so con-

---

* " Works of John Adams," vol. viii., p. 376.

spicuous upon all occasions, that I never wonder at any fresh proofs of it ; but your late purchase of an estate in the colony of Cayenne, with a view of emancipating the slaves on it, is a generous and noble proof of your humanity. Would to God a like spirit might diffuse itself generally into the minds of the people of this country." *

When Jefferson left France he left Lafayette struggling in behalf of civil liberty. The friends of the cause of liberty in France met with such success that Washington in a letter to Madam Graham, dated Jan. 9th, 1790, said : " The renovation of the French constitution is indeed one of the most wonderful events in the history of mankind, and the agency of the Marquis de Lafayette in a high degree honorable to his character. My greatest fear has been, that the nation would not be sufficiently cool and moderate in making arrangements for the security of that liberty, of which it seems to be fully possessed."

To Washington, Lafayette wrote a letter under date of March 7th, 1791, in which he thus spoke : " Whatever expectations I had conceived of a speedy termination of our revolutionary troubles, I still am tossed about in the ocean of factions and commotions of every kind ; for it is my fate to be attacked on each side with equal animosity ; on the one by the aristocratic, slavish parliamentary, clerical, in a word, by all the enemies to my free and lev- elling doctrine, and on the other by the Orleans factions, anti-royal, licentious, and pillaging parties of every kind ; so that my personal escape from amidst so many hostile bands, is rather dubious, although our great and good revolution is, thank Heaven, not only insured in France, but on the point of visiting other parts of the world, pro- vided the restriction of public order is soon obtained in

* " Works of Washington," by Sparks, vol. x., p. 177.

this country, where the good people have been better taught how to overthrow despotism, than they can understand how to submit to laws." On March 15th, 1792, Lafayette wrote to Washington thus: "The danger for us lies in our state of anarchy, owing to the ignorance of the people, the number of non-proprietors, the jealousy of every governing measure, all which inconveniences are worked up by designing men, or aristocrats in disguise, but both extremely tend to defeat our ideas of public order. * * * The Assembly is wild, uninformed, and too fond of popular applause. * * * The farmer finds his cares alleviated and will feel the more happy under our constitution, as the Assembly is going to give up its patronage of one set of priests. * * * Licentiousness, under the mask of patriotism, is our greatest evil, as it threatens property, tranquillity, and liberty itself." *

The madness of the French at the period of which Lafayette wrote, the manner in which they overthrew their Constitution and beheaded Louis XVI. and Marie Antoinette—whose lives Lafayette had once saved; the ease with which a Robespierre and a Napoleon ruled them; the terrible scenes which were enacted in Paris; the wars in which France engaged—wars in which Jefferson estimated that from eight to ten millions of lives were lost— need not here be dwelt upon. When the men known as Jacobins came into power Lafayette was obliged to give up his command in the army and to flee from France. While passing through Austria he was arrested and treated with cruelty worthy of a despotism. He was cast into a dungeon. In this dark Austrian place of confinement he was kept it is said nearly three years. The cell of the illustrious French patriot was three paces broad and five and a half long. Deprived of even a pen and ink he

---

* Sparks' "Life of Washington," vol. x., p. 502.

managed one day to mix some soot and water and with a toothpick to secretly write on a piece of paper which providentially came into his possession to a Princess who sympathized with him, the words: " I know not what disposition has been made of my plantation at Cayenne, but I hope that Madame Lafayette will take care that the negroes who cultivate it shall preserve their liberty." Pale and weak—a deeply suffering prisoner though he was—deprived of the air of heaven, his great soul did not wish the poor slaves which he had set free at his own expense, to be re-enslaved. A part of the time his wife, who was worthy to be the wife of a hero, shared his imprisonment. She was a woman who added lustre to his name. She was however but a tender woman and could not bear the suffering through which she was called to pass. Her devotion to her husband ultimately affected her health and cost her her life. Her mother, her grandmother, and her sister were executed by a ferocious populace on the gallows. She herself would have been executed had it not been for the death of Robespierre—a monster of iniquity, who had been educated by Jesuits as had an astonishingly large number of the men to whom France owed some of the worst features of this dreadful period in her history. Strange it was that the French at this time should have been so destitute of wisdom as to let a few leaders rivet upon them new chains of bondage, when in the United States three of the Presidents of the American Congress during the war for Independence were descended from the Huguenots, as was the distinguished Alexander Hamilton. Washington after having tried to effect Lafayette's liberation through American ministers at foreign Courts and by a special mission to Berlin finally wrote, not as the President of the United States but as George Washington—a man—to the Emperor of Germany, to whose jurisdiction Lafayette had been removed, a noble letter. Whether this letter received the courtesy of a reply, or whether it was instrumental in causing Germany, when she finally surrendered Lafayette at the command of Napoleon, to deliver him to an American Representative may not now be known. To Lafayette's son Washington opened his own home.

After his imprisonment Lafayette again became one of the most distinguished friends of liberty in France, and continued to exert himself in behalf of civil and religious freedom. Napoleon in vain tried to tempt him to side with him in the interests of despotism. Louis XVIII., who had secret designs respecting America and against the cause of liberty in Europe not generally known, ordered his Solicitor General to accuse Lafayette, who at the time was a member of the House of Deputies of France, of treason. The accusation was formally made. Lafayette rising demanded a public inquiry in the Parliament of France before the nation. He proposed that his accusers should lay before the nation their charges and that he should submit to France without reserve what he had to say of the charges and that he should single out his adversaries no matter what their rank. The Bourbon king quailed before the challenge and the accusation was dropped, but the Bourbon king succeeded in preventing Lafayette from being for a time re-elected to the French Parliament. Lafayette in the mean time visited the United States and received such an ovation as no man had ever before received. Congress insisted upon his receiving as a small return for the money which he had once expended himself on the people of the United States, two hundred thousand dollars, in addition to ten thousand dollars which it had sent him when in prison, and in addition to a whole county of land. At a formal reception given by Congress to this illustrious Frenchman, Henry Clay in the course of his address of welcome said: " The vain wish has been sometimes indulged, that Providence would allow the Patriot, after death to return to his country, and to contemplate the intermediate changes which had taken place—to view the forests felled, the cities built, the mountains levelled, the canals cut, the highways constructed, the progress of the arts, the advancement of learning, and the increase of population. General, your present visit to the United States is the realization of the consoling object of that wish." The distinguished orator, as he proceeded assured the guest of the Republic that in one respect he would find the people of America unaltered and that was in their affectionate and ardent gratitude to Lafayette and in their devotion to liberty. Lafayette in his feeling reply spoke of how the United States reflected " on every part of the world the light of a far superior civilization.

Lafayette after travelling three thousand miles in the United States returned to France, where he continued to exert himself in behalf of religious liberty, and in behalf of other great reforms. He became the acknowledged leader of the great revolution of 1830, and the Commander-in-chief of the National Guards. He placed Louis Philippe on the throne " a monarchy surrounded by republican institutions." He died full of honors and full of years and was buried beside the loving wife of his youth.

On Feb. 14th, 1815, Jefferson writing to Lafayette said: " A full measure of liberty is not now perhaps to be expected by your nation, nor am I confident they are prepared to preserve it. More than a generation will be requisite, under the administration of reasonable laws favoring the progress of knowledge in the general mass of the people, and their habituation to an independent security of person and property, before they will be capable of estimating the value of freedom, and the necessity of a sacred adherence to the principles on which it rests for preservation.   Instead of that liberty which takes root and growth in the progress of reason, if recovered by mere force or accident, it becomes, with an unprepared people, a tyranny still, of the many, the few, or the one.   Possibly you may remember, at the date of the *jeu de paume*, how earnestly I urged yourself and the patriots of my acquaintance, to enter then into a compact with the King, securing freedom of religion, freedom of the press, trial by jury, *habeas corpus*, and a national Legislature, all of which it was known he would then yield, to go home, and let these work on the amelioration of the condition of the people, until they should have rendered them capable of more, when occasions would not fail to arise for communicating to them more.   This was as much as I then thought them able to bear, soberly and usefully for themselves.   You thought otherwise, and that the dose might still be larger.   And I found you were right; for subsequent events proved they were equal to the constitution of 1791.   Unfortunately, some of the most honest and enlightened of our patriotic friends, (but closet politicians merely, unpracticed in the knowledge of man,) thought more could still be obtained and borne.   They did not weigh the hazards of a transition from one form of government to another, the value of what they had already rescued from those hazards, and might hold in security if they pleased, nor the imprudence of giving up the certainty of such a degree of liberty, under a limited monarch, for the uncertainty of a little more under the form of a republic.   You differed from them.   You were for stopping there, and for securing the constitution which the National Assembly had obtained.   Here, too, you were right; and from this fatal error of the republicans, from their separation from yourself and the constitution-alists in their councils, flowed all the subsequent suffer-ings and crimes of the French nation."

Again writing to Lafayette on May 14th, 1817, Jeffer-son said : " But although our speculations might be in-trusive, our prayers cannot but be acceptable, and mine are sincerely offered for the well-being of France. What government she can bear, depends not on the state of science, however exalted, in a select band of enlightened men, but on the condition of the general mind. That, I am sure, is advanced and will advance; and the last change of government was fortunate, inasmuch as the new will be less obstructive to the effects of that advance-ment. * * * I wish I could give better hopes of our Southern brethren. The achievement of their indepen-dence of Spain is no longer a question. But it is a very serious one, what will then become of them? Ignorance and bigotry, like other insanities, are incapable of self-government. They will fall under military despotism, and become the murderous tools of the ambition of their respective Bonapartes ; and whether this will be for their greater happiness, the rule of one only has taught you to judge. No one, I hope, can doubt my wish to see them and all mankind exercising self-government, and capable of exercising it. But the question is not what we wish but what is practicable? As their sincere friend and brother, then, I do believe the best thing for them, would be for themselves to come to an accord with Spain, under guarantee of France, Russia and the United States, allow-ing to Spain a nominal supremacy, with authority only to keep the peace among them, leaving them otherwise all the powers of self-government, until their experience in them, their emancipation from their priests, and advancement in information, shall prepare them for complete independence."

John Adams and Jefferson had not always thought alike regarding the ultimate success of the French Revolution. On July 13th, 1813, Adams thus wrote to Jefferson: " The first time that you and I differed in opinion on any material question was after your arrival from Europe; and that point was the French Revolution.

"You were well persuaded in your own mind that the nation would succeed in establishing a free republican government. I was as well persuaded in mine, that a project of such a government, over five-and-twenty millions of people, when four-and-twenty millions and five hundred thousand of them could neither read nor write, was as unnatural, irrational, and impracticable as it would be over the elephants, lions, tigers, panthers, wolves, and bears, in the royal menagerie at Versailles. Napoleon has lately invented a word which perfectly expresses my opinion at that time and ever since. He calls the project *Ideology;* and John Randolph, though he was, fourteen years ago, as wild an enthusiast for equality and fraternity as any of them, appears to be now a regenerated proselyte to Napoleon's opinion and mine, that it was all madness."

The venerable John Adams again wrote to Jefferson on Aug. 15th, 1823, and again alluding to France, said: " Not long after the *dénouement* of the tragedy of Louis XVI., when I was Vice-President, my friend, the Doctor,* came to breakfast with me alone. He was very sociable, very learned and eloquent on the subject of the French Revolution. It was opening a new era in the world, and presenting a near view of the millennium. I listened, I heard with great attention, and perfect *sang froid.* At

---

* Franklin.

last I asked the Doctor: 'Do you really believe the French will establish a free, democratic government in France?' He answered, 'I do firmly believe it.' 'Will you give me leave to ask you upon what grounds you entertain this opinion? Is it from any thing you ever read in history? Is there any instance of a Roman Catholic monarchy of five-and-twenty millions of people, at once converted into intelligent, free, and rational people?' 'No, I know of no instance like it.' 'Is there any thing in your knowledge of human nature, derived from books or experience, that any empire, ancient or modern, consisting of such multitudes of ignorant people, ever were, or ever can be, suddenly converted into materials capable of conducting a free government, especially a democratic republic?' 'No, I know of nothing of the kind.' 'Well, then, Sir, what is the ground of your opinion?'" Adams then, continuing his letter, gives a reference to Scripture, which Dr. Franklin significantly made, and a method which the philosopher suggested, to prevent a people's being troubled by kings. Doctor Franklin, however, himself suggested some reasons for doubting the success of the Revolution.

To this last letter Jefferson replied on Sept. 4th, 1823. " Your letter of August 15th," he wrote, " was received in due time with the welcome of everything which comes from you. With its opinions on the difficulties of revolutions from despotism to freedom, I very much concur. The generation which commences a revolution rarely completes it. Habituated from their infancy to passive submission of body and mind to their kings and priests, they are not qualified when called on to think and provide for themselves ; and their inexperience, their ignorance and bigotry make them instruments often, in the hands of Bonapartes and Iturbides, to defeat their own rights and

purposes. This is the present situation of Europe and
Spanish America. But it is not desperate. The light
which has been shed on mankind by the art of printing,
has eminently changed the condition of the world. As
yet, that light has dawned on the middling classes only of
the men of Europe. The kings and the rabble, of equal
ignorance, have not yet received its rays ; but it continues
to spread, and while printing is preserved, it can no more
recede than the sun return on his course. A first attempt
to recover the right of self-government may fail, so may
a second, a third, &c. But as a younger and more instructed race comes on, the sentiment becomes more and
more intuitive, and a fourth, a fifth, or some subsequent
one of the ever renewed attempts will ultimately succeed.
In France, the first effort was defeated by Robespierre, the
second by Bonaparte, the third by Louis XVIII. and his
holy allies: another is yet to come, and all Europe,
Russia excepted, has caught the spirit ; and all will attain
representative government, more or less perfect. * * *
To attain all this, however, rivers of blood must yet flow,
and years of desolation pass over ; yet the object is worth
rivers of blood, and years of desolation. For what inheritance so valuable, can man leave to his posterity?" Jefferson then speaks of the hope that he had, that the people
of Spain, Portugal, Italy, Prussia, Germany, and Greece,
would be blessed with a measure of liberty. Continuing,
he added : "You and I shall look down from another world
on these glorious achievements to man, which will add to
the joys even of heaven."

In a letter which Jefferson, under date of April 15th,
1811, wrote to Monsieur Pagonel he said: "I received
through Mr. Wardon the copy of your valuable work on
the French Revolution, for which I pray you to accept
my thanks. That its sale should have been suppressed is

no matter of wonder with me. The friend of liberty is too feelingly manifested, not to give umbrage to its enemies. We read in it, and weep over, the fatal errors which have lost to nations the present hope of liberty, and to reason the fairest prospect of its final triumph over all imposture, civil and religious. The testimony of one who himself was an actor in the scenes he notes, and who knew the true mean between rational liberty and the frenzies of demagogy, is a tribute to truth of inestimable value. The perusal of this work has given me new views of the causes of failure in a revolution of which I was a witness in its early part, and then augured well of it. I had no means afterwards, of observing its progress but the public papers, and their information came through channels too hostile to claim confidence. An acquaintance with many of the principal characters, and with their fate, furnished me grounds for conjectures, some of which you have confirmed, and some corrected. Shall we ever see as free and faithful a tableau of subsequent acts of this deplorable tragedy? Is reason to be forever amused with the *hochets* of physical sciences, in which she is indulged merely to divert her from solid speculations on the rights of man, and wrongs of his oppressors? It is impossible. The day of deliverance will come, although I shall not live to see it. The art of printing secures us against the retrogradation of reason, and information. The examples of its safe and wholesome guidance in government, which will be exhibited through the widespread regions of the American continent, will obliterate in time, the impressions left by the abortive experiments of France. With my prayers for the hastening of that auspicious day, and for the due effect of the lessons of your work to those who ought to profit by them, accept the assurance of my great esteem and respect."

As might be supposed the condition of the people of
Spain did not altogether escape Jefferson's notice.   In
that beautiful but benighted country but a very small
proportion of the population could read and write.   The
Roman Catholic Church and the State were united.   Only
one who has studied the results in such a country as
Spain can know what such a union means.   While the
people were miserably poor the wealth of the hierarchy
was almost beyond computation.   Wherever the eyes of
a traveller turned they would be apt to see oppression and
degradation.

Writing to Lafayette on Nov. 4th, 1823, Jefferson said:
"Alliances, Holy or Hellish, may be formed, and retard
the epoch of deliverance, may swell the rivers of blood
which are yet to flow, but their own will close the scene,
and leave to mankind the right of self-government.   I
trust that Spain will prove, that a nation cannot be con-
quered which determines not to be so, and that her success will be the turning of the tide of liberty, no more
to be arrested by human efforts.   Whether the state of
society in Europe can bear a republican government, I
doubted, you know, when with you, and I do now. * * *
But the only security of all, is a free press.   The force
of public opinion cannot be resisted, when permitted
freely to be expressed.   The agitation it produces must
be submitted to.   It is necessary to keep the waters
pure."

On Dec. 14th, 1813, Jefferson wrote a letter to Don
Valentine de Torunda Corunna, in which alluding to the
condition of Spain he said, "Give equal habits of energy
to the bodies, and science to the minds of her citizens,
and where could her superior be found?"

On April 28th, 1814, Jefferson wrote an encouraging
letter to his friend Le Chevalier de Onis, the Spanish

Minister, in which he dwelt upon the Constitution which
had been adopted by the Spanish patriots. After expressing a regret at the union of Church and State, for
which it provided and an aristocratic feature of the instrument which an American ought not to approve, he
continued : " But there is one provision which will im-
mortalize its inventors. It is that which, after a certain
epoch, disfranchises every citizen who cannot read and
write. This is new, and is the fruitful germ of the improvement of everything good, and the correction of everything
imperfect in the present constitution. This will give you
an enlightened people, and an energetic public opinion
which will control and enchain the aristocratic spirit of
the government. On the whole I hail your country as
now likely to resume and surpass its ancient splendor
among nations."

Jefferson's hopes for Spain's well-being were disap-
pointed. One of the first acts of Ferdinand VII. when
the so-called Holy Alliance again put upon his head a
crown was to decree, on May 4th, 1814, that the Cortez
should be abolished and that its acts should be considered
null and void, and that the Spanish Constitution should
be publicly burned.

Among Jefferson's correspondents as has been seen
was the learned diplomatist and brilliant writer on questions of political economy and agriculture—Monsieur
Dupont de Nemours. In 1772 this distinguished Frenchman, who had received various titles and decorations from
foreign princes, was invited to Poland by King Stanislas
Augustus, and made secretary of the council of public
education and governor of the king's nephew—Prince
Adam Czatoryski. Dupont, two years later, was recalled
to France by Turgot, the Comptroller General who
wished his learned countryman's assistance in the man-

agement of the finances of France. It is said that most
of the principles upon which the French Treasury is conducted to this day were derived from the measures which
Dupont attempted to carry out. He it was who negotiated with the English envoy, Dr. James Hutton, the
treaty of 1782, which recognized the independence of the
United States. In 1786 he also negotiated a highly
important commercial treaty. For these services the
French Government conferred upon him high distinctions.
He took a very interesting part in the French Revolution. In 1789 he was a member from Nemours to the
States General and later he was a member of the Constituent Assembly. Twice he was elected President of
that body. He, however, being opposed to the extreme
revolutionists came near being executed—his life being
saved by the downfall of Robespierre. As an illustration of the sad condition of affairs in the Assembly it
may here be stated that when the learned Dupont arose
to show the evil of a proposed measure respecting the
finances of France, he was mobbed on leaving the Chamber and his life was with difficulty saved. Although he
declined honors offered him by Napoleon he was instrumental in bringing about the treaty of 1803 by which the
vast territory of Louisiana was purchased by the United
States. He wrote various papers on highly important
scientific subjects for learned societies. In 1814 this distinguished man was Secretary of the provisional government
of France and at the restoration he became Chancellor of
the State.

About the time that Jefferson was President of the
United States, Monsieur Dupont visited America. At
Jefferson's especial request Dupont wrote and published
a plan of national education for the United States. In
the preface to his work he states that he had prepared

and published the work at the instance of, or to use his polite French expression, at the command of, Thomas Jefferson and in the closing lines of his volume he again alludes to Jefferson in a very complimentary manner and states that he had requested him to write the volume. This book is said to have exerted an important influence in France where its recommendations were partially adopted. Dupont enlarged with eloquence upon some of the principles which Jefferson had himself brought forward in the Assembly of Virginia in 1779. Dupont wished the President of the United States to add to his Cabinet a Secretary of Education, and had other plans which would be interesting to dwell upon. Some of the work which he probably would have had a Cabinet officer perform is, at the present day, accomplished by the admirable Bureau of Education in Washington, which was founded largely by efforts of General Garfield. Jefferson himself had a cherished plan for what may be called national education—a plan which it is proposed to unfold in another division of this volume—a plan which is designed to secure public education to all parts of even a continental republic.

In a letter to Dupont de Nemours, under date of April 24th, 1816, Jefferson wrote: "In the constitution of Spain, as proposed by the late Cortez, there was a principle entirely new to me, and not noticed in yours, that no person born after that day, should ever acquire the rights of citizenship until he could read and write. It is impossible sufficiently to estimate the wisdom of this provision. Of all those which have been thought of for securing fidelity in the administration of the government, constant reliance to the principles of the constitution, and progressive amendments with the progressive advances of the human mind, or changes in human affairs, it is the most effectual.   Enlighten the people generally, and tyranny and oppressions of body and mind will vanish like evil spirits at the dawn of day.   Although I do not, with some enthusiasts, believe that the human condition will ever advance to such a state of perfection as that there shall no longer be pain or vice in the world, yet I believe it susceptible of much improvement, and most of all, in matters of government and religion ; and that the diffusion of knowledge among the people is to be the instrument by which it is to be effected.   The constitution of the Cortez had defects enough ; but when I saw in it this amendatory provision, I was satisfied all would come right in time, under its salutary operation.   No people have more need of a similar provision than those for whom you have felt so much interest.   No mortal wishes them more success than I do.   But if what I have heard of the ignorance and bigotry of the mass be true, I doubt their capacity to understand and to support a free government ; and fear that their emancipation from the foreign tyranny of Spain, will result in a military despotism at home.   Palacios may be great ; others may be great; but it is the multitude which possesses force ; and wisdom must yield to that."

This letter of Jefferson's, there is reason to suspect, exerted an important influence in France.   Dupont was accustomed in Paris to meet a circle of pleasant and distinguished statesmen and Academicians—among whom was the learned Guizot, who, although a Protestant was at a later period made Minister of Public Instruction in France, and was able to accomplish more in establishing schools in his native land than had perhaps any Frenchman before his time.   This learned circle used to meet on Wednesdays at the home of the aged Madame d'Houdetot who received them at dinner.   One might almost fancy that Jefferson's letter was talked about at such a gathering. Guizot wrote a history of education in France. He also wrote a life of Jefferson in which he speaks in high terms of his devotion in the work of building up a school system in Virginia. Guizot before his death exerted his influence to induce France to adopt what are known as obligatory school laws. In March, 1852, the venerable Guizot, who had held peculiarly high stations in France, writing to his eldest daughter, said: "I shall certainly, if I live, allow myself the satisfaction of leaving a record, not only of what I did, but what I thought and proposed to do during the four years that I was Minister of Public Education. It is one of the passages of my life to which I attach the most importance, and I wish to leave a full and accurate account of it." Guizot must have been especially interested in the account which Dupont published in the year 1800 of the attention given to religious instruction outside of the schools of America. After paying a high compliment to the people of United States—indeed speaking of them too flatteringly—stating that there are not more than four people out of a thousand who cannot write legibly, and contrasting with their learning the astounding illiteracy of the people of Spain, of Portugal and of Italy and even of the people of Germany and France, and stating that in Poland not more than two men out of a hundred could write while in Russia not one out of one hundred could write, he remarks that the people of England, of Holland and of the Protestant cantons resemble the people of the United States because they read much in the Bible, and that parents consider it their duty to teach their children from its pages, and that youth are intellectually cultivated by sermons, by a liturgy in their own language, and by moral teachings and a worship

2

derived from the Bible, and also that the minds of
the people are even trained by argumentations of various kinds. He states that in the United States a
large proportion of the public read the Bible and the
newspapers. Dupont gave an interesting description of
family worship in the United States and of the opportunities which the people, and even the youth, enjoyed of
becoming acquainted, through periodicals, with observations on politics, philosophy ;—with the details of agriculture, and with the arts and with travels ;—with navigation,
and with extracts from all the good books which appear
in America and in Europe and with much other information. In a peculiarly happy French manner, however,
Dupont intimated that nevertheless public instruction in
the United States was not so good but that it could be,
and ought to be, improved. He wished to see a University established in which the studies would be higher and
even more useful than those pursued in the college. He
held that a University and colleges and common schools
would be helpful to each other and would support each
other. He spoke of the reward which Americans would
reap who established a University, and of the reward
which would be enjoyed by all who established colleges,
and then added that all who founded good primary
schools would receive the benediction of Heaven, the
veneration of posterity, and would have the joy of a
happy conscience. In the preface to his volume he
speaks of the great service which Monsieur Cuvier had
rendered France by publishing an account of the admirable primary schools which the people of Holland had
established, and evidently wished to himself render his
country a similar service by making known to them that
America might soon be expected to have schools rivalling
in excellence even the schools of Holland. He drew

attention to the importance of these institutions of America, and stated that they were worthy of the profound consideration of all men animated by a wish to promote the welfare of their nation.

What were Jefferson's views respecting the practicability of illiterate nations satisfactorily governing themselves? To state in a condensed form his conclusions, he believed as will be seen in a letter dated Jan. 16th, 1816, which will be more fully quoted in the next division of this volume, that, " If a nation expects to be ignorant and free in a state of civilization, it expects what never was and never will be." He believed, as has been seen in one of his letters to Lafayette, that, " Ignorance and bigotry, like other insanities, are incapable of self-government."

Believing as Jefferson did, it was natural for him to write—as it has already been seen that he wrote from Paris, under date of Jan. 4th, 1786, to Washington, who himself proposed to found some schools,—as follows: " It is an axiom in my mind, that our liberty can never be safe but in the hands of the people themselves, and that too, of the people with a certain degree of instruction. This it is the business of the State to effect, and on a general plan." In his book entitled " Notes on Virginia "—which Baron Humboldt characterized as a " classical work,"— after describing the school system which it was proposed to establish in Virginia, Jefferson states that, " Of the views of this law none is more legitimate, than that of rendering the people the safe, as they are the only legitimate guardians of their liberty." In a letter dated Nov. 29th, 1821,—as will be seen in due time—Jefferson drew attention to the innumerable blessings which nations reap from supporting in a worthy manner institutions of learning. He then said that " experience * * * teaches the awful lesson, that no nation is permitted to live in ignorance with impunity." * It may be proper to here again notice Jefferson's reasoning as contained in his bill " For the Better Diffusion of Knowledge," of 1779. It may in part be condensed thus: For various very weighty reasons the " public happiness " demands that a people who wish to enjoy the blessings of good government should be possessed of a very considerable amount of knowledge. If they are not, then men who are at once wicked and ambitious will impose upon their credulity and step by step steal from them their rights. " But," Jefferson adds, " the indigence of the greater number disabling them from so educating, at their own expense, those of their children, whom nature hath fully formed and disposed to become useful instruments of the public, it is better that such should be sought for and educated at the common expense of all, than that the happiness of all should be confided to the weak and wicked."

---

* " Early History of the University of Virginia," J. W. Randolph, Richmond, Va., 1856, p. 470.

II.

A STATE SHOULD HAVE A UNIVERSITY.

IT was a cherished conviction of Thomas Jefferson's that in a Commonwealth provision should be made for universities wisely suited to modern times, no less truly than for primary schools. As President of the United States he signed bills making large appropriations of land for the exclusive benefit of academies, seminaries and colleges. To Washington, who had in view the devoting of a quite large amount of money to the founding, or to the support of, institutions of learning, Jefferson wrote a letter on Feb. 23rd, 1795, in which he laid before him a plan for the transferring of a great European college to the national Capital. All the professors of the celebrated College of Geneva—an institution which after exerting a wide influence in Europe was temporarily suppressed during the French Revolution—wished to transplant the college to America. In this letter * Jefferson character-ized the College of Geneva as one of the eyes of Europe, the University of Edinburgh being the other.

In the year 1783, Jefferson, although bowed with grief owing to the recent death of his wife, had with others endeavored to established a grammar school in Albemarle county, Virginia. A charter was obtained for this acad-emy, in the year 1803, but it can hardly be said to have been fairly founded until the year 1814. In that year

* "Washington's Works," vol. xi., p. 473.

friends of education held a meeting and Jefferson, who was present, was elected one of the trustees of "Albemarle academy." At another meeting Jefferson was appointed a member of a committee to draught a petition to the Assembly of Virginia requesting that Virginia appropriate certain public lands in Albemarle county for the support of the institution. This he accordingly did, and also prayed the Legislature of Virginia to make a yearly appropriation of money for the support of this proposed seat of learning. He also requested that the institution should be allowed to call itself "Central College." The Assembly of Virginia granted only a part of the petition; but, Central College came into life with a Board of Managers which included James Monroe, who was at the time President of the United States, Ex-Presidents Jefferson and Madison, and Joseph C. Cabell who when Governor of Virginia—as Monroe when Governor before him had done—had encouraged the people to establish a good school system for the State. Jefferson and Madison and Monroe, although they could very ill afford to do so, gave each a thousand dollars to the infant institution. Six other gentlemen gave each a thousand dollars to the college and other friends gave smaller amounts. Towards the college thirty-five thousand dollars was subscribed and money was raised by other means than by subscription.

In a communication to the Legislature of Virginia, dated Jan. 6th, 1818,—written by Jefferson and signed by Madison and Monroe and Cabell and by Jefferson and two other officers of Central College,—the college was offered as a gift to the State of Virginia, providing the State would convert the college into a university. In this communication Jefferson pointed out that to found a university would require " funds far beyond what can be expected from individual contributions : "—funds for which, he added, " the revenues at the command of the Legislature would alone be adequate." He then continued: " And we are happy to see, that among the cares for the general good, which their station and the confidence of their fellow-citizens have made incumbent on them, this great political and moral want has not been overlooked. By a bill of the last session, passed by one branch, and printed by the other for public consideration, a disposition appears to go into a system of general education, of which a single University for the use of the whole State is to be a component part. A purpose so auspicious to the future destinies of our country, which would bring such a mass of mind into activity for its welfare, cannot be contemplated without kindling the warmest affection for the land of our birth, with an animating prospect into its future history. Well directed education improves the morals, enlarges the minds, enlightens the councils, instructs the industry, and advances the power, the prosperity, and the happiness of the nation. But it is not for us to suggest the high considerations, which their peculiar situation will naturally present to the minds of our law-givers, encouraging a pursuit of such incalculable effect ; nor would it be within the limits of our dutiful respect to them to add reasonings or inducements to their better understanding of what will be wise and profitable to our country." * The suggestion of the aged Jefferson and of his distinguished colleagues was adopted by the Legislature and thus was born " The University of Virginia." The Assembly did not act, however, before engaging in an earnest debate. It appointed Jefferson and Madison, and some other gentlemen, members of a Commission to report to

---

* " Early History of the University of Virginia." J. W. Randolph, Richmond, Va., 1856, pp. 402-3.

it a suitable location for the State University. Jefferson, as Chairman of the Commission, made a long and valuable report, in which he spoke of the benefits which a republic derives from establishing primary schools and institutions of different grades of learning. In this very able report he said: "The Commissioners were first to consider at what point it was understood that university education should commence." He then continued: "Certainly not with the alphabet, for reasons of expediency and impracticability, as well from the obvious sense of the Legislature." He then pointed out with great ability the high objects which tl e different grades of education were to subserve and the grand and beneficent results which a nation would reap from a good school system. The grammar schools or colleges, which he characterized as "institutions intermediate between the primary schools and University," he called "the passage of entrance for youths into the university." He sketched an outline of the studies which might be pursued with advantage in the different grades of institutions, and pointed out the great and peculiar benefits which each of the grades of learning would be instrumental in bestowing upon a people. In this long and singularly able report, he presented reasons for erecting the university in the centre of the Commonwealth on the site occupied by Central College. In the Legislature of Virginia Cabell held with Jefferson that the best interests of the cause of intellectual culture in Virginia would be subserved by erecting the buildings which were to be dedicated to learning, near to Charlotteville, which was near the home of Jefferson, and he labored with great ability to induce the Legislature to agree upon the proposed site. As the vote was being taken members of the Assembly spoke with warm eloquence. Judge Briscoe G. Baldwin, a member of the opposition to Cabell withdrew his objections, and: " In the name of Virginia, in the name of the dear land of his nativity, by that proud and dignified character which she had always borne," he conjured the members to " unite in the vote for the university. Great in arms," he declared, " great in character, she requires only to be great in science. Let us raise," he continued, " a pillar of fire to conduct her footsteps. If we make a retrogade movement now, if having accumulated a fund for education we refuse to appropriate it in this honorable way, we may, with the old Castilian, live to blush for our country. Let us, then, unite ; let us do our duty. He shall have lived to little purpose who does not know that in political matters delay breeds danger. There is a tide in the affairs of nations as of men. Let us, then, all unite—let us erect a temple in which our youths may assemble in honor of science. Virginia ! dear land of my birth ! protectress of my rights ! to thy glory let us consecrate the present hour ! " Cabell in a letter to Jefferson, under date of Jan. 18th, 1819, speaking of this debate said : " Having left the House before the critical vote on the site, to avoid the shock of feeling, which I should have been compelled to sustain, I did not hear Mr. Baldwin. But I am told the scene was truly affecting. A great part of the House was in tears ; and on the rising of the House, the Eastern members hovered around Mr. Baldwin ; some shook him by the hand : others solicited an introduction. Such magnanimity in a defeated adversary excited universal applause."

At the first meeting of the Board of Visitors, Jefferson was requested to become the Rector of the University. He consented to do so. He himself drew the plans for the edifices which were to be arranged in a parallelogram and connected with each other by piazzas. Each of the

---

* Ibid., p. 150.

buildings was to be of a different style of architecture and
to illustrate the styles of architecture of different ages.
The small village near where Jefferson lived was to become
an academic town.   The houses for the professors were
artistically located.   Every day when the weather was
fair and the venerable statesman was strong enough to do
so, he might be seen riding on horseback to inspect the
rising walls of the new centre of learning, or looking at
them through a telescope from a terrace near his mansion.
Sometimes he would give the workmen plans, drawn by
his own hand, to guide them in their work.

Ex-President John Adams, when about eighty-two
years of age, wrote letters of encouragement to the aged
Jefferson.   In one of these letters, dated May 26th, 1817,
he said : " I congratulate you, and Madison, and Monroe,
on your noble employment in founding a University.
From such a noble triumvirate, the world will expect
something very great and very new ; but if it contains
anything quite original, and very excellent, I fear the
prejudices are too deeply rooted to suffer it to last long,
though it may be acceptable at first."

During the years in which the buildings of the University of Virginia were being erected it would once in a
while happen that the Legislature would not appropriate
as much money for the fane of knowledge as the Board
of Visitors desired.   On April 9th, 1822, Jefferson wrote
to General Breckenridge, saying: " Our part is to pursue
with steadiness what is right, turning neither to right
or left for the intrigues or popular delusions of the day,
assured that the public approbation will in the end be
with us. * * * If, however, the ensuing session should
still refuse their patronage, a second or a third will think
better, and result finally in fulfilling the object of our
aim, the securing to our country a full and perpetual in-

stitution for all the useful sciences ; one which will restore us to our former station in the confederacy. * * * The public opinion is advancing. It is coming to our aid, and will force the institution on to consummation. The numbers are great, and many, from great distances, who visit it daily, as an object of curiosity. They become strengthened if friends, converted, if enemies, and all loud and zealous advocates, and will shortly give full tone to the public voice. Our motto should be, " Be not wearied in well-doing." Although Jefferson spoke thus encouragingly he had declared to Cabell, under date of Jan. 28th, 1819: " It is vain to give us the name of a University without the means of making it so."

In a paper to the Directors of the "Literary Fund," dated Nov. 29th, 1821, Jefferson, alluding to the architecture of the university buildings, said : " We had, therefore, no supplementary guide but our own judgments, which we have exercised conscientiously, in adopting a scale and style of building, believed to be proportioned to the respectability, the means, and the wants of our country, and such as will be approved in any future condition it may attain. We owed to it to do, not what was to perish with ourselves, but what would remain, be respected, and preserved through other ages, and we fondly hope that the instruction which may flow from this institution, kindly cherished, by advancing the minds of our youth with the growing science of the times, and elevating the views of our citizens generally, to the practice of the social duties and the functions of self-government, may ensure to our country the reputation, the safety and prosperity, and all the other blessings, which experience proves to result from the cultivation and improvement of the general mind ; and, without going into the monitory history of the ancient world, in all its quarters, and at all its periods, that of the soil on which we live, and of its occupants, indigenous and immigrant, teaches the awful lesson, that no nation is permitted to live in ignorance with impunity."*

The correspondence of Jefferson respecting the University of Virginia was large. A volume of five hundred and twenty eight pages, made up of letters and papers in large measure respecting the university, written by Jefferson, and J. C. Cabell, has been by the publisher J. W. Randolph, given to the public.

Who can estimate the value of academies, colleges, and universities to nations? In his sixth Annual Message to Congress, Jefferson, urging the founding of a great university at Washington, said : " A public institution can alone supply those sciences which, though rarely called for, are yet necessary to complete the circle, all the parts of which contribute to the improvement of the country, and some of them to its preservation." To these words of Jefferson's might be added words by John Adams in his " Principal Republics of the World " upon the imperative necessity to a republic to support public universities. The institutions of learning which were founded in America at a time when the people were poor, have by the statesmen which they have given to the world, more than repaid the United States, for all the money which has ever been expended upon them. In 1774 an American Congress convened at Philadelphia, to take into consideration the grave misunderstanding existing between England and her Colonies. This Congress issued State papers which will forever excite the admiration of the student of history. The important arguments which they contain were clothed in words which for their elegance and force would have done honor to a Cicero.

_____

* Ibid., p. 470.

Pitt, the celebrated English minister—one of the greatest statesmen of his age,—in a speech delivered in Parliament, among other remarks upon this distinguished Continental Congress, said: " I must declare and avow, that in all my reading and study,—and it has been my favorite study : I have read Thucydides, and have studied and admired the master states of the world,—that for solidity of reasoning, force of sagacity, and wisdom of conclusion, under such a complication of circumstances, no nation or body of men can stand in preference to the General Congress at Philadelphia."* These words of the eloquent Pitt might well have led members of Parliament to ask themselves how it happened that the statesmen of America were of such a high order of men. To such a question it might have been answered that in the Anglo-Saxon branch of the human family in America that society had not only been embellished and elevated but had been made stable, and in some degree wise, by means of institutions of learning ;—by means of the people wisely cultivating the minds which God had given them. Whoever will review the lives of the members of the Congress of 1776—the Congress in which the Independence of the Colonies from the Crown of England was declared,—will see that a large number of these distinguished men had studied within walls of learning of a high grade. Any one who will review the history of these men will be deeply impressed as he observes the educational advantages which many of them had enjoyed. Of the fifty-five men who were charged with the highly momentous work of framing the Constitution of the United States, at least nine had studied in Princeton College, four in Yale, three in Harvard, two in Columbia, one in the University of Pennsylvania, and five, six, or

---

* Hanyard's " Parliamentary Hist.," vol. xviii., p. 151.

seven in the University of William and Mary. In that
distinguished company Scotland had also a representative, who had studied in three of her universities. There
was one member who had studied in Glasgow, another
had been a student in Christ Church, Oxford, who with
three other of the members had been students of law in
the Temple—indeed, it is said that forty-five of the members of this Congress had received collegiate instruction. It
would be highly instructive to note how some, if not
indeed all, of the remaining number of these men had
studied in grammar schools or had indirectly received
benefits from institutions of the highest grades of learning. For instance, Benjamin Franklin had studied in a
grammar school in which it is not perhaps too much to
say that a higher course of secular instruction was given
than is to be obtained even in some institutions called
universities in Roman Catholic countries. He was a man
whose fame as a philosopher and man of letters was established in America and in Europe. He had moreover
studied in the library in Philadelphia which he had helped
to found—an institution which might be called a silent
university. He had been the means of founding, about
the year 1749, an academy in Pennsylvania which had
become the university of that commonwealth. He had
been an ardent scientific student. He had been made a
Fellow of the Royal Society in England and had received
the degree of Doctor from Oxford, Edinburgh and St.
Andrews—some of the greatest of the universities of
Great Britain:—not to speak of other honors which had
been conferred upon him. In a letter to the first President of King's College—now Columbia,—Franklin had
written: "I think, with you, that nothing is more important to the public weal than to form and train up
youth in wisdom and virtue. Wise and good men are, in

my opinion, the strength of the State,—much more so than riches and arms, which, under the management of ignorance and wickedness, often draw on destruction instead of providing for the safety of the people; and though the culture bestowed on many should be successful with few, yet the influence of the few, and the service in their power may be very great." Franklin's labors in behalf of education had been one of his noblest undertakings. Also in the Convention in which the Constitution of the United States was framed there was Roger Sherman, who had never been enabled to go to college. He had nobly learned the trade of a tallow chandler, and also that of shoemaker. Left an orphan in his youth he had provided for his mother during her long life. He had with his earnings provided for his younger brothers the blessings of college instruction. He had managed to study law and to be duly admitted to the bar. For years he had furnished the astronomical calculations for an almanac published in New York. In the church which he attended he had been made a deacon. As treasurer of Yale College he showed his interest in its welfare. He had served his State in various high capacities and had for many years been the Mayor of New Haven. For many years he had been a member of the Upper House of the Legislature of Connecticut. He had been a judge of the Court of Common Pleas and for twenty-three years, a judge of the Superior Court. He had been a member of the Continental Congress in 1774 and in every other Continental Congress except when prevented going to Congress by a law of rotation then in force. He had signed the Declaration of Independence and also the first Constitution of the States. Next to Franklin he was the most aged member of the Convention. It would be interesting to here pause to contemplate the culture

which each member of the distinguished assembly had
received through a wise policy which had been early
adopted in the colonies of fostering letters. George
Washington had only indirectly been helped in acquiring
knowledge through institutions of a high grade of learning. He had, however, acquired in many respects a
remarkably good education. Suffice it here to say that
many years before he became a member of the convention
he had had the title of LL.D. conferred upon him. As
I write I have before me a printed copy of the words
with which the learned faculty of Harvard College conferred the degree upon him. It was declared that he was
a man whose "knowledge and patriotic ardor are manifest to all," and that he "merits the highest honor, Doctor of Laws, the law of nature and nations, and the civil
law." Washington did not approve of titles of nobility,
which was perhaps one reason why he would not append
to his name his title of LL.D. His life-long interest in
the welfare of the University of William and Mary in
Virginia and of his connection with it for years as its
Chancellor need not here be dwelt upon. He was especially interested in the science of government and agricultural science. Before going to the Convention he had
written, or copied from papers which it has been claimed
were written by Madison, a description of the forms of
government of many lands. The Constitution of the
United States, formed though it was by a singularly gifted
body of men, was, before being adopted by the "people,"
examined by many assemblies, in which were a large
number of representatives of the seats of learning of the
new world.

In the highly valuable and quite lengthy Report
which Jefferson when in his seventy-seventh year, as
Chairman of a Commission to select a site for a State

University, with the concurrence of Madison and colleagues, wrote, or, finished, at an inn, on August 1st, 1818,
and sent to the Legislature of Virginia, after, in a learned
manner, dwelling on the very important objects which
would be attained by founding elementary schools, he
added: "And this brings us to the point at which are to
commence the higher branches of education, of which the
Legislature requires the development; those, for example, which are,

"To form the statesmen, legislators and judges, on
whom public prosperity and individual happiness are so
much to depend;

"To expound the principles and structure of government, the laws which regulate the intercourse of nations,
those formed municipally for our own government, and a
sound spirit of legislation, which, banishing all arbitrary
and unnecessary restraint on individual action, shall leave
us free to do whatever does not violate the equal rights
of another;

"To harmonize and promote the interests of agriculture, manufactures and commerce, and by well informed
views of political economy to give a free scope to the
public industry;

"To develop the reasoning faculties of our youth,
enlarge their minds, cultivate their morals, and instill into
them the precepts of virtue and order;

"To enlighten them with mathematical and physical
sciences, which advance the arts, and administer to the
health, the subsistence, and comforts of human life;

"And, generally, to form them to habits of reflection
and correct action, rendering them examples of virtue to
others, and of happiness within themselves.

"These are the objects of that higher grade of education, the benefits and blessings of which the Legislature

now propose to provide for the good and ornament of their country, the gratification and happiness of their fellow-citizens, of the parent especially, and his progeny, on whom all his affections are concentrated." *

The more one duly reflects upon the benefits which Jefferson pointed out will be reaped by nations who cherish the interests of useful learning, the more he will be astonished at the greatness of their value. It may be well to here consider some of the innumerable ways in which nations are paid back the money which they expend on institutions of a high grade of learning. When nations, needing on some great occasion the services of men of intelligence and culture, are enabled to call upon citizens who have passed through a high school, a college or a university, they have an assurance that the men whom they propose to entrust with momentous duties have at least received a certain amount of mental cultivation. In the year 1871, a highly interesting scene—a scene over which the historian may be expected to linger with pleasure, and to dwell with peculiar satisfaction upon the holy influence which it will exert upon the history of the world, was enacted in the attractive city of Geneva in Switzerland. The city of Geneva, over which sweeps the energizing air borne from the Alps or from the beautifully picturesque lake upon which it looks, has witnessed scenes upon which have hung, in large measure, the destinies of the cause of civil and religious liberty in the world, but one may doubt whether it has ever witnessed a single short act in the great drama of history, which has been followed by such momentous results, as the one which was enacted in the year 1871— a scene in which almost every—if not indeed every— actor was a graduate of some American, or English, or

* Ibid., p. 435.

European seat of learning. A band of men assembled to settle by arbitration a fearfully grave dispute upon the satisfactory settlement of which may be said to have perhaps hung the peace of the two Anglo-Saxon divisions of the human race,—indeed to no inconsiderable extent, the peace of the world. This is not the place to dwell upon the deep feeling with which the people of the United States viewed the injuries which they had received from Great Britain, or upon the vastness of the losses which the Republic had suffered, from armed vessels which the British Government, notwithstanding treaties, and obligations of peace and of honor, when the United States was engaged in a civil war—a war in which the most sacred interests of the human race were involved, —had permitted to be built, manned, and harbored in British ports, to do all the injury that they could to the Republic in its hour of sore trial. Nor is this the place to dwell upon all the horrors which might have followed if this ill-will had been allowed to smoulder until it should break out into flames of war—until the people of Great Britain and of the United States, upon whom the Almighty has stamped the lineaments of brotherhood, had done themselves the deadliest injury in their power. A calm and intelligent discussion before a Court of Arbitration—most of the members of which were disinterested and learned judges—whose decision was binding upon Great Britain and upon the United States—in a manner recognized by the world as just, wise and highly honorable to both nations, not only set at rest the cause of quarrel, but opened the way for a reconciliation between the two nations, at once impressive and sacred, and cleared a path for all the blessings which follow in the train of peace. Moreover, an example was given to all nations—an example which may be expected, in critical junctures which may arise in the history of any nation, to prevent the evils flowing from war.

It is certainly wise for republics to take all measures that need to be taken to secure such a diffusion of a high grade of knowledge as is demanded by their best interests. The youth who has been instructed in institutions of learning by the State may indeed perhaps win an honorable renown as a statesman which may be valuable to him personally, but in doing so he must become the servant of the people. By preserving the liberties, guarding the property, augmenting the happiness of communities, the statesman may render the commonwealth services of priceless value.

Leaving for the present the interesting contemplation of the grandeur of the work which colleges have been enabled to accomplish by helping to give wisdom to the patriotic representatives of nations, the connection between a high grade of culture and what may be called a certain class of inventions, may well attract the attention of the thoughtful philanthropist. As a youth who has studied in a common school will have in some respects a wider range of thought than one who has never been taught to read and write, so one who has been instructed in a grammar or high school, in a college or university, may be expected to have, in some respects, a wider sweep of thought than one who has simply received what is called a primary school education. It has often happened that a young man who has been enabled to study in a grammar school or in a university has had faculties developed which might never have manifested themselves to the world, had he simply been taught how to read and write and cipher. The services which men who have enjoyed the advantage of being instructed in learned centres of thought have rendered the world by applying the discoveries of science to the useful purposes of life is well worthy the careful consideration of the statesman.

No one can realize the indebtedness of the world to institutions of a high grade of learning, who has not traced the history of inventions which without the aid of science could never have been made. Innumerable consequences, direct and indirect, flow from every new truth respecting the properties of matter made known to man. The more one considers the extent to which the discoveries of science are applied to the affairs of every-day life, the more he will be amazed at the lofty mission in which institutions of a high grade of learning are engaged. Every citizen in the United States enjoys in one way or another, blessings which have come to him through the instrumentality of science. It is interesting to a thoughtful mind to consider the advantage it is to any nation to have among its citizens men capable of intelligently engaging in the work of making, with the aid of science, mechanical combinations, which multiply the products of industry, beneficially affect commerce, increase the comforts of life, and very greatly contribute to the prosperity and well-being of commonwealths.

It may here be instructive to pause to consider—even though but little effort be made to unfold them in their fulness,—a few of very many illustrations which might be given, of the services which institutions, of what may be called, a higher grade of learning, have, directly or indirectly, rendered the industrial arts. A contemporary of Jefferson's,—but four years his senior,—was James Watt, of Scotland. The father of this gifted man was a carpenter and shipwright. His mother was an estimable woman who herself gave much attention to the education of her son. The schools of Scotland were open to her youth—schools which were probably better than any in

Europe, unless the schools of Holland be excepted. In the exciting days of the great Reformation, John Knox had declared, in language now become quaint, " That no father, of what estate or condition that ever he may be, use his children at his own fantasie, especially in their youthhead, but all must be compelled to bring up their youth in learning and virtue." In 1696, Scotland had, as Holland had done before her, established a public-school system, which in innumerable ways proved to be an invaluable blessing to her people—indeed to the world. In due time, James Watt entered the grammar school of the town of Greenock, in which he lived. There he studied not only English and Mathematics, but also Greek and Latin and other studies which were destined to be useful to him in life. He also enjoyed the advantage of having at his command in his father's house some scientific books.

Young Watt finished his course at the grammar school, and, in accordance with his father's advice, undertook to learn a trade. He proposed to become a maker of mathematical instruments. With this end in view he went to Glasgow, but, in that city—now famous for its culture and wealth,—there was then found no one in business who could give him the instruction which he sought. Some relations he had in Glasgow were happy in enjoying the acquaintance of the highly learned Thomas Dick, Professor of Natural Philosophy in the University of Glasgow. This distinguished man whose eloquent and fascinating book, " On the Improvement of Society by the Diffusion of Knowledge," is not the least valuable of the services which he rendered the world, gave Watt excellent advice, which resulted in his spending some time in London in acquiring his trade. On his return to Glasgow Prof. Dick and his associate professors arranged that Watt should have a place in the university building in which he could make and sell mathematical instruments and in which he could repair the valuable instruments used in illustrating the lectures of the professors. The university even possessed a model of an engine which illustrated the very limited application which had been made of steam, up to that period, to the mechanic arts.

Watt enjoyed the great privilege of using the valuable library of the university, and the professors and students threw open what stores of books they themselves possessed to the poor yet energetic and already in some respects learned young man. He became a member of a club which numbered among its members the literati of Glasgow,—including Adam Smith who was for years a professor of the University of Glasgow as well as a distinguished writer on Political Economy,—Prof. Robert Simson, the celebrated restorer of the most important treatises of ancient geometers, the learned professors Anderson and Dick, and Prof. Joseph Black, the discoverer of latent heat, who in the opinion of the very distinguished scientist, Arago, should be classed among the most eminent chemists of the eighteenth century. These gentlemen used to visit Watt's room in the university. The bosom friend of the ingenious mathematical instrument-maker of the university was John Robison, who was a student but would have been, had it not been for his youth, made an assistant to Prof. Dick. John Robison became an eminent professor in the University of Edinburgh, but he is perhaps still more distinguished as the originator of the Encyclopedia Britannica. Students were accustomed to go to Watt, very much as though he were a professor, to be aided in their studies. In order to the better master scientific problems he studied German and Italian, so as to read what was written in those languages on scientific questions. His friend John Robison suggested to him, and counselled with him, on the feasibility of constructing a locomotive, or "fiery chariot" as it was playfully called by Watt.

Prof. Black having experimented with water had made a marvellous discovery out of which many very interesting consequences flowed. Little do people realize that even in ice there is, besides water, an imponderable substance, called *caloric*, so perfectly hidden and distributed that the most sensitive thermometer will not reveal its existence. Heat, imperceptible to known senses, one of the constituent principles of ice! No wonder that certain facts about steam puzzled Watt, who had been experimenting with the model of the so-called Newcomen engine owned by the university. Prof. Black, however, explained to him the interesting phenomena of latent heat, and in a remarkably kind manner encouraged the young man to continue to endeavor to construct a steam-engine which would be of practical utility to the world.

After spending six years in the university building Watt changed his abode, taking to himself a wife; still, however, keeping up his connection with the university and still being known for a number of years as its mathematical instrument-maker. The experiments which he continued to make with steam were so expensive, that he was obliged to borrow money from time to time from Prof. Black. The professor's salary in the university, however, was not large and his means were not sufficient to enable him to do all that it was necessary to do in constructing a steam-engine, especially in an age when making machinery was very much more expensive than it is at the present day. Dr. Black, happily, had a learned friend—Dr. Roebuck—who possessed considerable means and was of an enterprising disposition.   To Dr. Roebuck he explained the scientific principles on which Watt had planned a steam-engine.   Dr. Black finally succeeded in inducing Dr. Roebuck to become financially interested with Watt in his difficult undertaking.   Dr. Roebuck proved a kind friend to Watt and advanced quite a large amount of money to him, receiving for so doing an inter-est in the invention.   Watt's friend, Robison, has left on record the following statement: "I remember Mrs. Roe-buck's remarking one evening 'Jamie is a queer lad, and without the Doctor, his invention would have been lost; but Dr. Roebuck wont let it perish.'"   Watt's trial en-gine—owing in large measure to the difficulty, incidental to the period, in securing the services of workmen capable of making, with sufficient exactness, its various parts— was not a success.   Dr. Roebuck, becoming embarrassed in business, was not able to continue to bear his share of the expenses and Dr. Black had to loan Watt the money with which to secure his first patent for the steam-engine.   At this juncture, rendered peculiarly sad by a cause which need not here be dwelt upon, a gentleman—Prof. Small— who had been an instructor in the University of William and Mary, of Virginia, and had returned to Scotland, rendered Watt invaluable services.   Prof. Small had been very kind to Jefferson when at the university and the exalted esteem in which Jefferson when President of the United States held the worthy Scotchman, who had brought to America Scotch learning, may be inferred from a long letter of affectionate counsel to his grandson, Thomas Jefferson Randolph, dated Nov. 24th, 1808.   The statesman, after speaking of the great temptations through which he had, as an orphan, passed, continued: "I had the good fortune to become acquainted very early with some characters of very high standing, and to feel the incessant wish that I could ever become what they were. Under temptations and difficulties, I would ask myself what would Dr. Small, Mr. Wythe, Peyton Randolph do in this situation? What course in it will insure me their approbation? I am certain that this mode of deciding on my conduct tended more to its correctness than any reasoning powers I possessed. Knowing the even and dignified line they pursued, I could never doubt for a moment which of two courses would be in character for them." If it was happy for Jefferson to have Prof. Small as his instructor and warm friend it was especially happy for Watt to have him as his bosom friend to whom he could confide every burden of his heart. Prof. Small offered to help Watt to the extent of his means, and finally induced his friend and partner, Matthew Boulton, an accomplished manufacturer, to purchase Dr. Roebuck's interest in Watt's,—as yet unsuccessful,—invention of a steam-engine. Very many scientific facts had to be examined before the wonderful contrivance which was in the inventor's mind could be completed. The thoroughness of the experiments made are attested by the specifications of the various patents which were granted Watt. Prof. Small who was in reality a partner of Boulton and Watt, died just as Watt had succeeded in making a successful steam-engine. One of his last acts was to draw a Bill, petitioning Parliament to give Watt certain rights without which he could not go to the expense of putting up works in which to build steam-engines.

The esteem which Watt felt for the learned friends which he had made in the University of Glasgow may be illustrated by some incidents recorded by Samuel Smiles in his fascinating biography of Watt.* There were men who attempted to deprive Watt of the rewards which

---

* "Lives of Boulton and Watt," p. 464.

were justly his, for having after very many years of labor, given to the world,—one might almost say,—his magical contrivance. Watt wrote to his old friend Dr. Black, that Prof. Robison had left his class of Natural Philosophy in the University of Edinburgh and had travelled a long distance to testify respecting the invention of the steam-engine and had done "wonders." It may be added that when Prof. Robison returned to Edinburgh his natural philosophy class received him with three cheers. The professor gave them a short account of the trial, characterizing it as, "not more the cause of Watt *v.* Hornblower, than of science against ignorance." "When I had finished," the professor added in a letter to Watt, "I got another plaudit, that Mrs. Siddons would have relished." * When Dr. Black heard of the issue of the trial, tears coursed down his face. "It 's very foolish," he said, "but I can't help it when I hear of anything good to Jamie Watt." Dr. Black, not long after he had received a letter from Watt, was found sitting in his chair, dead. Watt sorrowfully wrote to Prof. Robison respecting Prof. Black: "I may say that to him I owe, in a great measure, what I am; he taught me to reason and experiment in natural philosophy, and was a true friend and philosopher, whose loss will always be lamented while I live. We may all pray that our latter end may be like his; he has truly gone to sleep in the arms of his Creator, and been spared all the regrets attendant on a more lingering exit. I could dwell longer on this subject but regrets are unavailing, and only tend to enfeeble our own minds, and make them less able to bear the ills we cannot avoid. Let us cherish the friends we have left, and do as much good as we can in our day!" †

One of the galaxy of learned men who may be said to

---

* Ibid., p. 64.   † Ibid., p. 465.

have aided Watt in solving some of the great problems with which he had to deal in his attempt to apply some profound discoveries of various sciences to the mechanic arts, was an American philosopher and statesman. Benjamin Franklin was representing the United States in Europe when Watt was endeavoring to construct a steam-engine. Franklin introduced by letter Prof. Small to Mr. Boulton. The learned Matthew Boulton—who was a distinguished manufacturer, associated with him Prof. Small and the professor's friend Watt. Boulton had before Prof. Small prevailed upon him to become interested in Watt's steam-engine—indeed at one of the darkest hours in Watt's life—sent to Franklin a model of a steam-engine requesting Franklin to give an opinion to him respecting the possibility of perfecting on scientific principles such a mechanical contrivance as the proposed engine. Franklin had received in a free grammar school in New England, a better education than could be obtained in his day in quite a large number of European universities. He was recognized as one of the most eminent scientists of his age and was connected with the Academy of Sciences of France. Although his reputation as a philosopher may be considered as having been somewhat cast into the shade by his distinction as a statesman, his influence as a philosopher has been remarkably far-reaching. To Boulton, Franklin wrote a very encouraging letter and made suggestions which have been very widely, —if not universally,—adopted in the fire-places of steam-engines. This letter was not only valuable on account of its wise suggestions, but was highly interesting for the encouragement which it gave to Boulton to believe that science could overcome the difficulties in the way of constructing a steam-engine,—indeed, had it not been for this letter, Prof. Small might never have been enabled to

induce Boulton, who may be said to have been one of the
most gifted and able manufacturers in very important
respects, in England, to become interested with Watt in
carrying to a successful issue, his highly useful invention.

Watt lived to be eighty-three years of age and received
many honors. The University of Glasgow conferred
upon him the title of LL.D. and educated for him a
son. During the very many years in which he had been
engaged in the work of reducing steam to man's servitude, he had made many and great sacrifices. Although
he had in the meantime made quite a large number of
valuable inventions, and although he had become distinguished as an engineer and had presented to the city of
Glasgow, in whose service he had been at times engaged,
a plan by which the Clyde River, which was then but a
trout stream, has been made into one of the busiest
water-highways of the world, yet he had been kept so impoverished by his experiments with steam that he had to
borrow from his friend Prof. Black the means with which
to secure the papers for his first patent for a steam-engine.
Although his friend Robison had secured for him a
position as engineer by the Russian Government at such
a large salary that wealth was within his grasp, he had
declined the position in order to serve the world by giving
to man a mechanical combination of inestimable value,
which he believed science capable of constructing. Watt
in a sad hour had felt that he was not accomplishing any
good for his fellow-man. When he had unbosomed this
feeling to Prof. Small he had been encouraged to go on,
and when his darkest hour had come upon him the kind
professor had offered to help him to the extent of his
means and had followed up his words by acts of great
kindness. But if Watt felt that he was doing no good
when he was engaged in applying profound principles of

science to the mechanic arts, not so thought the world when his great mission in life was ended.

Scarcely a fortnight after Watt's death Lord Jeffrey in an Edinburgh paper* voiced a feeling ascription of praise to a great benefactor of the human race. In the course of his warm tribute to James Watt, he said: " This name fortunately needs no commemoration of ours, for he that bore it survived to see it crowned with undisputed and unenvied honors ; and many generations will probably pass away, before it shall have gathered " all its fame." We have said that Mr. Watt was the great *Improver* of the steam-engine ; but, in truth, as to all that is admirable in its structure, or vast in its utility, he should rather be described as its *Inventor.* * * * By his admirable contriv-ance, it has become a thing stupendous alike for its force and its flexibility,—for the prodigious power which it can exert, and the ease, and precision, and ductility, with which that power can be varied, distributed and applied. The trunk of an elephant, that can pick up a pin, and rend an oak, is as nothing to it. It can engrave a seal, and crush masses of obdurate metal before it—draw out, with-out breaking, a thread as fine as gossamer, and lift a ship of war like a bauble in the air. It can embroider muslin and forge anchors,—cut steel into ribands, and impel loaded vessels against the fury of the winds and waves.

" It would be difficult to estimate the value of the benefits which these inventions have conferred upon this country. There is no branch of industry that has not been indebted to them ; and, in all the most material, they have not only widened most magnificently the field of its exertions, but multiplied a thousand-fold the amount of its production. It was our improved steam-engine, in short, that fought the battles of Europe, and

---

* *The Scotsman*, Sept. 4th, 1819.

exalted and sustained, through the late tremendous contest, the political greatness of our land. It is the same great power which now enables us to pay the interest of our debt, and to maintain the arduous struggle in which we are still engaged [1819], with the skill and capital of countries less oppressed with taxation. But these are poor and narrow views of its importance. It has increased indefinitely the mass of human comforts and enjoyments; and rendered cheap and accessible, all over the world, the materials of wealth and prosperity. It has armed the feeble hand of man, in short, with a power to which no limits can be assigned; completed the dominion of mind over the most refractory qualities of matter; and laid a sure foundation for all those future miracles of mechanic power which are to aid and reward the labours of after generations. It is to the genius of one man, too, that all this is mainly owing! And certainly no man ever bestowed such a gift on his kind. The blessing is not only universal but unbounded; and the fabled inventors of the plough and the loom, who were deified by the erring gratitude of their rude contemporaries, conferred less important benefits on mankind than the inventor of our present steam-engine."

If Lord Jeffrey, as early as the year 1819, could say that the steam-engine had multiplied the productions of British industry a thousand-fold, how should one describe at the present day, its value to mankind? Suffice it to say that machinery in modern times accomplishes probably more and better work in England alone—to say nothing of what it performs in other divisions of the globe,—than could the hands of all the men and women, and the labor of all the beasts of burden, in the world, before the invention of the steam-engine. While in the last century some nations, under sadly mistaken views of economy, or for other equally unhappy reasons, refused to support grammar schools or universities, Scotland has no reason to regret the money which she expended in supporting public primary and grammar schools, and on maintaining a university. It was more natural that Scotland with its free schools should give to the world such a cultured intellect as that of Watt's, than it would have been for any other country in Europe to have done so,—Holland—a land of heroic history, to whom Scotland herself may be regarded as indebted for her public school system—alone excepted.

It would be well to compare the puny strength of man with that of the steam-engine—to make an estimate of the money value of a single invention to Great Britain. To make such a calculation would require a vast array of astonishingly instructive figures. Suffice it to say that these figures, when summed up, would make a grand total which would eloquently illustrate the wisdom of that statesmanship which guards well the interests of high culture—which provides as did Jefferson's educational bill of 1779, that youth especially gifted with genius and virtue—as often found in families of the poor as in those of the rich—"should be rendered by liberal education * * * without regard to wealth, birth, or other accidental condition or circumstance," if they so desired, "useful instruments of the public." * In an able defence of such a wise policy Jefferson in his "Notes on Virginia," added, to use his own words, that "by our plan which preserves the selection of the youth of genius from among the classes of the poor we hope to avail the State of those talents which nature has sown as liberally among the poor as the rich, but which perish without use, if not sought for and cultivated." I will here incidentally say

* Jefferson's "Bill for the Better Diffusion of Knowledge," of 1779.

that Jefferson had perhaps been helped by Prof. Small, whom Scotland had given for a time to the United States, to duly appreciate the importance to nations of right views respecting the wisdom of securing to the people the far-reaching blessings of a wise intellectual culture.

Watt when endeavoring to subject to man's servitude the mysterious power which steam was capable of exerting had at times fancied that he was doing no good in the world and had sorrowfully confided to Prof. Small his sorrow. But if Watt at times thus looked upon his great work, not so, at the last, did the people of Great Britain. At his death it was deemed eminently fitting that a monument should be erected to his memory in Westminster Abbey—among the statues of many of Great Britain's most illustrious sons. On the colossal statue erected to his honor, is written, the following epitaph: " Not to perpetuate a name which must endure while the peaceful arts flourish, but to show that mankind have learned to honor those who best deserve their gratitude, the King, his Ministers, and many of the Nobles and Commoners of the realm, raised this monument to James Watt, who directing the force of an original genius early exercised in philosophic research to the improvement of the steam-engine, enlarged the resources of his country, increased the power of man, and rose to an eminent place among the most illustrious followers of science, and the real benefactors of the world. Born at Greenock, 1736. Died at Heathfield, in Staffordshire, 1819."

Westminster Abbey was not to be the only place which was to have a statue of Watt. In Greenock, Scotland, where Watt received a free education, is a library in which are books which Watt presented to the town. The visitor as he enters this treasury of knowledge sees a statue of

3

the illustrious mechanician which was erected in his honor by the citizens of Greenock who assuredly did not regret having maintained a free grammar or high school in their midst.   In Glasgow a grand colossal statue in bronze on a beautiful granite base testifies to the honor which Glasgow feels at having been the place in which the great idea of giving to mankind the modern steam-engine was conceived.

Thinking of James Watt, Sir Walter Scott broke, one might almost say, into rapture.   " It was my fortune," he says, " to meet him, whether in the body or in spirit it matters not.   There were assembled about half a score of our Northern Lights.   *   *   *   Amidst this company stood Mr. Watt, the man whose genius discovered the means of multiplying our national resources to a degree perhaps even beyond his own stupendous powers of calculation and combination ; bringing the treasures of the abyss to the summit of the earth ; giving the feeble arm of man the momentum of an Afrite ; commanding manufactures to rise, as the rod of the prophet produced water in the desert ; affording the means of dispensing with that time and tide which waits for no man ; and of sailing without that wind which defied the commands and threats of Xerxes himself.   This potent commander of the elements, the abridger of time and space, this magician whose cloudy machinery has produced a change on the world, the effects of which, extraordinary as they are, are perhaps only now beginning to be felt, was not only the profound man of science, the most successful combiner of powers and calculator of numbers as adapted to practical purposes, was not only one of the most generally well informed, but one of the best and kindest of human beings."

Without dwelling longer on the praise bestowed on James Watt by his contemporaries, suffice it to say that the more one reflects upon the vastness of the service which the man who invented the modern steam-engine rendered to the human race the more it will be realized that the world has reason to be thankful that Scotland adopted the wise policy of securing to her youth the blessing of something more than merely, what is commonly called, a primary education.

It may here be remarked that Watt and Prof. Robison and others had attempted to construct a travelling engine—or, as it is called in modern times, a locomotive, —indeed Watt had taken out a patent for such an invention. During Watt's life and for some years after his death, the so-called steam-carriage was but a rude, unwieldy, machine, that withal travelled at such a snail's-pace as to be profitably used for few, if for any purposes. One might doubt whether Watt and his learned associates ever pictured to themselves the fiery-horse of modern times—a mighty industrial agency effecting a revolution in the domain of human industry,—capable of even tirelessly dragging comfortable coaches, almost as fast, if not indeed faster, than the eagle flies, between distant cities, or across continents,—doing more work than tens of millions of human laborers and horses could perform. The locomotive unites States and Territories, some of which might have remained separated forever, while others might have been to this day deserts, but for its useful aid. Indeed, the locomotive may yet be instrumental in nationalizing—of uniting in a common citizenship—the people of continents. The gentlemen around whose heads gathers much of the fame of having invented the modern locomotive were George Stephenson and his son Robert Stephenson. I had prepared an historical sketch of these mechanicians and engineers illustrating somewhat minutely ways in which indirectly and directly they were indebted to institutions of higher learning for much of their success in life.   Suffice it, however, to say that the indirect influence exerted by institutions of higher culture, such as academies and libraries and universities, is sometimes even vaster and more interesting than is their direct influence.   One who will trace the sacrifices made by George Stephenson to give his son Robert a high education will be apt to feel that there is a silent eloquence in the noble structure in England known as the Stephenson Memorial which, with its surrounding grounds, marks the spot where stood the humble cottage in which Robert Stephenson was born,—a structure in which youth of both sexes receive school instruction and in which there is a reading-room for mechanics.

A visitor to the great building in Washington in which are preserved the models of the thousands of inventions which have been given letters-patent by the Government · of the United States, will see quite a good many simple contrivances which might have been invented—in some instances perhaps have been made,—by men or women who did not even know the letters of the alphabet.   He would also see many inventions which he would recognize as the work of men, or of women, possessed of an intimate acquaintance with scientific truths.   He would see surgical articles, engineering, astronomical, and other contrivances, which he would instinctively feel were made by men or women possessed in no ordinary degree of scientific knowledge.   Should the visitor examine, for example, such a piece of mechanism as that of the first electric telegraph instrument which Prof. Morse gave to the world, he could infer with certainty that such a scientific invention could not have been made by any one unable to read and write.   What a part that instrument has already played in the history of the world !   Its work is like unto those of magic! It is impossible to estimate fully the value of such a scientific invention to mankind!

The part which institutions of higher learning have acted in giving to the world the electric telegraph will be found by the careful student of Political Economy to be the more interesting, and the greater, the more searchingly it is examined. He will find that many, if not indeed every philosopher whose scientific experiments contributed to make it possible for man to sufficiently understand the mysterious powers which are brought into exercise in the electric telegraph, had been indebted for much, if not for all, of his education to institutions of higher learning. That certain phenomena, such as that amber and some other bodies when rubbed possess singular properties, attracted the attention of some learned men of two thousand and more years ago. The mysterious force which could be awakened by friction came to be called electricity. Its study and that of kindred phenomena became in time an abstruse science. Electricity is an imponderable, subtle agent which may be even said to pervade all matter and to be ever ready, if excited, to display its existence. Much that one would wish to know respecting electricity, science has not yet disclosed. She has even long declined to satisfy the curiosity of man by telling him whether electricity is a material agent, or merely a property of matter, or whether the secret of its power is due to the vibrations of an ether. She has secrets for those who serve her which may be as interesting as are any that she has yet disclosed.

The inventor of the first electric telegraph instrument was Samuel Finley Breese Morse. One of his grandfathers had been President of Princeton College and his father was a clergyman of wide learning who when a youth had graduated at Yale College. In due time

Finley 'Morse—as he was sometimes called—was sent to Yale College. The Legislature of Connecticut had from the year 1701 taken a deep interest in providing for the support of its college. Although in the year 1755 the yearly appropriation of funds was for a time discontinued on account of financial embarrassment brought upon the Colony by the Canadian war, yet this loss to the college had been in some degree made good by the Legislature making a larger appropriation in the year 1792 for its principal seat of learning than it had ever made before. The institution which had received many gifts from citizens was also more closely identified with the government of Connecticut than it had ever been before. With the handsome fund which the State appropriated for the college, real estate was bought, three new academical buildings and a house for its president were erected, and a handsome addition made to its already valuable library. New professorships were established, and what is perhaps at present most worthy of notice " a complete philosophical and chemical apparatus " was provided for this already celebrated centre of learning. Among the studies to which young Morse was introduced in college was the interesting science of electricity. The professor of natural philosophy in Yale College was the learned Prof. Jeremiah Day. In his lectures, Dr. Day dwelt carefully on electricity.* Mr. Irenæus Prime, in a very interesting biography of the distinguished inventor of the electric telegraph, states, after giving a record of the lectures delivered and the text-books used on electricity, by Prof. Day, that one of the professor's experiments with electricity " was the germ of the great invention that now daily and hourly astonishes the world, and has given

---

* Testimony given by Prof. Day in a court of law in the highly interesting " Life of Samuel F. B. Morse," by Samuel Irenæus Prime, p. 19.

immortality of fame to the student who twenty years afterward, conceived the idea of making this experiment of practical value to mankind." Morse himself, alluding to one of the professor's experiments thus spoke : " It was the crude seed which took root in my mind, and grew up into form and ripened into the invention of the Telegraph.". Morse's able biographer adds : " But there was at the same time, in the faculty of Yale College, another illustrious man, to whom more than to Dr. Dwight or Dr. Day, Mr. Morse was indebted for those impressions which resulted finally in his great invention. Benjamin Silliman long held front rank among men of science." After paying a graceful tribute to Prof. Silliman's learning the biographer presents some highly interesting testimony delivered in a court of law by Prof. Silliman, respecting the care and thoroughness with which Morse had pursued the study of certain branches of electrical science. To the Rev. Mr. Morse,—the father of Samuel F. B. Morse, —Prof. McLean, of Princeton College, had sent for publication a paper on electricity which might well excite the mind of the young man. After leaving college young Morse continued to pursue his studies in electricity studying under Prof. Dana of the University of New York and under Prof. Renwick of Columbia College.

Morse, however gifted in intellect, was poor. His father had had his scanty means swept away by having indorsed for a friend. Thus to his sons he had bequeathed a debt instead of a fortune. After leaving college young Morse having taken lessons in painting was enabled to earn a subsistence by painting portraits. In order to acquire training as an artist he spent some years in Europe taking lessons of celebrated painters. In the year 1832 when on his way from France back to his native land, while conversing upon Benjamin Franklin's experiments with electricity, a great thought came to him—a great thought respecting electricity which deeply agitated him. Henceforth, his mind was to be in travail until the electric telegraph should be born. He withdrew from every one and noted in his pocket-book the wonderful plan which he had conceived. At night when he retired, sleep refused to throw her kindly mantle on him. He felt that the Deity had suddenly called him to act a great part in the history of civilization. From this period for many years, Morse was to heroically labor to impress upon the public mind, less gifted in some respects than his own, the value to the human race of an electric telegraph. He was poor. Although he believed that he possessed the secret of bringing the inhabitants of distant parts of the world into instantaneous communication, and, although he might well feel that wealth and fame were hovering about him, he was too poor to make the costly experiments which the incredulous public required before it would credit the new surprise which science had in store for mankind. His situation became forlorn, and he had a family of three motherless children to provide for. Sad-hearted,—day after day was passing over his head. Should death overtake him all his labors for the human race might be lost to the world. Let a curtain here hide the sorrows and struggles of unrecognized genius.

Happily, in the year 1835, Morse was appointed Professor of the Literature of Design in the University of the City of New York. This university fronts Washington Square. It would be highly interesting to notice, in passing, the services which this noble seat of learning has rendered the world. The Rev. John Hall, of New York, —a graduate of Belfast College, Ireland,—whose devotion to the cause of true learning and whose high Christian character may well remind one of the noblest virtues of the Puritans,—is the Chancellor of the university—a university which is still rendering the Empire State and the world inestimable service. May it long be blessed with prosperity!

Prof. Morse was enabled—especially living as he did in a university building—to make, in spare hours many experiments with his electric telegraph instruments. He was enabled to improve the system of telegraphic signs, and alphabet and sounds which his highly trained mind had devised.

Prof. Morse, in a letter * in which he alluded to his going to the university, said : " There I immediately commenced, with very limited means, to experiment upon my invention." He then, after describing the apparatus which he employed in his experiments, continued : "With this apparatus, rude as it was, and completed before the first of the year 1836, I was enabled to and did mark down telegraphic intelligible signs, and to make and did make distinguishable sounds for telegraphing ; and having arrived at that point, I exhibited it to some of my friends early in that year, and among others to Prof. Leonard D. Gale who was a college professor of the University. * * * Up to the autumn of 1837 my telegraphic apparatus existed in so rude a form that I felt a reluctance to have it seen. My means were very limited—so limited as to preclude the possibility of constructing an apparatus of such mechanical finish as to warrant my success in venturing upon its public exhibition. I had no wish to expose to ridicule the representative of so many hours of laborious thought."

Not the least of the advantages which Morse as a Professor in the University of the City of New York enjoyed was that of the fellowship, to some extent, of men of

---

* Ibid., p. 292.

science. Prof. Gale became his confidential friend and partner. In 1837, Prof. Daubney of the University of Oxford, being on a visit to the United States, and some friends, including the learned Henry A. Tappan who was one of the faculty of the university, and at a later date President of the University of Michigan, were invited to see experiments on the telegraph. Among the students who were privileged to see the experiments was a Mr. Alfred Vail, who recognizing to some extent the value of the telegraph, induced his father and brother to advance funds with which to make experiments of such a nature as would make it impossible for the public not to recognize the value of the invention. He also became a partner of Prof. Morse's—a partnership which he had in after years reason to value in the highest degree and to return ardent thanks to the professor for the blessing which he had been instrumental in conferring upon him.

In the meantime rumors having got abroad of the wonders which could be performed by telegraphy, Mr. Levi Woodbury, Secretary of the United States Treasury, issued a circular to naval officers and to men in certain departments of the civil service of the United States, and to others, to furnish him with reliable information respecting the services which the best telegraphic system which had as yet been devised in any part of the world might be made to render the Republic. To the circular which Prof. Morse received he replied in a long letter in which he unfolded the wonderful possibilities of the electric telegraph. Secretary Woodbury replied under date of Dec. 6th, 1837, that he was satisfied that the telegraph would be valuable to commerce as well as to the government. He added: "It might most properly be made appurtenant to the Post-Office Department; and during war, would prove a most essential aid to the military operations of the country."

Prof. Morse showed his invention to many scientists and was always attentive to any suggestions which they made. Thus, he may not only be said to have called to his aid whatever suggestions he might thus obtain, but to have also received the indorsement of so many men of science that a dignity surrounded his invention which necessarily commanded a consideration at the hands of the United States Government. For example, the Franklin Institute of Philadelphia—a learned Society which Franklin had helped to found—appointed a Committee to carefully examine the invention and to report to the Society its conclusions. One of them, Robert M. Patterson had been a correspondent of Jefferson's, to whom the aged statesman had contributed some highly philosophic thoughts pointing out improvements of vast importance to civilized nations which might be made in the system of weights and measures in general use in the transactions of commerce. Patterson was the Professor of Natural Philosophy, of Chemistry, and of Mathematics in the University of Pennsylvania—a university which, as has been said, owed its origin to Franklin. At a later period he was one of the professors of the University of Virginia. He was also President of the American Philosophic Society as well as a member of the Franklin Institute. Another member of the Committee was Roswell Park, a professor in Natural Philosophy of the University of Pennsylvania. Prof. Walker of the Philadelphia High School, Isaiah Lukens who was a very able mechanician, and two other scientists connected with the United States mint,—one of them being at a later period at the head of the Department of Weights and Measures of the United States,—made a body of men whose conclusions might well command the attention of the most incredulous minds. This learned Committee reported to the Institute with high admiration that not only had electricity, by

Morse's invention, been reduced to subserviency to man's wishes, but that the invention was capable of being made of such value to the Republic, that the National Government should advance the means with which to test its possibilities on a large scale. When Prof. Morse informed by letter one of his brothers of the action of the Franklin Institute his accomplished brother wrote back to him, saying: "Your invention, measuring it by the power which it will give man to accomplish his plans, is not only the greatest invention of the age, but the greatest invention of any age. I see, as an almost immediate effect, that the surface of the earth will be net-worked with wire, and every wire will be a nerve, conveying to every part intelligence of what is doing in every other part. The earth will become a huge animal with ten million hands, and every hand a pen to record whatever the directing soul may dictate. No limit can be assigned to the value of the invention." Young Mr. Vail, Prof. Morse's former student who had become his partner, on hearing what the Franklin Institute had said about the telegraph though it was but in miniature form, wrote on March 19th, 1837, to him saying: "I feel, Professor Morse, that if I am ever worth anything, it will be wholly attributable to your kindness—I now should have no *earthly* prospect of happiness and domestic bliss had it not been for what you have done, which I shall ever remember with liveliest emotions of gratitude, whether it is eventually successful or not. I can appreciate your reasonable and appropriate remark that there is nothing certain in this life; that it is a world of care, anxiety, and trouble, and that our dependence must be placed upon a higher power than of earth." *

The high confidence reposed in Prof. Morse by the Franklin Institute, and the letters from distinguished

---

* Ibid., p. 338.

scientiests, helped to open the way for the inventor to bring the electric telegraph to the attention of the Federal Government. When he visited the national Capitol, the Congressional Committee of Commerce, to whom Congress, acting on an official communication of the Secretary of War, had referred the consideration of the electric telegraph, treated him with much consideration, placing the private room of the Committee at the disposal of the inventor. The President of the United States and the members of his Cabinet visited Morse to see a telegraph in operation. The Chairman of the Committee—Mr. J. O. F. Smith—reported favorably on the electric telegraph, and then in order to be enabled to do so honorably, tendered his resignation to Congress, and bought himself an interest in the patent and went with Morse to Europe to obtain patent-rights in the old world. In Europe Prof. Morse astonished even the *Savants* by the scientific and ingenious manner in which he applied electricity to the practical purposes of life. In the Academy of Sciences of France he was treated with high consideration. To the members of that distinguished society he showed his invention, receiving their criticisms and admiration. In Europe he met the learned and venerable Humboldt. This celebrated scientist had himself experimented with electricity and had published to the world the secret of the power exerted by a species of fish—that which is sometimes in modern times, called the electric eel. He had given a graphic account of the combats which are sometimes waged by the *gymnoti*—or the so-called electric eel,—which reaches a size of five or six feet in length,— and the wild horses in the vicinity of the Colabozo, South Africa,—a combat in which the formidable denizen of the water would occasionally strike terror into the hearts of the horses and paralyze or kill the poor brutes. Morse

also met at the same dinner table with Humboldt, the
illustrious Arago who had also made valuable experiments
with the mysterious forces of electricity.   In a letter
which Morse wrote from his sick-room at the unveiling of
a statue of Humboldt he recalled his experience in the
Academy of Sciences of France.   He wrote: "I sat at a
short distance from Baron Humboldt and I can never
forget the feelings of encouragement, in those anxious
moments, when, after the lucid explanation of my Telegraph to the Academy by M. Arago, the Baron Humboldt
arose, and, taking my hand, congratulated me and thanked
me before them all."   Morse then alluded to his last conversation with Humboldt in which the venerable sage
spoke with enthusiasm of American science and expatiated
with warmth upon the scientific labors of Maury and
Dana—characterizing one of Dana's books as one of the
most valuable contributions to science of the age.   It was
natural that such a society as that of the Academy of
Sciences of France should look with great gratification
upon Morse's electric telegraph.   Mr. Smith, Morse's
partner, when thinking of how little the Government of
the United States was doing in the meantime, in the
matter of practically encouraging Morse, recalled a scene
which had once taken place in the Academy of Sciences of
France.   On March 20th, 1800, Volta the philosopher, had
explained to the Academy a discovery which he had made
respecting electricity.   When a committee announced the
result of their examination of the discovery, Napoleon,
who as President of the Academy was at the time pre-
siding, at once arose from his chair, and moved to suspend
the rules of the learned Society respecting the formalities
it was accustomed to observe, and to at once confer a
gold medal on the illustrious scientist.   The proposition
was carried by acclamation, and Napoleon on the same

day presented the philosopher with two thousand crowns. It may here be added that Napoleon offered a prize of sixty thousand francs to any one who would make as valuable a discovery respecting electricity as had Franklin or Volta. Napoleon also provided for a yearly prize of three thousand francs for the best experiments with what is called the galvanic fluid. This is not the place to linger to give an account of the experience of the American inventor in Europe. In France the patent which he procured was practically worthless. The despotic government of the period was afraid to allow the people to employ an agent which might be useful to them in combining at a given instant against the government. A time was to come when Napoleon III. was to act in some respects in a highly generous manner to Morse and was to unite with other governments in making him a pecuniary return for his invention, but in the meanwhile Prof. Morse was becoming poorer and poorer. When he finally, after making an arrangement with the Russian government which in time might be worth something to him, returned to America he found that during the years that he had been absent from his native land his government had given little or no attention to the telegraph.

Without pausing to dwell upon the professor's struggle with poverty,—or of the new testimonials which men of science presented to him respecting his invention,—or of the electrical experiments which Prof. Henry of Princeton College,—who in his department had perhaps no superior in the world,—made for Prof. Morse, it is interesting to note that Congress finally—amidst jeers in the House of Representatives—appropriated by a majority of but six votes, thirty thousand dollars to enable Prof. Morse to construct a telegraph on a scale which would prove to the world whether it was or was not of value to a great nation.   In the United States Senate the bill passed in silence as the clock was about striking midnight on the last night of a session.   Prof. Morse was a man of deep Evangelical convictions.   He had sat in the gallery of Congress when his invention had been treated with derision.   From the Senate chamber he had retired on Feb. 24th, 1842—the last day of the session—as night was settling on the Capitol of the United States.   A Senator had informed him that between one and two hundred measures would have to be passed upon before the appropriation for a telegraph could be taken up and that it was impossible for the Senate to act upon an electric telegraph bill.   Sad-hearted and with only twenty-five cents in his pocket—without money with which to return to New York,—Morse retired to enjoy a tranquil slumber. He firmly believed that a Divine providence would not forsake him.

There has been a temptation felt on the part of some of Morse's biographers to consider the pleasantly affecting manner in which the news of what had been done for him in the Senate just before midnight, was conveyed to him by a young lady, as being romantic.   The truth is, however, that the young lady was very young and the daughter of an old college friend at whose house he was a guest—a friend who was the United States Commissioner of Patents and who had labored among his friends in the Senate while Morse was asleep and had had the pleasure of seeing the bill to give the telegraph a trial, pass just as the Senate was about being dissolved.   His daughter Miss Ellsworth, was doubtless a kind-hearted girl who broke the news to the professor in a peculiarly kind manner and it was fitting that Prof. Morse should give to the world a proof of the beautiful friendship which existed between himself and Miss Ellsworth by engaging that she should be the first one to send a message on the telegraph when it should be formally tested in the presence of the world. In due time President Polk, who was a graduate of the University of North Carolina, signed the bill which was to appropriate thirty thousand dollars to enable Prof. Morse to ultimately prove to the world not only that man could instantaneously correspond with his fellows though separated by fifty or one hundred miles, but that he could in a fraction of a second correspond with friends who might be living in the most distant tropics or in either of the hemispheres.

Well it was that the Government of the United States had not longer delayed to give due attention to the electric telegraph. To a friend Prof. Morse wrote: "My personal funds were reduced to a fraction of a dollar, and, had the passage of the bill failed from any cause, there would have been little prospect for another attempt on my part to introduce to the world my new invention." With energy Prof. Morse set to work to connect by telegraph Baltimore and the national capital. He made many experiments with electricity on a scale which had before been beyond his means to make. On Aug. 10th, 1843, he wrote to John C. Spencer, Secretary of the Treasury, that he had proved the truth of a law of electricity which was destined to be of the grandest consequence in telegraphy. After describing his experiments he informed the Secretary of War that his experiments had been performed in the presence of Professors Renwick, Draper, Ellet and Schaeffer and his assistants Professors Fisher and Gale; and that Professors Silliman, Henry, Torrey and Dr. Chilton would have been present had they not been detained by their official duties. He added: "The practical inference from this law is, *that a telegraphic communication on the Electric Mag-*

netic plan may with certainty be established ACROSS
THE ATLANTIC OCEAN!" Prof. Morse further added:
"Startling as this may now seem, I am confident the
time will come when this project will be realized." The
Secretary of War replied that he was gratified with the
results of his experiments and that he trusted that the
country would have reason to be satisfied with his labors.
In the meanwhile the heaviest trial in some respects which
Prof. Morse had yet had to bear settled upon him. He
had intended to cover the telegraph wires with a coating
of lead and to lay them under ground all the way from
Washington to Baltimore. After spending in so doing
about twenty-three thousand dollars of the government
appropriation of thirty thousand dollars he had made the
startling and at first very sad discovery that the electric
current would not take kindly to his arrangement for
underground wires. His friends about him feared that his
mind and strength would give way. Years before he had
suggested to Secretary Woodbury a plan for using posts
to support the wires. He decided to try such a plan, but
he had to encounter the difficulty of doing so in a way
which would keep captive the electric current until it had
performed his bidding. The professor had to decide upon
a practicable plan by which the wires when they touched the
posts would be insulated. Two plans were suggested to
him, one, by Alfred Vail, and the other by Mr. Ezra
Cornell—who afterwards founded the University which is
called by his name and is now one of the wealthiest universities in the great State of New York. Mr. Cornell
was a man of energy and of remarkable business and
practical intelligence. He had studied at a public school
and had at one time of his life been a school teacher. He
had acquired habits of thought which were to be very
useful to Mr. Morse. Mr. Cornell, who was engaged by

Morse to help him in various ways, showed remarkable intelligence. He also privately studied about electricity in the Congressional library. The plan for insulating the wires with the aid of glass where they were supported by poles did not receive the preference by Prof. Morse, over the plan suggested by Mr. Vail. The sorely tried professor gave directions that expensive measures which the new plan demanded should be taken. Happily at this critical juncture Morse visited Prof. Henry of Princeton College. Prof. Henry showed him that he had made a mistake in adopting the plan for insulating the wires which he had decided to adopt, and that the mistake must end in disaster as had his first plan of covering the wires with lead and earth—but that if he would adopt the one of the two plans which he had rejected he would be enabled to accomplish his purpose. Prof. Morse returned to his work, countermanded the expensive measures which he had decided to apply to the wires, and adopted the plan endorsed by Prof. Henry. Sad indeed it would have been for Morse had he been obliged to spend on costly experiments so much money as not to have enough left with which to complete his telegraph between Washington and Baltimore.

On May 24th, 1844, under circumstances peculiarly exciting and agreeable, the telegraph was formally opened. Miss Ellsworth was called upon to send to Prof. Morse the first message. She knew that he was imbued with the faith of the Puritans and that through all the trials through which he had passed he had looked for the support and the blessing of the Almighty. With great delicacy she selected a part of a verse from the Bible to flash over the wire to her friend. Her message was: "What has God wrought?" A member of Congress named Seymour, who was afterwards Governor of Connecticut, at once claimed the slip of paper on which the first message was received, on the ground that Miss Ellsworth was a native of Hartford. The mystic paper was deposited in the Hartford Museum or Athenæum, where it is still preserved. It is not necessary to here dwell upon the services rendered to the people of the United States by the first telegraph line built in America. Congress soon after its completion passed a second appropriation to keep it in operation. If about this period one could have been permitted to look into Miss Ellsworth's diary he would have seen in it a little poem in Prof. Morse's handwriting. The words read:

TO MISS A. G. E.

THE SUN-DIAL.

" Horas non numero nisi serenas."
" I note not the hours except they be bright."

The sun when it shines in a clear cloudless sky
   Marks the time on my disk in figures of light.
If clouds gather o'er me unheeded they fly,
   " I note not the hours except they be bright."

So when I review all the scenes that have past
   Between me and thee, be they dark, be they light,
I forget what was dark, the light I hold fast,
   " I note not the hours except they be bright."

WASHINGTON, March, 1845, SAMUEL F. B. MORSE.

In Prof. Morse's character there were many features which were highly praiseworthy. There was one idea which he long cherished and would not sacrifice until compelled to do so by a hasty act of a Congress which was strangely-long incredulous respecting the value of

his wonderful invention. Prof. Morse believed that in a
republic the telegraph should form part of a postal system. It would be instructive to here dwell upon the
danger to which the liberties of a people are exposed by
monopolies. In the daily business of life the merchant
could perhaps be ruined by having rivals in trade favored
in transmitting intelligence. Circumstances might arise
in which a telegraph or railroad company might ignore
the interests of a community—isolating it even from the
rest of the world until it reduced it to abject submission
to its will. In a well-ordered government a civil service
wisely organized by law, could attend to certain interests
of the people in a way which is perhaps little imagined
by ordinary citizens. So many evils had Jefferson known
to occur in Europe from the power wielded by secular
and religious corporations—even travelling when in the
old world in lands in which one fourth or much more of
all the real estate was exempt from taxation on the
ground that it was owned by a Romish ecclesiastical corporation—by which arrangement the poor were obliged
directly or indirectly to pay not only their own taxes but
also the taxes of this corporation,—and in various ways
to be to a great extent controlled and impoverished by
legislation which enriched corporations by placing the
people at their mercy;—that he, when the Constitution
of the United States was about being adopted, expressed
the opinion in one or more of his letters that a provision
should be inserted in the Constitution of the Republic
by which the people would be protected from the evils
flowing from the existence of monopolies. Morse was
unwilling to sell to private parties the invention of the
electric telegraph until the United States Government
had considered the propriety of accepting the invention
at a price trifling compared with its real value to the

United States. Morse's proposition to add the telegraph to the United States postal system was referred by Congress to the Postmaster General the Hon. Cave Johnson. This gentleman did not at once realize the wonderful value of a well-developed telegraph system to a nation. In his Report to Congress he said : " Although the invention is an agent vastly superior to any other ever devised by the genius of man. * * * yet the operation of the telegraph between this city [Washington] and Baltimore has not satisfied me that under any rate of postage that can be adopted, its revenues can be made to cover its expenditures." On receiving this report Congress declined the valuable offer made by Morse to give it a finer postal service than had ever been adopted by any nation. The postal service of the United States has a far higher mission to perform than merely to raise a revenue by means of postage stamps. The great truth that the postal system of the United States by promoting the circulation of knowledge and by enabling people to communicate with each other on innumerable subjects promotes the dissemination of knowledge no less truly than do institutions of valuable learning in the land, is not, it is to be feared, as widely realized as it should be even to this day. Thus Morse was compelled to become interested with private companies and soon, one might almost say, a princely income commenced to flow to him.

This is not the place to dwell upon the honors which were conferred upon Prof. Morse by learned societies and by many governments. It is doubtful whether any American scientist had ever before received as many medals and honors of various kinds as were bestowed upon the inventor of the electric telegraph. It would be highly interesting and would still further illustrate the ·connection which exists between the services rendered by the sciences taught, and the breadth of mind encouraged, by institutions of a high grade of learning, should one point out the part acted by the energetic Cyrus W. Field and Prof. Morse, in uniting the hemispheres by telegraph —a work the grandeur of which may well impress one's mind more and more, as one attempts to realize it in its true greatness.

It was a happy moment in the life of Prof. Morse when in 1859, to an assembly in the University of New York— at which were present the Prince of Wales, who was visiting the United States, and the Duke of Newcastle,—he made an address in the course of which he thus spoke: "The infant Telegraph, born and nursed within these walls, had scarcely attained a feeble existence, ere it essayed to make its voice heard on the other side of the Atlantic. I carried it to Paris in 1838. It attracted the warm interest not only of the Continental philosophers, but also of the intelligent and appreciative among the eminent nobles of Britain, then on a visit to the French capital. Foremost among these was the late Marquis of Northampton, then President of the Royal Society, the late distinguished Earl of Elgin, and in a marked degree the noble Earl of Lincoln. The last named nobleman in a special manner, gave it his favor; he comprehended its important future, and, in the midst of the skepticism that clouded its cradle, he risked his character for sound judgment in venturing to stand godfather to the friendless child. He took it under his roof in London, invited the statesmen and the philosophers of Britain to see it, and urged forward with kind words and generous attentions those who had the infant in charge. It is with no ordinary feelings, therefore, that after the lapse of twenty years I have the singular honor this morning of greeting with hearty welcome, in such presence, before such an assemblage, and in the cradle of the Telegraph, this noble Earl of Lincoln, in the person of the present Duke of Newcastle." *

Of all the many titles and honors which were showered upon Prof. Morse there was perhaps none which gave him greater pleasure than did the title of LL.D. conferred upon him by Yale College. To President Day of Yale College, who had been one of his college professors and had on Aug. 27th, 1846, communicated to him the action of the college, Morse wrote: "Permit me to return, through you, my sincere thanks to the honorable corporation for the high honor they have conferred upon me at the last commencement, in bestowing upon me the degree of Doctor of Laws. I esteem it doubly valuable as emanating from my much-loved and venerated *alma mater*. In the success with which it has pleased God to crown my telegraphic invention, it is not the least gratifying circumstance that you consider the invention as reflecting credit on my collegiate instruction, and I may therefore say that, in reviewing the mental processes by which I arrived at the final result, I can distinctly trace them back to their incipiency, in the lessons of my esteemed instructors in natural philosophy and in chemistry. Later developments in electro-magnetism in the lectures of Prof. J. F. Dana were, indeed, the more immediate sources whence I drew much of my material, but this was dependent for its efficacy on my earlier college instruction. Be pleased to accept my sincere thanks for the flattering and friendly manner in which you have communicated to me the act of the corporation. In common with all the friends of learning, I sincerely deplore the necessity, which you conceive to exist, of your resignation of the Presidency of the college over whose interests you have so

---

* "Life of S. F. B. Morse." By S. I. Prime, pp. 392–3.

long watched. May the blessing of God accompany you in your retirement!"

Not only by inventing an electric telegraph did Morse endeavor to serve his country. His literary labors were very interesting. As professor in the University of New York his lectures to the students have been regarded as "models of graceful rhetoric and elaborate argument." He published many papers in periodicals on various subjects. There was one subject to which he gave special study and endeavored to bring to the attention of American citizens. When in Rome and in some other parts of Europe he had seen a vast amount of illiteracy, superstition and deep degradation, which he believed was caused by the teachings of Roman Catholicism. He had been led by knowledge which he had acquired in Europe to firmly believe that the form of government of the vast Italian corporation ruled by the Pope and Cardinals—the Popes having for hundreds of years been Italians and so arranged affairs that a vast majority of the Cardinals, who elect the Pope, should be Italians,—was in the worst sense of the word despotic and opposed to the teachings of the Bible, and that it looked with especial hatred upon liberty in Church and State in America,—and that it had decided to war against the public schools and institutions of higher learning in the United States and to employ whatever talent it could command to prejudice,—by arguments sometimes so subtle that they would not always be recognized as emanating from priestcraft,—the people of America against the principles of government held sacred by Washington and Jefferson and their colleagues,—principles of the greatest value to the most important interests of useful learning and of civil and religious liberty. Thus believing he wrote a great many valuable papers on Romanism—papers which were calculated to set right any one who had wavered in judgment respecting the value of free institutions to American citizens. Many of these instructive contributions to the press were ultimately edited in book-form, under the title of "Foreign Conspiracy against the Liberties of the United States: revised and corrected, with Notes by the Author." This volume passed through numerous editions. In the year 1837, he edited, and published with an introduction by himself, a book entitled: "Confessions of a French Catholic Priest, to which are added Warnings to the People of the United States, by the same Author." On the title-page Morse put a sentence which he had heard from the lips of Lafayette—a sentence which, when its authenticity was questioned, he proved to be true by producing the written testimony of living witnesses in whose presence Lafayette had made the remark. The sentence read: "American liberty can be destroyed only by the Popish clergy."—"Lafayette." In 1841, Morse published a volume of papers which he had first given to the world through a daily paper, entitled: "Our Liberties defended; the Question discussed; is the Protestant or Papal System most favorable to Civil and Religious Liberty?" Another book which he published was entitled: "Imminent Dangers to the Free Institutions of the United States through Foreign Immigration, and the Present State of the Naturalization Laws. By an American." He also published other learned papers to which attention need not here be particularly drawn. Morse also introduced into the United States the wonderful method of taking pictures by the aid of the sun and subtle chemical combinations. He may be said to have taken the first photographic picture ever taken in America. He and his distinguished colleague in the University of the City of New York, Prof. John William

Draper, realized that while Daguerre's marvellous invention of photogenic drawing could give pictures of statu-
ary and architectural objects it could not be applied to
landscape scenery or used in a satisfactory manner in
taking portraits. Prof. Draper conducted a series of
very learned and highly interesting experiments in the
laboratory of the university and succeeded in vastly improving the already wonderful invention. The wonders
wrought by photography and its inestimable value to the
astronomer and its value in many ways to the civilized
nations would open an interesting subject for contemplation. In recent times electricity is often employed in
photography. Photographic pictures of the interior of
mines and of caverns as well as of landscapes and of innumerable objects often in modern times in an instant speak to
one in a way which surpass the powers of the most eloquent orator or the most labored pages of the most elegant author.

Prof. Morse was a member of the Presbyterian Church
and was a man of decided religious convictions. He gave
liberally of his means to charities. To a grandson he
wrote in 1868: "The nearer I approach to the end of my
pilgrimage, the clearer is the evidence of the Divine origin of the Bible, the grandeur and sublimity of God's
remedy for fallen man are more appreciated, and the
future is illumined with hope. and joy." In the same
year he wrote to his brother: "The Saviour daily seems
more precious; his love, his atonement, his divine power,
are themes which occupy my mind in the wakeful hours of
the night, and change the time of 'watching for the morning' from irksomeness to joyful communion with him."

The last public act of the inventor of the electric telegraph was to be present, although eighty years had combined to make his head snowy white, at the unveiling of

a statue to Franklin. He ended an address by saying of Franklin : " May his illustrious example of devotion to the interest of universal humanity be the seed of further fruit for the good of the world !"

On April 2d, 1872 Prof. Morse's spirit was summoned into the presence of its Creator. This is not the place to dwell upon the high honors paid to the illustrious dead. It may be stated that his imposing obsequies caused sadness not only in the great city of New York. The Legislatures of Massachusetts and of New York paid him especial honor. His death was held to be a national bereavement. On April 16th, both Houses of Congress, the President of the United States and his Cabinet, the Judges of the Supreme Court of the United States and the Governors of the different States assembled in the national Capitol. After James G. Blaine, who was assisted by the Vice-President of the United States and presided at the impressive scene, had made an address he was followed by other speakers whose words deepened the solemnities of the day. A large portrait of the great inventor of the telegraph, which occupied a place in the legislative hall of the Republic, brought to the minds of the great assembly of statesmen the figure of Prof. Morse. Around the painting were written the words, " What hath God wrought ?" Telegrams of sympathy during the impressive services were received from many parts of the world and were read aloud by Mr. Cyrus W. Field. After the service had been opened by prayer, Speaker Blaine said : " Less than thirty years ago, a man of genius and learning was an earnest petitioner before Congress for a small pecuniary aid, that enabled him to test certain occult theories of science which he had laboriously evolved. To-night the representatives of fifty million people assemble in their legislative hall to do homage

and honor to the name of ' Morse.' Great discoverers
and inventors rarely live to witness the full development and perfection of their mighty conceptions, but to
him whose death we now mourn, and whose fame we
celebrate, it was in God's good providence vouchsafed
otherwise. The little thread of wire placed as a timid
experiment between the national capital and neighboring
city grew and lengthened, and multiplied with almost
the rapidity of the electric current that darted along its
iron nerves, until, within his own lifetime, continent was
bound unto continent, hemisphere answered through
ocean's depths unto hemisphere, and an encircled globe
flashed forth his eulogy in the unmatched elements of a
grand achievement." When Blaine ceased speaking he
announced the names of eminent statesmen who were to
take part in the solemn memorial service. James A. Garfield, when his name had been announced, impressively
said : " The grave has just closed over the mortal remains
of one whose name will be forever associated with a
series of achievements in the domain of discovery and invention the most wonderful our race has ever known,—
wonderful in the results accomplished, more wonderful
still in the agencies employed, most wonderful in the
scientific revelations which preceded and accompanied
their development." As Garfield approached the close
of his remarks, he spoke of electricity as "that chainless
spirit which fills the immensity of space with its invisible
presence,—which dwells in the blaze of the sun, follows
the path of the farthest star, and courses the depths of
earth and sea,—That mighty spirit," he added, "has at
last yielded to the human will. It has entered a body
prepared for its dwelling. It has found a voice through
which it speaks to the human ear. It has taken its place
as the humble servant of man, and through all coming

time its work will be associated with the name and fame of Samuel F. B. Morse. * * * The future of this great achievement can be measured by no known standards. Morse gave us the instrument and the alphabet. The world is only beginning to spell out the lesson, whose meaning the future will read."

One might ask what truths would Garfield have had the world learn from such an invention as that given to the world by Prof. Morse? He would have had statesmen observe the wisdom of nations cherishing the interests of the arts and sciences. But a very short time before taking part in paying the last sad honors to Prof. Morse, he had in Congress urged with eloquence the wisdom of the United States Government extending aid to the cause of education throughout the Republic—especially in some of the States of which a majority of the voters could not read and write. When speaking at the service in memory of Prof. Morse, Garfield justly exclaimed: "The electro-magnetic telegraph is the embodiment—I might say the incarnation—of many centuries of thought—of many generations of effort to elicit from Nature one of her deepest mysteries. No one man, no one country, could have achieved it. It is the child of the human race,—'the heir of all the ages.' How wonderful were the steps which led to its creation!" Garfield then proceeded to review with high eloquence the steps which had ushered into the world the discoveries respecting electricity until, as he expressed it, "the work of the inventor began." He mentioned by name the illustrious scientists whose philosophic experiments had made it possible to apply electricity to telegraphy. Almost every one—if not indeed every one—of the great men whose names he mentioned, had made the acquaintance of science in State institutions of higher learning,—and a goodly number of the men whose names he named had been themselves university professors.

It is interesting to here notice that while Morse was laboring in the United States to give to the world an electric telegraph a somewhat similar effort was being made in Europe. A student at the University of Heidelberg had seen an experiment performed by one of his German professors which had suggested to him a kind of electric telegraph. He and Prof. Wheatstone had formed a partnership and had invented an electric telegraph, which, though much inferior to Prof. Morse's invention, deserves honorable mention. Even if they had never adopted any of Prof. Morse's ideas their invention would doubtless have subserved some useful purposes.

It would be instructive to dwell on many of the highly interesting applications of electricity to some of the arts and sciences. By Prof. Graham Bell's invention of the telephone—an invention which has been improved by Prof. A. E. Dolbear,—articulate speech can be transmitted for even hundreds of miles, so that one can have whispered into his ear the low notes of good-will and affection in the familiar tones of his most cherished friend,—can literally converse with distant dear ones. Suffice it, however, to conclude these remarks about electricity by saying that if Yale College, which has given to the world hundreds of useful men, had never educated any other youth than Morse she would have returned to Connecticut more than all the money which that State has ever expended on her high schools and on Yale College.

It would be interesting to dwell upon the money value of useful inventions to nations. Even the incidental ways in which the members of a community are benefited by the electric telegraph and by photography, is worthy of the consideration of the student of social science. For example, classes of workmen receive employment in making magnetic telegraph instruments and in manufacturing from ore wire ; another class of people are employed as telegraph operators, or as photographers. In this latter class of citizens are to be found, in some instances, women. In the present stage of civilization the thoughtful statesman may well view with concern the condition of many of the gentler sex who are thrown upon their own exertions for support. In a selfish world they have often sadly few ways of earning for themselves an honorable subsistence. In at least some instances women are employed as telegraph operators, or assume, without compromising a single womanly feeling, the beautiful and appropriate avocation of taking photographs. Suppose that one hundred thousand men and women are employed as telegraph operators receiving for their work, on an average, five hundred dollars a year, fifty millions of dollars are thus yearly divided among an estimable class of citizens. Surely the poor have an incidental, no less truly than a direct interest, in nations cherishing the interests of the arts and sciences !

To place a just money value on inventions which promote the happiness and comfort of communities—even sometimes save life,—would be almost, or quite, impossible. Yet approximations, valuable to the student of social well-being, can justly be made. John Marshall,— the second Chief-Justice of the Supreme Court of the United States,—once calculated that the cotton-gin, invented by Eli Whitney—a young man who after studying in the public schools of Connecticut, graduated in Yale College, became a school teacher, and died in the year 1825,—had saved the United States, five hundred millions of dollars. George Sewall Boutwell, who as a financier and statesman, occupies an honorable place in American history, computed the value to the United States of Whitney's invention up to about the year 1859, at one thousand millions of dollars. Should this calculation be extended to the year 1880, the figures would become so immense as to make it difficult for one to appreciate their vastness. A basis on which to estimate the value of such an invention as the cotton-gin can be afforded in part, in the following manner. When Whitney, in 1792, after graduating at Yale College went to Georgia it took an ordinary slave about one day to clean up a pound of green-seed cotton. Whitney was happy in enjoying the acquaintance of the gifted widow of Gen. Greene—one of the most distinguished generals of the war for Independence. She, having urged him and encouraged him in the kindly manner which is one of the charms of the gentler sex, to endeavor to invent some contrivance for freeing the fleecy material from its undesired attendants, he invented a machine which would do many hundreds of times as much work as could the most skilful fingers of any human being. In the year 1880 there were at least several times as many millions of bales of cotton produced in the United States as there were pounds before Whitney's invention enriched the world.

When science creates new and useful industries she deserves to be credited by the thoughtful citizen with the wealth which she thus bestows upon the human race. For example, in recent years petroleum, or rock oil, has been made valuable to mankind by the achievements of scientists and of ingenious inventors. This singular oil had been known and looked upon with wonder by the ancient Egyptians and by the Assyrians. Even Herodotus, Pliny and Dioscorides were interested enough in its

4

mysterious appearance to allude to it in their writings. It was to be found in ancient times, as it is to be found to-day, in Italy, on the borders of the Caspian Sea, on the slopes of the Caucasus in Burmah, and from the Atlantic coast of the American continent to the Pacific Ocean. Even the mariner might have seen it as it bubbled up in the ocean in sight of the crater of Vesuvius, or as it glistened on the waters off the coast of what is now known as Venezuela and Southern California. Some of the American Indians were acquainted with some of its mysterious properties. In the night, rendered more sombre by the shadow of over-hanging trees, the Indians have been known to gather on the banks of a stream whose bosom was covered with oil. They would, when about to engage in war, mix with the oil a paint and anoint their dusky bodies or triumphantly shout as they illumined the dark stream by setting fire to the oil which floated on its waters. For a long period even American citizens were to see rivers of oil going to waste, content with occasionally bottling a little of it as medicine.

In 1855, the learned Benjamin Silliman, Jr., who after graduating in Yale College became one of its professors and added to the lustre already shed upon the name of Silliman by his distinguished father, was engaged by Messrs. Eveleth and Bissell of New York, to scientifically examine rock oil. Prof. Silliman produced, as the result of his scientific experiments, a paper in which he pointed out the value of petroleum to the arts and the mode of treatment to which the crude oil should be subjected to make it yield results useful to man. Not, however, until the year 1859, did people awake, even to a limited degree, to a realization of the vastness of the mineral wealth which science had just revealed to the world. When in the year 1859, oil wells commenced to yield princely fortunes to their owners, a scene of wild excitement was enacted in Pennsylvania. Thousands of people rushed to fields and hills in whose depths were subterranean rivers of wealth. Villages were called into existence one might almost say instantaneously. Men got rich suddenly and often parted with their newly acquired gold as though it had been a plaything. In time, however, the excitement subsided and a new, yet an immense, industry recovered from its intoxication. The invention of lamps suited to the use of the new kind of oil gave a great impetus to the petroleum industry. The first patent for lamps was made in 1859 and during that year some forty inventions for lamps and patent burners and for appliances in general for using oil, were patented. In 1860, although the mutterings of the approaching storm of civil war much occupied the minds of thoughtful people, seventy-one such inventions were made. In 1861, fifty three new patents were granted at Washington, and in 1862 one hundred and one patents were issued to facilitate the employment of petroleum in lamps. Each succeeding year increased the number of inventions by which the refined oil is made useful to the human race. To speak of the valuable inventions which have been made for transporting petroleum great distances, and the innumerable ways in which the refined oil, —or kerosene as it is called,—and of the way in which the products that remain when the oil is refined, are applied to the arts, would be to write a chapter which might well excite the interest of the student of political economy. In twenty years' time the petroleum industry became a source of vast wealth to the United States. Many thousands of men have been enabled to support their families by the means which have flowed to them through the newly opened industry. Pennsylvania alone received up to the year 1879,—to say nothing of what it and different parts of the United States, have received since 1879, and to say nothing of the lowness of the price at which it at times sold vast quantities of oil,—$293,872,-162. Up to 1879, at least $488,079,842 worth of oil was exported from the United States to different parts of the world—to say nothing of the value of the oil used in the United States. But these figures represent but a small part of the benefit received by mankind from the service rendered by scientists and by inventors in making petroleum useful to the nations of the earth. The art of refining petroleum has been introduced from the United States into different lands. One may almost say that wherever mercantile enterprise can make itself felt there kerosene is apt to be found. Light has been brought to millions of people who had once to spend their evenings in partial, if not in complete, darkness.—Thus the hours of day have been lengthened to many households. The old, often unprofitable and dreary, winter evenings of many homes, have become hours of happy recreation or of study and improvement. Many bold whalers whose ships were wont to vex every sea and to dare even the perils of the Arctic regions, have been, in a measure, relieved from their arduous toil, and the persecuted yet inoffensive whale has been left in some degree in peace. The substitution of the light of kerosene for the ancient pine-knot or tallow dip is one of the many revolutions which science has been instrumental in bringing about in recent years. The wealth which petroleum since it was touched by the hand of science has given to the United States, was all the more valuable, coming as it did when the Republic was impoverished by civil war.

It would be interesting to dwell upon what science has done in the last century in metallurgy:—to show, for example, how the manufacture of iron—a metal of price-less value to mankind—has been wonderfully aided by the chemist, and how even the iron age—interesting as it is in the history of civilization—is giving way to a steel age, and how by a chemical discovery steel rails are made which endure more than thirty times the wear and tear that iron rails can bear, thus enabling the locomotive to travel with a safety and speed and with an economy scarcely to be hoped for in times when rails were made of iron;—and how ships by being built of steel are made lighter, stronger and in various ways safer in case of col-lision as well as capable of carrying a greater amount of freight than the finest ships of their size of iron. Let it suffice, however, to say that if science has cost nations something for her maintenance she has returned to all who have cherished her many times that cost even in money.

Many of the services rendered by men whose minds have been broadened in centres of learning have more than a money value. Wonderful discoveries in medicine have been made by which the ravages of desolating epidemics are stayed and by which literally many millions of lives have been saved. Every new discovery of such a nature, has a value which is interesting alike to all the citizens of a land. In every country there is an amount of preventable sickness that is very costly to the public. This sickness, much of which could be prevented by sanitary science, was estimated by Chadwick in 1842 to amount even in England alone to £14,000,000 sterling per annum—not to speak of indirect losses. In England, France and Germany it is calculated that in 1880 the people on an average lived, six years longer than they did fifty years earlier.*

---

* " The Progress of the World," by M. G. Mulhall, F.S.S., 1880, p. 3.

The science of navigation is deeply indebted to the universities of a past age. The astronomer—as for example Prof. Galileo,—who scanned through the telescope —an instrument which has a very interesting history— the star-lit depths of space and penetrated some of the secrets of the immeasurable abysses of the heavens, gathered material for making a mystic guide-book and for converting the moon and·stars into lighthouses, by which the mariner is to-day enabled to make his way across the trackless waste of waters. By his subtle calculations the astronomer has made discoveries which affect every operation of trade in which the navigator has a part to perform. If Columbus, as is claimed by many of his biographers—including a member of his own family— studied in the University of Pavia, the fact is interesting inasmuch as that university was celebrated for the attention given in it to the science of navigation. It was a university that might well prepare a youth to render the world a priceless service. The discovery of the American continent was not merely valuable to the old world because of its precious metals. Its agricultural products alone—including plants new to Europeans—was an invaluable blessing to the old world. Even the quinine tree, valuable as it is in medicine, is probably vastly less valuable to Europeans than is the American potato—a vegetable which in innumerable cases has banished the sad sickness known as scurvy from the habitations of the poor. The potato is found to yield thirty times in weight to the acre as much as does wheat. Next to wheat it may be said to rank as a food product in the world. It is in short the bread of very many millions of people.

It has already been noticed that Jefferson believed that one of the greatest blessings which institutions of a high grade of learning render nations is that of educating youth to become statesmen. A few statistics may here illustrate in some faint degree the indebtedness of the United States to high schools and colleges for legislative wisdom. At the annual commencement of the somewhat unknown University of North Carolina in 1855, it was found that among its alumni gathered together, there were six Governors. It was found that among the alumni of the institution had been a President and a Vice-President of the United States, a Secretary of the Navy, a Minister to France, a Treasurer and a Comptroller of the State, two of the three Supreme, and six of the seven Superior Court Judges, the Attorney General, and nearly a fourth of the members of the General Assembly of the State of North Carolina. Up to about the year 1884, among the graduates of Princeton have been at least one President of the United States, two Vice-Presidents, one Chief-Justice, four Associate Justices, five Secretaries of State, four Secretaries of the Navy, five Attorney Generals, more than one hundred and twenty Judges of the State courts, more than one hundred and fifty Members of Congress and twenty foreign Ambassadors. It has already been noticed that of the fifty-five statesmen who at one of the most critical periods of American history, were charged with the momentous work of framing a Constitution for the United States, at least nine of them had studied in Princeton College. Probably the history of very many other seats of learning in the old world and in America would illustrate, more forcibly than have the statistics which have just been presented, the silent influence which institutions of a high grade of learning exert upon communities and upon the world. It has been estimated that at least about one fourth of all the members of Congress, during the first one hundred years of the Republic's history were once college students.

Colleges, as has been seen, do not merely educate men to be statesmen. They give to the world engineers, authors, lawyers, physicians, chemists, and men with faculties so trained that they are prepared to cast light upon various questions of deepest interest to the human race. Many of these men are better qualified to serve the communities in which they reside than it would have been possible for them to be had there been no generous provision made for their mental culture. Of all the services which institutions of a high grade of learning have rendered the world there is none more interesting and important than the blessing which they have rendered by qualifying men to examine and appreciate the claims of the Christian religion and to put a just value upon the pretensions and superstitions of false religions. One may well observe with ever increasing interest, how large is the number of the ministers of Evangelical Christianity who have studied and taught in universities. Among these men, to whom in the Divine providence the world owes the deepest gratitude, might be mentioned Wickliff, who translated the Bible into English; the martyrs John Huss and Jerome of Prague; Luther, who did a work in Germany, which the more it is examined the grander and more important to mankind it is found to be; Calvin who as a Reformer successfully contended for many of the great truths of Christianity; and a host of learned ministers of the Gospel whose eloquence has been consecrated to one of the most important objects which can enlist the affections of noble souls.

One of the many incidental advantages which a university renders a State which has a school system similar to the one which Jefferson labored to secure in Virginia, is that it helps to maintain, or to raise, the standard of

study in the common schools and in the high schools or
colleges. A youth realizing that one of the rewards
which he will obtain by being faithful in his studies, is
the privilege of entering the grammar school and of
ultimately entering the university, has a reward for
faithfulness in his employment set before him which.
encourages him in the happiest manner to cheerfully and
earnestly endeavor to attain at least a certain standard of
excellence in all his studies.

Although Jefferson had never seen many of the great
scientific inventions which are of priceless value to civilized nations,—had never seen a locomotive, or heard of
employing electricity as an agent to bear messages under
the ocean or around the world in an instant, yet the
venerable statesman had seen science accomplish many
wonders. In the able paper which he sent to the
Legislature of Virginia in August, 1818, respecting a suitable site for a University in Virginia, he, after alluding to
rewards which a commonwealth may be expected to reap
from such an institution, continues : " The commissioners
are happy in considering the statute under which they
are assembled as proof that the Legislature is far from
the abandonment of objects so interesting. They are
sensible that the advantages of well-directed education,
moral, political and economical, are truly above estimate.
Education generates habits of application, of order and
the love of virtue ; and controls, by the force of habit,
any innate obliquities in our moral organization. We
should be far, too, from the persuasion that man is fixed,
by the law of his nature, at a given point ; that his improvement is a chimera, and the hope delusive of rendering himself wiser, happier or better than our forefathers
were. As well might it be urged that the wild and uncultivated tree, hitherto yielding sour and bitter fruit

only, can never be made to yield better; yet we know
that the grafting art implants a new tree on the savage
stock, producing what is most estimable both in kind and
in degree. Education, in like manner, ingrafts a new man
on the native stock, and improves what in his nature was
vicious and perverse into qualities of virtue and social
worth. And it cannot be but that each generation succeeding to the knowledge acquired by all those that
preceded it, adding to it their own acquisitions and discoveries, and handing the mass down for successive and
constant accumulation, must advance the knowledge and
well-being of mankind, not *infinitely*, as some have said,
but *indefinitely*, and to a term which no one can fix and
foresee. Indeed, we need look back half a century, to
times which many now living remember well, and see the
wonderful advances in the sciences and arts which have
been made within that period. Some of these have
rendered the elements themselves subservient to the
purposes of man, have harnessed them to the yoke of his
labors, and effected the great blessings of moderating his
own, of accomplishing what was beyond his feeble force,
and extending the comforts of life to a much enlarged
circle, who had before known its necessaries only. That
these are not the vain dreams of sanguine hope, we have
before our eyes real and living examples. What, but
education, has advanced us beyond the condition of our
indigenous neighbors? And what chains them to their
present state of barbarism and wretchedness, but a
bigoted veneration for the supposed superlative wisdom
of their fathers, and the preposterous idea that to look
backward for better things, and not forward, as it should
seem, to return to the days of eating acorns and roots,
rather than indulge the degeneracies of civilization? And
how much more encouraging to the achievements of

science and improvement is this than the desponding
view that the condition of man cannot be ameliorated,
that what has been must ever be, and that to secure
ourselves where we are, we must tread, with awful reverence, in the footsteps of our fathers. This doctrine is
the genuine fruit of the alliance between Church and State ;
the tenants of which, finding themselves but two well in
their present condition, oppose all advances which might
unmask their usurpations, and monopolies of honors,
wealth and power, and fear every change, as endangering
the comforts which they now hold. Nor must we omit to
mention among the benefits of education, the incalculable
advantage of training up able counsellors to administer
the affairs of our country in all its departments, legislative,
executive and judiciary, and to bear their proper share in
the councils of our national government ; nothing more
than education advancing the prosperity, the power and
the happiness of a nation.* In this same paper, Jefferson
said : "Some good men, and even of respectable information, consider the learned sciences as useless acquirements ;
some think that they do not better the condition of man ;
and others that education, like private and individual
concerns, should be left to private individual effort ;
not reflecting that an establishment embracing all the
sciences which may be useful and even necessary in the
various vocations of life, with the buildings and apparatus
belonging to each, is far beyond the reach of individual
means, and must either derive existence from public
patronage, or not exist at all. This would leave us, then,
without those callings which depend on education, or
send us to other countries to seek the instruction they
require."

---

* "Early History of the University of Virginia," J. W. Randolph, Richmond, 1856, pp. 432–7.

Without pausing to dwell upon all the arguments which Jefferson, from time to time, incidentally urged respecting the value of colleges and of universities to the United States, it may be well to somewhat briefly notice that if colleges were not public, the rich could indeed send their youth to whatever fanes of knowledge they pleased, no matter how expensive it was to do so, but youth in moderate circumstances in life would, to a great extent, be excluded from such halls of learning. If the rich alone should enjoy the advantages of a collegiate education they might, to too great an extent, become practically an aristocracy. The statesmen who framed the Constitution of the United States provided that titles of nobility should not be given to any citizen of the Republic. At the close of the war for Independence the officers who had taken part in the war formed themselves into an organization which they named "The Cincinnati." They had medals struck for the members of the Society. The decorations were perhaps especially prized by the foreign officers who had taken part in the war. Washington laboriously, and with great earnestness, exerted his influence to cause the Society to dissolve, or, at least, to provide that under no circumstances should it be permitted to contain a germ which might develop into an Order of nobility. Washington conferred again and again with Jefferson regarding this Order. I will here present an extract from a letter which Jefferson wrote to Washington from Paris on Nov. 14th, 1786. Jefferson thus spoke of the Society of the Cincinnati: "What has heretofore passed between us on this institution, makes it my duty to mention to you, that I have never heard a person in Europe, learned or unlearned, express his thoughts on this institution, who did not consider it as dishonorable and destructive to our governments ; and that every writing which has come out since my arrival here, in which it is mentioned, considers it, even as now reformed, as the germ whose development is one day to destroy the fabric we have reared. I did not apprehend this, while I had American ideas only. But I confess that what I have seen in Europe has brought me over to that opinion; and that though the day may be at some distance, beyond the reach of our lives perhaps, yet it will certainly come, when a single fibre left of this institution will produce an hereditary aristocracy, which will change the form of our governments from the best to the worst in the world. To know the mass of evil which flows from this fatal source, a person must be in France; he must see the finest soil, the finest climate, the most compact State, the most benevolent character of people, and every earthly advantage combined, insufficient to prevent this scourge from rendering existence a curse to twenty-four out of twenty-five parts of the inhabitants of this country. With us, the branches of this institution cover all the States. The Southern ones, at this time, are aristocratic in their dispositions; and, that that spirit should grow and extend itself, is within the natural order of things. I do not flatter myself with the immortality of our governments, but I shall think little of their longevity unless this germ of destruction is taken out." It is pleasant to be able to state that this Society which Washington and Jefferson looked upon with misgiving, finally dissolved and gave the money which it had acquired, amounting to a good many thousands of dollars, to a college that had been named after Washington—a college to which Washington himself had given a handsome donation. Some of the evils connected with the existence of an aristocracy are the following. The aristocracy control the Government. Laws are too often enacted which, however favorable to the aristocracy, are injurious to the interests of the common people. For example, 'the nobles in France before the Revolution, managed to enact laws by which the property of nobles could not be taxed. The common people were thus obliged not only to pay their own taxes but the taxes of the nobles as well. The nobles invested themselves with peculiar honors. For instance no one could be an officer in the army who was not a noble of a certain grade. The history of every nation teaches that, under certain circumstances which may arise, an aristocracy is capable of enacting laws which may effect the destruction of the happiness, of the liberties, and even of the lives of the common people—may even be tempted to endeavor to reduce their fellow-citizens to a state of vassalage—may even be betrayed into thinking of themselves as a superior species and into assuming offensive pretensions. The history of every nation in the world teaches that, no matter how lovely in character some members of an aristocracy may be, the existence of an order of nobility in a land is responsible for direful evils,—is an infringement on human liberty and a greater evil than benefit even to the favored few:—is a system which can justly claim no encouragement from the spirit of the Christian religion and is at war with just principles of good government.

In a nation in which all men are equal the people enjoy the advantage of the talents of the poor as well as of the rich. When the people of the United States declared to the world, as they did when they adopted their National Constitution, that no order of nobility should exist under the United States flag, they presented a strange spectacle to the nations of the world who had become accustomed to seeing the innumerable evils which ever result from creating wrong artificial distinctions among men. A Government "of the people, by the people, for the people," * was indeed, a hundred years ago, an interesting sight to the world.

In a very able and eloquent discourse, delivered in Chautauqua county, New York, July 26th, 1837, on the importance of raising the standard of education throughout the land, William H. Seward said : " The aristocracy with which the world has been scourged was never one that was produced by science and learning. * * * If at this day, wealth sometimes usurps the place of intellect and appropriates its honors, it is only because public sentiment is perverted, and requires to be corrected by a higher standard of education. But, although education increases the power and influence of its votaries, it has no tendency like other means of power to confine its advantages to a small number; on the contrary, it is expansive and thus tends to produce equality, not by levelling all to the condition of the base, but by elevating all to the association of the wise and good."

Seward's sentiments regarding creating, in some respects, an equality among citizens are certainly noble and wise. Is it not so plain as scarcely to need illustration, that if halls of learning are ever open to the sons and daughters of all American citizens, that youth will have opportunities to qualify themselves to guard their own interests, the cause of learning, of liberty, and of good government, in their country; but, that if institutions of learning are closed to the youth of parents in moderate circumstances, no matter how talented and noble they may be, and opened only to the rich, that the State would deprive itself of the advantages of the wisdom and services of a class of people from whom have arisen a host of patriots who have been one of the glories of the nation.

---

* Abraham Lincoln's speech at the dedication of the Cemetery at Gettysburg.

In a republic there cannot be a surplus of wisdom and true learning. The prosperity and strength of a State depend more upon having intelligent and virtuous citizens than it does upon possessing valuable mines of gold and silver. If only the rich were privileged to send their youth to colleges then, inasmuch as riches are confined principally to chief cities, there would sadly often be a dearth of highly educated men in small towns and villages and in rural districts. The successful working of a republican government requires that there should be few districts devoid of high intelligence. Free colleges and universities disseminate over a State men of culture who directly or indirectly help in guarding the important interests of the commonwealth and in diffusing knowledge. It is a mistake to suppose that the only ones benefited by free institutions of learning are those who attend them. The good physician who ministers to the sick and blesses his neighbors in their hours of severest need and suffering, or by advice on sanitary matters saves a community from an epidemic, is not the only one who is blessed by the university. The engineer who builds bridges and works of invaluable utility to generations repays to the State many times the cost of his instruction in the public shrine of learning. The lawyer who maintains the dignity of law without which savagery would characterize a community—without which the widow and the orphan would in many cases have no protector,—helps to distribute to others than himself the blessings of higher education. Can a more unjust objection to high schools, academies and colleges be conceived than that their benefits are monopolized by those who study within their walls? These monuments of learning in which the lamp of knowledge is kept trimmed and burning give light to minds which in their turn diffuse intelligence, and blessings flowing from knowledge, in all parts of the Republic. Why should the blessings of knowledge be curtailed by being confined only to the sons of wealthy families? Would the intelligent and patriotic poor be pleased at having these institutions of liberal culture closed to their youth? Let the fountains of learning be ever free to the children of citizens in moderate circumstances who are to be a blessing, it may be, to the nation no less truly than are the children of parents blessed with wealth. All honor to the many noble-hearted people of wealth who have shown themselves friends of letters and of the human race by giving of their means and time to found and maintain the cause of learning on the earth! What would science have done without this class of friends!

'When Jefferson was in Europe he had observed with a statesman's eye the condition of its people. Writing from France to his distinguished friend and former instructor, George Wythe on April 13th, 1786,* he spoke feelingly of the "ignorance, superstition, poverty, and oppression of body and mind, in every form" which he declared was firmly settled on the mass of the people." He then, from the condition of the countries of Europe, derived a warning for the people of the United States. He said: "I think by far the most important bill in our whole code, [Code for Virginia] is that for the diffusion of knowledge among the people. No other sure foundation can be devised, for the preservation of freedom and happiness. If anybody thinks that kings, nobles, or priests are good conservators of the public happiness, send him here. It is the best school in the universe to cure him of that folly. He will see here, with his own eyes, that these

---

* " Memoirs and Writings of Jefferson," edited by Thomas Jefferson Randolph, vol. ii., p. 43.

descriptions of men are an abandoned confederacy against the happiness of the mass of the people. The omnipotence of their effect cannot be better proved, than in this country, particularly, where, notwithstanding the finest soil upon earth, the finest climate under heaven, and a people of the most benevolent, the most gay and amiable character of which the human form is susceptible; where such a people, I say, surrounded by so many blessings from nature, are loaded with misery, by kings, nobles, and priests, and by them alone. Preach, my Dear Sir, a crusade against ignorance; establish and improve the law for educating the common people. Let our countrymen know, that the people alone can protect us against these evils, and that the tax which will be paid for this purpose is not more than the thousandth part of what will be paid to kings, priests and nobles, who will rise up among us if we leave the people in ignorance."

Jefferson believed that strong-minded, well informed, and moral men were needed in a republic. He believed, as can be seen by the " Bill for the Better Diffusion of Knowledge " which he introduced into the Assembly of Virginia in 1779, that in all classes of citizens worthy and virtuous youth were to be found who could be fitted by education, to, as he expressed it, " guard the sacred deposit of the rights and liberties of their fellow-citizens." * He added: " It is better that such should be sought for and educated at the common expence of all, than that the happiness of all should be confided to the weak and wicked."

---

* " And to avail the Commonwealth of those talents and virtues which nature has sown as liberally among the poor as rich, and which are lost to their country by the want of means for their cultivation. Be it further enacted as follows," etc., etc.   The heading of a division respecting grammar schools or colleges, in a very lengthy bill which Jefferson in his old age, framed. See " Early History of the University of Virginia," J. W. Randolph, Richmond, Va., p. 426.

He then in his bill made especial provision by which this class of youth should be enabled to receive collegiate and university instruction.

While dwelling for a moment on the interest which citizens in moderate circumstances in life—indeed, all lovers of liberty—should have in supporting public institutions of learning it may here be interesting to supplement the remarks by Jefferson which have just been quoted, by noticing the views of James Madison and of William H. Seward on the wisdom of the people of a republic providing high grades of instruction for their youth. Madison's public declarations, when, as President of the United States, he repeatedly recommended to Congress the erection of a national university, and his sentiments on the value of colleges and universities to nations, as expressed in the reports of the University of Virginia in his official connection with its management, need not here be repeated. A letter of his dated Aug. 4th, 1822, to W. T. Barry, may here however be noticed. After briefly acknowledging a letter and circular which he had received, he said:

" The liberal appropriations made by the Legislature of Kentucky for a general system of education cannot be too much applauded. A popular Government, without popular information, or the means of acquiring it, is but a prologue to a farce or a tragedy ; or, perhaps, both. Knowledge will forever govern ignorance ; and a people who mean to be their own governors must arm themselves with the power which knowledge gives.

" I have always felt a more than ordinary interest in the destinies of Kentucky. Among her earliest settlers were some of my particular friends and neighbors. And I was myself among the foremost advocates for submitting to the will of the ' District ' the question and the time of its becoming a separate member of the American family. Its rapid growth and signal prosperity in this character have afforded me much pleasure; which is not a little enhanced by the enlightened patriotism which is now providing for the State a plan of education embracing every class of citizens, and every grade and department of knowledge. No error is more certain than the one proceeding from a hasty and superficial view of the subject: that the people at large have no interest in the establishment of academies, colleges, and universities, where a few only, and those not of the poorer classes, can obtain for their sons the advantages of superior education. It is thought to be unjust that all should be taxed for the benefit of a part, and that, too, the part least needing it.

"If provision were not made at the same time for every part, the objection would be a natural one. But, besides the consideration, when the higher seminaries belong to a plan for general education, that it is better for the poorer classes to have the aid of the richer, by a general tax on property, than that every parent should provide at his own expense for the education of his children, it is certain that every class is interested in establishments which [give] to the human mind its highest improvements, and to every country its truest and most durable celebrity.

"Learned institutions ought to be favorite objects with every free people. They throw that light over the public mind which is the best security against crafty and dangerous encroachments on the public liberty. They are the nurseries of skilful teachers for the schools distributed throughout the community. They are themselves schools for the particular talents required for some of the public trusts, on the able execution of which the welfare of the people depends. They multiply the educated individuals, from among whom the people may elect a due portion of their public agents of every description ; more especially of those who are to frame the laws; by the perspicuity, the consistency, and the stability, as well as by the just and equal spirit of which the great social purposes are to be answered.

"Without such institutions, the more costly of which can scarcely be provided by individual means, none but the few whose wealth enables them to support their sons abroad can give them the fullest education; and in proportion as this is done, the influence is monopolized which superior information everywhere possesses. At cheaper and nearer seats of learning, parents with slender incomes may place their sons in a course of education, putting them on a level with the sons of the richest. Whilst those who are without property, or with but little, must be peculiarly interested in a system which unites with the more learned institutions a provision for diffusing through the entire society the education needed for the common purposes of life. A system comprising the learned institutions may be still further recommended to the more indigent class of citizens by such an arrangement as was reported to the General Assembly of Virginia, in the year 1779, by a committee appointed to revise laws in order to adapt them to the genius of Republican Government. It made part of a ' Bill for the more general diffusion of knowledge,' that wherever a youth was ascertained to possess talents meriting an education which his parents could not afford, he should be carried forward at the public expense, from seminary to seminary, to the completion of his studies at the highest.

"But why should it be necessary in this case to distinguish the society into classes, according to their property? When it is considered that the establishment and endowment of academies, colleges, and universities, are a provision, not merely for the existing generation, but for succeeding ones also; that in Governments like ours, a constant rotation of property results from the free scope to industry, and from the laws of inheritance; and when it is considered, moreover, how much of the exertions and privations of all are meant, not for themselves, but for their posterity, there can be little ground for objections from any class to plans of which every class must have its turn of benefits. The rich man, when contributing to a permanent plan for the education of the poor, ought to reflect that he is providing for that of his own descendants; and the poor man, who concurs in a provision for those who are not poor, that at no distant day it may be enjoyed by descendants from himself. It does not require a long life to witness these vicissitudes of fortune.

" It is among the happy peculiarities of our Union, that the States composing it derive from their relation to each other and to the whole a salutary emulation, without the enmity involved in competitions among States alien to each other. This emulation, we may perceive, is not without its influence in several important respects; and in none ought it to be more felt than in the merit of diffusing the light and the advantages of public instruction. In the example, therefore, which Kentucky is presenting, she not only consults her own welfare, but is giving an impulse to any of her sisters who may be behind her in the noble career.

" Throughout the civilized world nations are courting the praise of fostering science and the useful arts, and are opening their eyes to the principles and the blessings of Representative Government. The American people owe it to themselves, and to the cause of Free Government, to prove, by their establishments for the advancement and diffusion of knowledge, that their political institutions, which are attracting observation from every quarter, and are respected as models by the new-born States in our own Hemisphere, are as favorable to the intellectual and moral improvement of man as they are conformable to his individual and social rights. What spectacle can be more edifying or more seasonable than that of liberty and learning, each leaning on the other for their mutual and surest support?"

As the aged Madison proceeded in his letter to his Kentucky friend, he spoke of the difficulties which Virginia had encountered in the establishment of a satisfactory school system, and advised his friend to give attention to the example set by the Eastern States which had less to contend with than had Virginia in the work of education. He ventured to suggest that in Kentucky the grade of instruction given to the poor might be raised by adding to reading, writing and arithmetic "some knowledge of geography; such as can easily be conveyed by a globe and maps, and a concise geographical grammar." He then continued: "And how easily and quickly might a general idea, even, be conveyed of the solar system, by the aid of a planatarium of the cheapest construction. No information seems better calculated to expand the mind and gratify curiosity than what would thus be imparted. This is especially the case with what relates to the globe we inhabit, the nations among which it is divided, and the characters and customs which distinguish them. An acquaintance with foreign countries in this mode has a kindred effect with that of seeing them as travellers, which never fails, in uncorrupted minds, to weaken local prejudices and enlarge the sphere of benevolent feelings. A knowledge of the globe and its various inhabitants, however slight, might, moreover, create a taste for books of travels and voyages; out of which might grow a general taste for history—an inexhaustible fund of entertainment and instruction. Any reading not of a vicious species must be a good substitute for the amusements too apt to fill up the leisure of the laboring classes." The venerable Madison then with a kind and graceful conclusion brought his letter to a close.

On the 16th of February, 1829, when Madison lacked one month of being seventy-eight years of age, he wrote a note to Samuel S. Lewis, President of the " Washington College Parthenon" Association. In this note, while tendering his acknowledgments for the honorary membership which had been conferred upon him, he took occasion to say that his " lengthened observations " made him " more and more sensible of the essential connection between a diffusion of knowledge and the success of Republican institutions." On September 6th, 1830, Madison wrote to Thomas W. Gilmer regarding the University of Virginia and the primary schools of the State. He wished there to be " a sympathy between the incipient and the finishing establishments provided for public education." He spoke of " a satisfactory plan for primary schools " as being " a vital desideratum in our Republics." He spoke also of the difficulties which had to be encountered in establishing a satisfactory school system in the Southern States. The aged patriot declared that he " should be proud of sharing in the merit " of devising improvements that would make the common-school system of Virginia more effective. He wished every one associated with the University of Virginia " to take a warm interest in the primary schools." In this letter Madison spoke of his age and of his infirmities, and expressed his belief that the work to be done for the cause of education would be taken up by abler hands than his own.

William H. Seward, who as a statesman in some respects much resembled Jefferson, in a discourse on
" Education," delivered in 1837, in Chatauqua county,
New York, stated that : " It is obvious that there must
always be various grades of education, and corresponding
grades in the institutions in which it is obtained; and
that all these will flourish only when all shall be duly
maintained : "—that, " They must and will have a recipro-
cal influence upon each other."

One may well feel hesitation in presenting extracts
from Seward's eloquent deliverances on the educational
needs of the Republic when he reflects that only when the
great New York statesman's discourse is seen in full, can
justice be done to the eloquence of his language. He
held that the standard of education in the common schools
and in the academies and colleges of the State of New
York should be raised. He thought that " an undue
feeling of contentment and self-complacency," regarding
the subject pervaded the community. He declared that
citizens of the Republic ought " to possess a measure of
knowledge, not only as great as is enjoyed by the citizens
or subjects of other States, but at least as much superior
as their power and responsibilities are greater." He held
that youth were generally dismissed from school " at the
very period when their education has only commenced."
Seward, after sketching a high grade of instruction which
seemed to him feasible to give to every youth in the
United States, continued : " All this education at least
must have been contemplated by the founders of this
government. Do you think they regarded the scarcely
more than mechanical acquirements of reading and writing as constituting that standard of education which was
to sustain this exquisitely organized, yet most liberal of all
governments? No ; I understand them rather as requiring, that the people could well comprehend and justly

approve or condemn, all the measures of administration."
Seward declared that "Great as the undertaking to
establish such a standard of education seems to be, it is
inconsiderable, compared with what has already been
accomplished.   It is only about three hundred years since
a Bible, now so cheap as to be found in the hands of the
most humble of the race for whom it had been promulgated more than fifteen hundred years, was obtained only
by the tedious and laborious multiplication of manuscript
copies, and was sold at a price that rendered it a sealed
book to all but the affluent.   Books of the bewildered sciences and arts, that had been obtained, were
still more rare, and were more valuable than a thousand times their present cost.   Even the ability to read
and write was a qualification so rare, that it entitled its
fortunate possessor to be the counsellor of kings, and to
an exemption from the capital punishment adjudged
against felony.   If at that period some philanthropist had
predicted that in the close of the eighteenth century, in a
country then undiscovered, a race would exist among
whom the Bible would be found in every family ; and a
greater number of books in a single city than the world
then contained ; that all the population of a great empire
would be able to read and write their native language ;
that the boasted mysteries of all science then known to
the few, who pursued their solitary studies in cloisters,
would be revealed to all the world, with ten thousand
discoveries never yet "dreamed of in their philosophy" ;
would not the prophecy have been thought more vision-
ary than my present belief, that with the aid of earnest
and wisely-directed effort, all the acquirements of academical and collegiate education of this day, may, within
less than half a century, constitute the ordinary proficiency
acquired in our (common) schools. * * * It is certain that,

by means of persevering improvement in the system of instruction, the standard of knowledge that has obtained among us may be continually elevated. * * * Let us imagine this whole people educated to the extent that I have supposed practicable ; and then can we conceive the immense and glorious change which would have come upon the condition of our country! Then indeed would our public councils be worthy the dignity of a race that has asserted and maintained their capability of self-government." Seward said that it was his belief that it was " a measure quite as indispensable and of as great efficiency, to elevate the standard of our colleges and academies, and to increase the number of students received in them " as it was to care for " our common schools."

It may here be incidentally noticed that Seward wrote quite a history of public education in the State of New York. The words of such thoughtful and learned statesmen as Jefferson and Seward respecting the provision for the education of youth which should be made in a republic, are interesting to the student of political economy— especially inasmuch as a certain class of people, prominent among whom are to be mentioned the Roman Catholic hierarchy,—especially Jesuits,—are endeavoring to persuade, sadly often with success, American citizens to give up their public-school system, or to at least be satisfied with a low grade of public education.

And now to return to Jefferson's labors in the cause of education in his native State. It was natural that one who wished as truly as he did a good educational system to be made " the key-stone of the arch of our Government," * should be deeply interested in the founding of the University of Virginia. He wished the organization

---

* Jefferson's letter to Adams, Oct. 28th, 1813 (In " Memoirs of Jefferson," by Thomas Jefferson Randolph).

of the school system of Virginia to be so thorough that the common schools and the University could, as he expressed it in a letter to Gen. Breckenridge, dated Feb. 15th, 1821, "go on hand in hand forever." In this same letter he said: "Nobody can doubt my zeal for the general instruction of the people. * * * I never have proposed a sacrifice of the primary to the ultimate grade of instruction. Let us keep our eye steadily on the whole system."* To Joseph C. Cabell, Jefferson wrote on Jan. 13th, 1823: "Were it necessary to give up either the Primaries or the University I would rather abandon the last, because it is safer to have a whole people respectably enlightened, than a few in a high state of science, and the many in ignorance. This last is the most dangerous state in which a nation can be. The nations and governments of Europe are so many proofs of it." † Writing to Cabell again on the following 28th of January he proposed to secure the necessary means with which to complete the *university* and then to push the interests of the common schools and to have provision made "systematically and proportionally," for "all the other intermediate academies." Under date of Jan. 22d, 1820, writing to Cabell, Jefferson had thus spoken: "Kentucky, our daughter, planted since Virginia was a distinguished State, has a University with fourteen professors and upwards of 200 students; while we, with a fund [the Literary Fund] of a million and a half of dollars, ready raised and appropriated, are higgling without the heart to let it go to its use. If our Legislature does not heartily push our University, we must send our children for education to Kentucky or Cambridge. * * * All the States but our own are sensible that knowledge is

---

* Ibid.

† "Early History of the University of Virginia," J. W. Randolph, Richmond, 1856, p. 267.

power. * * * The efforts now generally making through
the States to advance their science, is for power; while we
are sinking into the barbarism of our Indian aborigines, and
expect, like them, to oppose by ignorance the overwhelming mass of light and science by which we shall be surrounded. It is a comfort that I am not to live to see
this." In another letter to Cabell, under date of Dec.
25th, 1820, Jefferson pointed out the fact that knowledge
is power. "I lately saw in a newspaper," he said, "an
estimate in square miles of the area of each of the States,
of which the following is an extract: "Virginia 70,000
square miles, Massachusetts 7,250, Connecticut 4,764,
Delaware 2,120, Rhode Island 1,580." By this it appears
that there are but three States smaller than Massachusetts; that she is the twenty-first only in the scale of size,
and but one tenth of that of Virginia; yet it is unquestion-
able that she has more influence in our confederacy than
any other State in it. Whence this ascendency? From her
attention to education, unquestionably. There can be no
stronger proof that knowledge is power, and that ignorance is weakness. *Quousque tandem* will our Legislature
be dead to this truth?"

Jefferson was aided in the great work of founding the
University of Virginia by a number of friends of learning.
For instance the learned Rev. John Rice of Virginia—a
distinguished Presbyterian minister and the editor of a
literary and religious periodical in Richmond—took up his
gifted pen in behalf of the policy of founding the university. One of the points to which he drew attention
was that Virginia was incurring pecuniary losses by not
having suitable institutions of learning of her own. He
charged her with being guilty of the "most culpable
negligence" in the matter. He pointed out that instead
of saving money by not having institutions of learning of

her own and thus compelling youth to go to other States for instruction, she gained less than she lost. He then dwelt upon one of the ways in which she lost by such a policy. He said : " This is no light matter. *Ten years ago* I made extensive enquiries on the subject, and ascertained to my conviction, that the amount of money annually carried from Virginia, for purposes of education alone, exceeded $250,000. Since that period it has been greater. Take a quarter of a million as the average of the last eight and twenty years, and the amount is the enormous sum of $7,000,000. But had our schools been such as the resources of Virginia would have well allowed, and her honor and interest demanded, it is by no means extravagant to suppose, that the five States which bind.on ours would have sent as many students to us as under the present wretched system we have sent to them. This, then, makes another amount of seven millions! Let our economists look to that. Fourteen millions of good dollars lost to us by our parsimony!! Let our wise men calculate the annual interest of our losses, and add to this principal! They will then see what are the fruits of this precious speculation. In the language of the craft, it may well be said ' Verily, it is a losing job.' " * In addition to the Rev. Mr. Rice's appeal for the university another gifted writer published an able paper respecting the university, which he signed " A Friend to Science." The author's real name was Joseph C. Cabell. He ended the article by paying an eloquent tribute to Jefferson. After dwelling upon the interest taken in public education by Jefferson, he said : " Where is the man with heart so cold as not to glow at the recital of views so generous and so exalted? The name of this great and good man will

---

* "Early History of the University of Virginia," J. W. Randolph, Richmond, Va., p. 157.

descend with his works to the latest times, and will be hailed with rapturous enthusiasm by the friends of liberty and learning in every quarter of the civilized globe." It may be doubted whether even the distinguished writer who signed himself a "Friend of Science" knew how devotedly Jefferson had labored in the cause of education for nearly or quite half a century.

Jefferson realized in some degree the grandeur of the work in which the people of the United States were engaged in establishing a Republic which should illustrate to the world the blessings of liberty and of self-government. He keenly realized that if the citizens of all parts of the United States did not cherish the cause of learning, the Republic,—notwithstanding its hopes of grandeur and of happiness,—would be exposed to humiliation, to disgrace, and in many respects to degradation. He would sometimes forecast with sadness the future of the United States. He could almost see, at times, the horizon growing black with coming ruin and with the approach of desolating calamities. While he would indeed sometimes thank God that the evil day would not come in his generation yet he did not give way altogether to hopeless, enervating fear. On the contrary, he would rally his energies and seek to help the youth of the land to become intelligent enough to successfully cope with the dangers which he saw that they might some day have to encounter. He felt that the life or death of the Republic depended upon whether or not she cherished the interests of learning. It is told of a soldier who while the battle of Gettysburg was in progress lay wounded on a height from which he could overlook the scene of battle. As the soldiers surged backwards and forwards the scene became to him grand and overwhelming. He felt that the destiny of the great Republic of the new world, hung trembling in the balance ! It was with somewhat similar feelings that Jefferson watched the efforts of the friends of education in Virginia,—and the opposition which they encountered,—as they endeavored to establish a good school system in the Commonwealth. As a statesman he not only believed that " well directed education improves the morals, enlarges the minds, enlightens the councils, instructs the industry, and advances the power, the prosperity, and the happiness " * of a nation,—as nothing could do better †—but that " no other sure foundation can be devised for the preservation of freedom and happiness." ‡ He believed, as has been seen, not only that the sciences, "advance the arts, and administer to the health, the subsistence, and comforts of human life," § but that the most important laws which were on the statute books of Virginia were her laws having in view the instruction in useful learning of her youth, and that the money she would expend in maintaining a good school system would be money well spent. He believed, as has been seen, " That the tax which will be paid for this purpose is not more than the thousandth part of what will be paid to kings, priests, and nobles, who will rise up among us, if we leave the people in ignorance." In short, Jefferson had noticed—and only those who have thoughtfully studied the history of nations can fully understand the force of his words,—that the history of every nation and of every age " teaches the awful lesson, that no nation is permitted to live in ignorance with impunity."

* Report to Legislature of Virginia Jan. 6, 1818.—See " History of the University of Virginia as Contained in Letters of Jefferson and Cabell," pp. 402.   † " Early History of the University of Virginia," p. 437.

‡ Letter to George Wythe, April 13, 1786. In " Memoirs and Writings of Jefferson." By Randolph.

§ Report to Legislature of Virginia, Aug. 1st, 1818.—" Early History of the University of Virginia." J. W. Randolph, 1856, p. 435.

It was with deep feeling that the aged Jefferson wrote, under date of Jan. 31st, 1821, to Cabell, who had written to him that he thought of retiring from the Assembly of Virginia: "But the gloomiest of all prospects is the desertion of the best friends of the institution, for desertion I must call it. I know not the necessities which may force this upon you. Gen. Coke, you say, will explain them to me; but I cannot conceive them, nor persuade myself they are uncontrollable. I have ever hoped that yourself, Gen. Breckenridge, and Mr. Johnson would stand at your posts in the Legislature until everything was effected, and the institution opened. If it is so difficult to get along with all the energy and influence of our present colleagues in the legislature, how can we expect to proceed at all, reducing our moving power? I know well your devotion to your country and your foresight of the awful scenes coming, on her, sooner or later. With this foresight, what service can we ever render her equal to this? What object of our lives can we propose so important? What interest of our own which ought not to be postponed to this? Health, time, (labor,) on what in the single life which nature has given us, can these be better bestowed than on this immortal boon to our country? The exertions and the mortifications are temporary; the benefit eternal. If any member of our college visitors could justifiably withdraw from this sacred duty, it would be myself, who *quadragenis stipendiis jamdudum peractis*, have neither vigor of body nor mind left to keep the field; but I will die in the last ditch, and so I hope you will, my friend, as well as our firm-breasted brothers and colleagues, Mr. Johnson and Gen. Breckenridge. Nature will not give you a second life wherein to atone for the omissions of this. Pray then, dear, and very dear Sir, do not think of deserting us, but view the

5

sacrifices which seem to stand in your way, as the lesser duties, and such as ought to be postponed to this, the greatest of all. Continue with us in these holy labors until, having seen their accomplishment, we may say with old Simeon, ' *nunc dimittas, Domine.*' "

This pathetic exhortation of the aged statesman of Monticello to Cabell was not without effect. Gen. Dade,* in the Senate of Virginia in 1828, speaking of Joseph C. Cabell's connection with the University of Virginia, said: "In promoting that monument of wisdom and taste [he] was second only to the immortal Jefferson."

---

* See "Life of Thomas Jefferson," by Henry S. Randall, LL.D., p. 464.

III.

JEFFERSON'S IDEAL UNIVERSITY.

THE amount of thought and the self-sacrificing labor which Jefferson gave to the great work of breathing a noble spirit into the university which was to add new honors to the name of Virginia, was an eloquent proof of his conviction of the priceless worth of useful knowledge to citizens of a republic.

What studies will be most useful in laying the foundation of the acquirements and habits of mind which will be most valuable to American citizens is a question worthy of far greater consideration by thoughtful parents and statesmen than, it is to be feared, it in many cases receives The question becomes all the more perplexing when one bears in mind how limited is the time that youth can attend educational institutions.

When colleges and universities were first established in Europe they were adapted, as a rule, to a condition of society very different from that of the people of the United States in the nineteenth century. Jefferson lived in an age when great revolutions and changes convulsed the civilized world. He had seen empires and kingdoms rise and fall. He had seen States in the old world dismembered, overrun with armies and revolutionized in some degree, by various political causes. He had breathed an air which emboldened thoughtful men of learning to fearlessly review the errors and virtues of past gener-

ations. He felt that educational establishments in
America might be modelled on a broader, a better, a
much nobler basis than were some of the so-called
seminaries of learning of the old world. He recognized
the great truth that on some parts of the globe it may be
wise to pursue various branches of learning unneeded in
others. A time had been in Europe when if the universities rendered the world invaluable service, they did so
in spite of a certain spiritual and temporal despotism to
which they were in many instances subjected—a despotism which dreaded the results which impartial historical
and scientific investigation would lead to and looked
with displeasure and with threats of persecution upon
professors such as Galileo and some of his most learned
associates, and which even insisted that if the Bible was
studied at all it should be interpreted by many and often
contradictory and unreliable writers—some of whom were
styled " the Fathers,"—rather than that the student
should with a fearless and honest spirit seek untrammelled
and unvexed with despotic rules, for truth. As a man of
independent character Jefferson realized that the mischievous relics of the dark ages should not be allowed a
place needed by the proper demands and improvements
of a progressive age. He realized that new and vast
regions of knowledge were being explored, and that
discoveries were being made which were worthy of the
regard of statesmen who were interested in the founding of
good educational establishments, and that American citizens should be encouraged to attain higher and yet higher
degrees of useful culture. He wished the great Republic
of the new world to be enriched with every blessing which
the noblest gifts of useful learning could bestow upon her.

William E. Gladstone—whose name may with all the
more freedom be mentioned as he is justly held in singu-

larly high esteem in America as well as in England and
Europe—has declared that "The proper work of universities, could they perform it, while they guard and
cultivate all ancient truth, is to keep themselves in the
foremost ranks of modern discovery, to harmonize continually the inherited with the acquired wealth of mankind, and to give a charter to freedom of discussion, while
they maintain the reasonable limits of the domain of
tradition and of authority." * Jefferson could not but
have agreed with much that the learned and eloquent
Gladstone has said about great educational establishments. If he was as bold, or bolder, than the great
English statesman in introducing improvements and in
cherishing noble views respecting the grandeur of the
mission of universities, he was yet very cautious and careful in the work of grouping together liberal and judicious
courses of instruction in the new university which he was
taking a prominent part in securing to his native State.

Among the many questions which the Virginian statesman had to consider was, "How much time should be
devoted by students to the study of Greek and Latin?"
It is a question upon which to this day distinguished
statesmen and men of letters have expressed different
opinions. Jefferson planned that students should have
much liberty in choosing for themselves the courses of
study which they should be led to believe would be most
useful.to them in after life. He would have a young man
have, to at least a certain extent, an aim in life. He
wished him to be helped by wisely arranged courses of
instruction provided by the university, to form broad and
intelligent views respecting useful learning and to a certain
extent to anticipate right ambitions of a mature manhood.

---

* "The Might and Mirth of Literature," by W. E. Gladstone, John De
Roy, collector, p. 25.

To certain departments of the temple of knowledge he would allow young men to enter without any knowledge of the Greek and Latin languages. While he did not expect young men having many different aims in life to engage in a common course of study he, for a numerous class of young men, considered an acquaintance with Greek and Latin to be of high importance. It is widely known that in modern times some thoughtful men have felt that in many American colleges an unwisely large proportion of time is given to the study of the dead languages. I was once pleasantly surprised to receive through a book-store which had printed a book entitled " Our National System of Education," which I had published in 1877, a kind note from James Abram Garfield and a couple of pamphlets which he had himself published. One of these pamphlets was an able address which he had delivered on " College Education " at Hiram College on June 14th, 1867. In this address, while he spoke in high terms of the value of an acquaintance with the classics and alluded to the pleasure with which he himself, as a professor, had taught them, he yet freely and strongly expressed the conviction, that a larger proportion of time, as a rule, was given to classical studies in American colleges than was consistent with the highest wisdom. He pointed out some of the many branches of knowledge with which it is of very great importance that American youth should be acquainted, and spoke of the impossibility of their receiving due instruction in various very important branches of learning if they were compelled to give an unfair proportion of their time to dead languages. Garfield illustrated his address with very weighty proofs of the truth of the position which he maintained and declared that in American colleges, the dead languages held a place, " in obedience to the tyranny of custom," which was not defensible. He declared further that "each new college is modelled after the older ones, and all the American colleges have been patterned on an humble scale after the universities of England." Of course Garfield was careful to make evident that he did not mean that the study of Greek and Latin was not of very great usefulness to cultivators of literature and especially to ministers of the Gospel. He meant, however, that so many useful studies had claims on the attention of youth that it was not wise to insist that half their time and more, up to manhood should be exclusively devoted to the study of the classics. He further pointed out that there were "a family of modern languages almost equal in force and perfection to the classic tongues, and a modern literature, which, if less perfect than the ancient in æsthetic form, is immeasurably richer in truth, and is filled with the noblest and bravest thoughts of the world." He added that "When universities were founded, modern science had not been born." He maintained that the place which classical studies bear to other learning should be readjusted. Garfield was careful to add, however, that "There are most weighty reasons why Latin and Greek should be retained as a part of a liberal education." He then made in behalf of these studies an eloquent and able plea. "These studies then," he continued, "should not be neglected : they should neither devour nor be devoured. I insist," he added, "they can be made more valuable, and at the same time less prominent, than they now are. A large part of the labor now bestowed upon them is not devoted to learning the genius and spirit of the language, but is more than wasted on pedantic trifles." Before presenting Jefferson's views on the wisdom of giving the classics an honorable place in the course of study of a certain class of youth, it may here be noticed that Mr. Charles Francis Adams Jr., and other able writers have expressed opinions respecting the value to youth of a knowledge of Greek and Latin which will be found to contrast in some respects with those which were ardently held by Jefferson.

The value of an acquaintance with the dead languages when contrasted with much that it is desirable that American youth should know, has been attacked by wit. The Rev. J. D. Beugless, in a very interesting paper entitled, "What Our Universities should Teach," which was published in the July number of the entertaining and ably edited *Overland Monthly*, 1869,—a Californian magazine,—takes what may be called radical ground against youth devoting much time to the study of the classics. In his entertaining style, he writes: "Just here we recall an incident which aptly illustrates this whole controversy. Some years ago, in a time famous for steamboat racing on the Mississippi, two travellers, A and B, fell into a conversation. Said A to B: 'Have you ever studied Latin?' 'No, Sir,' was the reply. 'Then you have lost one fourth of your life, sir.' 'Did you ever study Greek?' 'No, sir.' 'There is another quarter of your life lost.' 'But you have studied mathematics?' 'No, sir.' 'Another quarter'—In the midst of this last sentence the boiler burst. 'Have you ever learned to swim?' shouted B. 'No, no, sir, I have n't,' exclaimed A. 'Then there is *all* of your life lost,' rejoined B, and swam ashore."

However highly Jefferson esteemed for a certain class of youth an acquaintance with Latin and Greek, he did so in a way in which Garfield would probably have agreed with him. The study of such languages as Hebrew, Greek and Latin give a certain discipline to the intellect and give a student a profounder comprehension, than people generally acquire, of the meaning of many English words. In this last respect an acquaintance with these languages may indirectly be of singular value to the statesman when called upon to frame enactments and to lawyers and judges when settling questions of law. It has been estimated that at least thirty per cent of the words in the English language are derived from Latin. Even to pure English roots of words Latin suffixes are found joined. In a thousand incidental ways an acquaintance with the classical languages may prove of very great value to the jurist and to the statesman. In a large library in which these words are being written is a department of law. In this division of the library are great volumes which are collections of the Bulls of the Popes in Latin. Some of these missives have made nations tremble. They have at times played a strange, sad part in history. They have given law to millions of those who have regarded with awe whatever issued from the lips of a Roman Pontiff. The titles of various nations to a large part of the continent of America have been based upon Papal missives. If Protestants have regarded as a superstition worthy of pity or contempt many of the claims of the Papacy not so have a vast number of people. The student of International law— indeed every statesman and citizen,—should know far more about these dusky volumes than is generally known. Then would they know how to act wisely in various controversies which are likely to occur wherever the hierarchy of the religion of Rome has power. One can but apprehend that, as a rule, Ecclesiastical law is not taught in American law schools as its importance demands that it should be and as it is taught in some of the great universities of Germany. The thoughtful American citizen and statesman who turns his gaze upon the conflict between Church and State, which has long raged and is still in ex-

citing progress in Europe and in South America, will feel
that it may at any moment be of the highest importance
that the jurists and statesmen of every land which values
civil liberty should be acquainted with the great principles
involved in the issue.   In Germany no one is allowed to
be a lawyer who is unacquainted with Latin and has
passed through a university.   Indeed, in Germany one
may often find students consulting in the original Latin
the celebrated Institutes of Justinian, which have been
for centuries the basis of the systems of jurisprudence in,
one may say, many lands.   It has been declared by the
widely known scholar Dr. Max Müller,—and Dr. Eliot,
President of Harvard College agrees with the declaration,
—that, " In Latin we have the key to Spanish, Portuguese, French and Italian.   Any one who desires to learn
the modern Romance languages—Italian, Spanish and
French—will find that he actually has to spend less time
if he learns Latin first, than if he had studied each of the
modern dialects separately and without this foreknowl-
edge of the common parent."   If, however, Dr. Müller
deems it just to thus speak of the Latin language, how
shall one speak of the value of a knowledge of Greek,
which language has been regarded as bearing, to at least
some extent, the same relation to German that Latin
does to some other languages?   An intelligent Christian
with even a limited acquaintance with the Greek grammar
may be helped much in obtaining an intelligent acquaintance with some of the expressions which he finds in the
New Testament.   Matters respecting questions of religion
are so important that Christians may well gladly welcome
knowledge which may help them to the better understanding what the Almighty has caused to be written for the
instruction of his children.   The Greek language has, independently of many other claims to consideration, that of

being the speech in which the New Testament has been written. Even to a cultured heathen the Bible, as a book which exerts a vaster influence for good than any other book in the world, can but have a peculiar interest.

The revival of the study of Greek and Hebrew—from which latter language English is indebted for many of its beautiful idioms,—marks a very important epoch in the history of the world. An historical incident may here be presented which has exerted a vast influence upon the human race and is intimately united with a series of mighty events of singular interest to the student of the history of civilization and to lovers of liberty. Just before and in the early part of the sixteenth century, in the shades of Oxford University,—an educational establishment already venerable with age, and worthy of world-wide honor, because of the statesmen, and the saintly Wickliff,—who has been called " The Morning Star of the Reformation,"—whom it had given to the world,—might have been seen a group of highly cultivated professors, each one of whom would daily be a central figure around which would gather some scholars who were one day to leave the impress of their lives upon the history of civilization. In the group of great teachers might have been seen William Grocyn, Thomas Linacre, and Thomas Colet. Without pausing to describe each one of the learned men who shed lustre upon the great University of Oxford,—a home of learning which might be characterized as one of the most important of all the centres of intellectual activity in Great Britain, if not indeed of the world at that period,—it may here be stated that Thomas Colet was the eldest son of Sir Henry Colet, who was several times Lord Mayor of London. Sir Henry had had twenty-one children, all of whom had died except Thomas—who was one day to be called " the good Dean Colet." Thomas being rich and longing to see the youth of London instructed, founded a school—which is still in existence—for one hundred and fifty-three young people, and endowed the establishment with what would be equal in modern times to about $150,000 to $200,000.   In the instruction of its scholars he took a personal interest.   It was, however, as one of the instructors,—and as the Dean—of the University of Oxford that he was to accomplish much of the noblest work of his life.   Among the students who listened at times to Colet's instructive lectures was Sir Thomas More who was to give to the world his singularly able work entitled " Utopia,"—a book in which he was to describe an ideal Republic with such eloquence and ability that it was to exert for centuries a singularly wide and beneficent influence on the thoughts of many statesmen in America and in England, where some of the suggestions which it contained were to be realized.   Although Sir Thomas More was never, as far as is known, sufficiently under the influence of Colet to join with him in longing to see Europe enjoying an open Bible and to see Roman Catholicism converted into a regenerated and pure religion, yet a time was to come when even More—a persecutor though he was—was to declare of Colet that " For centuries there hath not been among us any one man more learned and holy."

Among Colet's students was to be found a youth who had a peculiarly sad history, and whom even the exhortations of the kind Dean were not to be successful in causing to take a far bolder stand in favor of Evangelical religion than he did take.   Not a little however, of what was good in the life of Erasmus has been attributed to the influence of Colet.   Erasmus indeed had had a sad life.   Before he was born his father, supposing—owing to a falsehood that had been told him—that she who was about to be-

come a mother had died, in a fit of melancholy became
a monk. Although he was not allowed by his Church to
recognize his almost more than orphan son, yet, despite
all the difficulties in his way, he succeeded in securing
him in some respects, a very high education. Although
Erasmus was to bitterly grieve the old professor at Oxford by acting a timid part in the arena of history, and to
fail sadly in taking the stand which he should have taken
respecting some great religious questions, yet he was to
give the public a revised text of the new Testament in
Greek which was to do much towards thoroughly awaken-
ing Europe from the spell cast upon it by the dark ages.
While at Oxford Erasmus wrote : " Here I have met with
humanity, politeness, learning not trite and superficial,
but deep, accurate, true old Greek and Latin learning,
and withal so much of it, that, but for mere curiosity, I
have no occasion to visit Italy." Erasmus then speaking
of one of the professors said that in him he admired " an
universal compass of learning." Of another he said, his
"acuteness, depth, and accuracy are not to be exceeded."

Among the students who were to listen with deep
attention to the eloquence of Colet—rendered especially
impressive by its earnestness—was a youth named William Tyndale. With a profound faith in the truths of
Christianity and a fearless faith in the revelations of
science Colet labored to inaugurate true biblical study.
He pointed out with sadness the ignorance of Bible
truth, and the wickedness wofully common, among the
clergy of his day. On Feb. 12th, 1512, a great convocation gathered in the Cathedral of St. Paul's in London.
The convocation had practically been assembled by Cardinal Wolsey's direction, partly with a view of suppressing by persecution heretics—as all who did not believe
in Roman Catholicism were called. Dean Colet was

requested to preach the sermon. His first words fell like
a thunderbolt upon the ears of haughty bishops. His
sermon was wonderfully bold as he spoke of reforms
which were needed in the Romish church. Had it not
been for the protection of his friend, the Archbishop of
Canterbury and of the King of England, the hatred of foes
might have quickly wrought his ruin. At once learned,
eloquent, bold and earnest in Christian work, of a beautiful and winning character, ever ready to encourage youth
to act a truly noble part in life, Colet's influence in the
circle in which he moved and gave instruction was to be
felt at times in the happiest manner. Well might William
Tyndale listen with the generous responsiveness of a
noble heart to the words of the venerable Dean.

William Tyndale, however humble was his demeanor,
was descended from a noble family. His grandfather,
Baron de Tyndale, had been involved in the wars between the proud houses of York and Lancaster. Having
escaped from a disastrous field of battle, he had lived for
a time in concealment. The gentle Alicia, the daughter
and sole heiress of a wealthy family, had married the dis-
guised Baron. A son had been born to the happy pair,—
a son who in time inherited the family wealth and became the father of two sons—one of whom became a distinguished merchant and the other, who was William,
was to make the name of Tyndale historic. Although
several branches of the Tyndale family were honored
with knighthood, it is not upon them but upon the life of
William that the historian is wont to especially linger.

William Tyndale was born about the year 1477. From
a child he was instructed in grammar, logic and philosophy. At a very early age he entered the already venerable University of Oxford and became so proficient in the
Greek and Latin languages that he was enabled to read

to his fellow-students in St. Mary Magdalen Hall, and to the students of Magdalen College, the New Testament. William not only studied in Oxford but also entered the celebrated University of Cambridge where he is said to have taken a degree. After leaving the university, William formed a lasting friendship with the noble John Frith, who, although his junior in years also studied at Cambridge and was possessed of rare scholarly attainments, of deep piety, and was characterized by beautiful and noble manners. He was withal a very earnest-hearted reformer, and was to be associated with Tyndale in giving to the world many a valuable contribution to religious literature.

William Tyndale became a friar and was set apart as a Roman Catholic priest to the nunnery of Lambley. The question has sometimes been asked whether one can ever expect reforms to originate among Roman Catholic ecclesiastics. It should be remembered that again and again it has happened that reforms have been inaugurated even among this description of men. It has been seen that Tyndale before becoming a Romish ecclesiastic had obtained a knowledge of Greek, which was to be to him a key to the weightiest secrets of the Bible.

Tyndale was invited to become a chaplain in the hall of Sir John Welch, a knight of Gloucestershire, and also to act as the tutor of the knight's children. At the table of the lord of the manor Tyndale would at times meet the prelates and clergy of the country—would meet,—to use the words of an historian,—" abbots, deans, archdeacons, with divers other doctors and great beneficed men." He was grieved and humiliated to see how ignorant these men often showed themselves of the truths of the Bible. He was even sometimes betrayed into urging them to at least acquaint themselves with the truths contained in the New

Testament. At last the clerical visitors to Squire Welch preferred to resign the good cheer of the knight's table rather, as it was expressed by Fuller, " than to have the sour sauce of Master Tyndale's company." Tyndale's demeanor was at times singularly gentlemanly and prudent. For example, when the knight's lady, somewhat ruffled at seeing the prelates unable to hold a satisfactory argument with the learned tutor, asked him whether it was probable that she would prefer his judgment to that of the wealthy prelates, he politely refrained from replying. When, however, he soon afterwards translated from Latin into English a valuable religious work, he dedicated the manuscript to Sir John and his gentle partner. This handbook, called " The Pocket-dagger of the Christian Soldier," which he thus translated into the English language, taught that Christianity does not consist in the reception of certain dogmas taught by certain ecclesiastics of the Romish Church, or in the observance of ceremonies, but in yielding service to the Saviour. The work was read with interest and the knight and his gentle helpmate were converted to Evangelical Christianity. Tyndale, however, did not always succeed in holding his peace. Once when conversing with a Romish ecclesiastic respecting the Pope, his clerical friend exclaimed : " We had better be without God's laws than the Pope's." Tyndale, who believed that the Pope was a man who made unchristian pretensions, indignantly replied : " I defy the Pope and all his laws; and, if God give me life, ere many years the ploughboys shall know more of the Scriptures than you do." Naturally having made such a speech he became an object of persecution. Leaving the mansion of his kind friend Sir John Welch, he preached, it is said, to crowded houses in Bristol. But his name was to become historic, not because of his eloquence, however noble that was to be, but because of the mighty influence he was to be instrumental in exerting by giving to the Anglo-Saxon race a translation of the New Testament and a part of a translation of the Old Testament, in language which will probably for ever, in great measure, leave its impress upon—or mould—the English tongue and beneficially affect the character of the Anglo-Saxon race.

Without pausing to here dwell upon the thrillingly interesting lives of Tyndale and of his noble helper Erith,—lives which became the more interesting as they neared their martyrdom,—or to notice the strangely interesting history of the various translations of the Bible into English,—suffice it to say that the more the well-informed American citizen contemplates the influence of the widely familiar English Bible,—in which, if the English reader misses some of the beauty of the language as it was first given by God to man, he can still in his own language hear the words of the Eternal as he speaks to his children,—the more he will realize how happy it has been for the human race that the study of the dead languages has been given an honorable place in the universities of Great Britain. What Tyndale did for the English-speaking race a professor in the great Sorbonne in Paris was to do for the French, a professor of the University of Wurtemberg was to do for the Germans and professors of other universities were to do for different divisions of the human race.

Luther in the year 1524, in a very forcible and eloquent address which he sent to all the councillors of all the cities of Germany, pointing out the duty of magistrates interesting themselves in securing to youth the blessing of school instruction, urged upon his countrymen, with a force to which Germans to this day respond, that the study of Greek and Latin and Hebrew should be intro-

duced into the German schools. "What use," said the
great Reformer, "is there, it may be asked, in learning
Latin, Greek, and Hebrew? We can read the Bible very
well in German." "Without language," he declared, "we
could not have received the Gospel. * * * Languages
are the scabbard which contains the sword of the Spirit ;
they are the casket that contains the jewels. * * * If
we neglect the languages, we shall not only eventually
lose the Gospel, but be unable to speak or write in Latin
or in German. No sooner did men cease to cultivate
them than Christendom declined until it fell under the
power of the Pope ; but, now that languages are again
honored, they shed such light that all the world is astonished, and every one is forced to acknowledge that our
Gospel is almost as pure as that of the Apostles themselves." *

That Luther and the Reformers should have looked
upon the cultivation of such languages as Hebrew and
Greek and even of Latin as rendering a priceless service
to the cause of Christianity, was natural. That many
statesmen, feeling that in every land there must be among
the people an intimate relationship between intelligent
views respecting religious truths and of good government
believe that, independent of various other considerations, if the study of any languages is helpful in aiding
people to form right religious views, it indirectly renders
a State a great service. As the soldiers of an army
must be disciplined and prepared to do effective work
by being made to go through evolutions and to take part
in military manœuvres in many cases of no particular
use in themselves save for the possible benefit which the
State may some day realize from having a well-instructed

* "History of Reformation in Sixteenth Century" by J. H. Merle
D'Aubigné, pp. 173, 174.

army at its disposal, so the minds of a certain class of American citizens should be disciplined and prepared for usefulness in various ways to the State. " The learning Greek and Latin," Jefferson wrote in his book entitled " Notes on Virginia," " is going into disuse in Europe. I know not," he continued, " what their manners and customs may call for ; but it would be very ill-judged in us to follow their example in this instance. * * * I do not pretend that language is science. It is only an instrument for the attainment of science. But that time is not lost which is employed in providing tools for future operation." To these condensed views of Jefferson's let it here suffice to notice a letter which he wrote, under date of Aug. 24th, 1819, to John Brazier, a Greek scholar, respecting the value of a knowledge of the Greek and Latin languages to American youth. The letter illustrates some of the feelings which the venerable statesman experienced when providing instruction in Latin and Greek for a certain class of the youth of Virginia. He said : " Among the values of classical learning, I estimate the reading the Greek and Roman authors in all the beauties of their originals. And why should not this innocent and elegant luxury take its preëminent stand ahead of all those addressed merely to the senses. I think myself more indebted to my father for this than for all the other luxuries his cares and affections have placed within my reach ; and more now than when younger and more susceptible of delights from other sources. * * * To the moralist they are valuable, because they furnish ethical writings highly and justly esteemed. * * * To these original sources he must now, therefore, return, to recover the virgin purity of his religion. The lawyer finds in the Latin language the system of civil law, most conformable with the principles of justice of any which has ever yet been established among men, and from which much has been incorporated into our own. The physician as good a code of his art as has been given us to this day. * * * The statesman will find in these languages history, politics, mathematics, ethics, eloquence, love of country, to which he must add the sciences of his own day, for which of them should be unknown to him? And all the sciences must recur to the classical languages for the etymon, and sound understanding of their fundamental terms. For the merchant I should not say that the languages are a necessity. Ethics, mathematics, geography, political economy, history, seem to constitute the immediate foundations of his calling. The agriculturist needs ethics, mathematics, chemistry and natural philosophy. The mechanic the same. To them the languages are but ornament and comfort. I know it is often said there have been shining examples of men of great abilities in all the businesses of life, without any other science than what they had gathered from conversations and intercourse with the world. But who can say what these men would have been had they started in science, on the shoulders of a Demosthenes, or Cicero, of a Locke or Bacon, or a Newton? To sum the whole therefore, it may truly be said that the classical languages are a solid basis for most, and an ornament to all the sciences.

"I am warned by my aching fingers to close this hasty sketch, and to place here my last and fondest wishes for the advancement of our country in the useful sciences and arts, and my assurances of respect and esteem for the Reviewer of the Memoire on Modern Greek."

However often taught in a way subject to just criticism, Jefferson wished the study of the classics to be neither condemned nor eulogized save with discrimination.

The study of mathematics Jefferson held in high esteem. This important science has a history whose commencement goes backward for thousands of years. That a goodly number of cultured Greeks had made interesting progress in mathematical knowledge is well established. The Grecians, it is supposed by some writers, were indebted for this knowledge to the Egyptians. Others would suggest that there is a strong probability that the people of Hindustan and of China had possessed valuable mathematical knowledge in a remote age and that modern civilization is probably especially indebted to the Orient for its knowledge of algebra. The historic Roman Empire having become a wreck and various revolutions sweeping over a large part of Europe, the science of mathematics was ultimately led to seek, for some centuries, refuge from barbarism and neglect in the bosoms of Mussulmans. The professors of Islam, after conquering a territory twice or thrice the size of all Europe,—committing deeds of woful and almost incredible cruelty,—turned their furious zeal into the cause of learning. Without pausing to dwell upon the great universities and vast libraries which Mahometans, in the golden age of their religion reared, suffice it to say that the followers of Mahomet recognized the value to mankind of the science of mathematics. The great Caliph Almamon caused the relics of Grecian science to be sought for and translated into Arabic. As an absolute sovereign he exhorted his subjects to acquire an acquaintance with the volumes which he provided for their welfare. If the Arabians did not add as much to mathematical science as they did to some departments of useful learning, yet it is to them that modern civilization is supposed to be indebted for the mystic numerals—sometimes called Arabic figures—used in arithmetic and to a great extent

in all branches of mathematics. In the Arabic seats of
learning youth of various religious beliefs were sometimes
to be found enjoying a scholarly fellowship. Even Pope
Sylvester II., whom some Roman Catholic historians are
wont to regard as having been an uncommonly learned
man for his age, and who was even accused, by the ignorant populace by whom he was surrounded, of using magical arts, when a youth acquired a part of his education
at one of these Mahometan establishments of learning.
Even young women were to be seen in these universities
enjoying the same advantages as did their brothers.
Indeed it is recorded that the devoirs paid by the most
distinguished men to the ladies of their choice were often
as truly in homage of their intelligence as to the charms
of their beauty and of their virtue.* Unhappily, the
Saracens, after suffering greatly by the wars of the Cru-
sades, which misguided, so-called Christians waged against
them,—wars in which millions of lives were lost,—and
after enduring in Spain bitter persecution culminating in
half a million of them—at the instance of the Inquisition—being compelled to leave by way of the sea under
circumstances of cruelty so awful that the historian may
well shudder as he contemplates its enormity,—the impoverished Mussulmans made the fatal mistake of not adequately providing institutions of learning for their youth.

Without pausing to dwell upon the improvements which
have been made during recent centuries in mathematical
science, suffice it to say that in all lands and by all intelligent communities, the inestimable value to nations of an
acquaintance with the science of mathematics is in a good
degree appreciated. To the astronomer who turns his
telescope towards the abyss of space ; to the navigator who
recognizes the sun in its meridian splendor, and many of the

---

* Philobiblius' " Hist. of Education."

stars, as friendly sign-boards in the heavens to point out to him his way across the waters of the deep; to the engineer who builds any one of a thousand different structures useful to man; to the mechanician who makes inventions, sometimes of priceless worth to mankind,— and indirectly to every one who enjoys the privilege of living surrounded with the advantages of modern civilization,—the science of mathematics is a blessing worth preserving.

The University of Virginia was to have a department of mathematics in which youth, who chose to do so, could — sometimes laboriously indeed — prepare themselves for future usefulness to the world. There, the student's mind, if given to idle wandering, was to be disciplined and invigorated and given an exactitude of judgment on various subjects, while at the same time it was to be furnished with mystic knowledge which would aid it, sometimes, in philosophic enquiries of deep concern to humanity.

In the University of Virginia the various useful sciences which are embraced under the name of natural philosophy —including chemistry—were to be fearlessly, honestly, and earnestly taught. The authority of no man, whether he was celebrated, and had been held in as high esteem in mediæval institutions of learning as was Aristotle, or whether he was arbitrary and powerful as were certain hierarchs, was to be valued beyond its worth. Sciences were also to be taught about which Aristotle and Italian Pontiffs had been as ignorant as babes. Students were to be taught how to examine in an intelligent and just manner, by philosophical experiments, various phenomena worthy of the consideration of the godlike mind of man.

It is wonderfully strange that men and women, surrounded for thousands of years by the wonders of creation, should not have studied more closely than they have the handiwork of the Almighty and his ordainings, commonly called laws, respecting the government of the material universe. In all ages, doubtless, there have been enquiring minds who have looked with mysterious inquisitiveness at various phenomena. They have become fascinated as they have made, and in many instances recorded and classified, observations of one kind and another respecting the materials of which the world is composed. Thus each generation has added to the knowledge of mankind respecting the mysteries of creation. There have been, perhaps indeed, wonderful arts and sciences lost to the world because past generations have not always been as considerate as they should have been about providing for their transmission to their posterity, or, because the iron hand of despotism has been permitted to hold a withering sway over the best interests of the human family, yet the world to-day owes a debt of gratitude to many a student of bygone ages.

Millions upon millions of men and women have looked on clear nights at the glories of the varied heavenly canopy over them, as by ones and twos a vast assemblage of worlds have, to a certain extent, illumined the night. That the sun as it shone in its splendor in the day had certain peculiarities ;—that, for example, its rays warmed the earth and enabled the husbandman to accomplish much that without its friendly aid could not be accomplished by man, would be noticed and in time recorded. Though man with all his wonderful dormant capabilities lived until comparatively recent times without a telescope and without other marvellous instruments with which the civilized nations of to-day are blessed, and could not with the unaided eye know how orderly and interesting are the wonderful movements of the celestial bodies, could not, perhaps, realize the greatness of the distances from the earth to the planets and mighty suns—so-called fixed stars—upon which he gazed ; indeed though man before the invention of the telescope and other astronomical instruments could not know of many of the wonders of the illimitable heavens which are known at the present day to science, yet he could and did make and record many an observation which has added to the intellectual wealth of his fellow-man. Thoughtful men engaged in pastoral employment and looking at times after their flocks at night, or travellers obliged to sleep under the starry skies, would learn to note the time of night when certain brilliant luminaries would arise above the horizon or assume certain positions in the great heavens, and thus be enabled to assure themselves from time to time of the number of hours which would pass ere the welcome sun would cast his golden light upon their way. They would learn to welcome the brilliant star which heralded the morning. In their admiration of its beauty they would name it Venus. By collecting and intelligently grouping together facts respecting the celestial, bodies, valuable knowledge would be obtained. These studies would in time be called the science of astronomy. Age after age new and wonderful facts respecting the great orbs which sweep through space would be noted. For various reasons some of these observations would require hundreds or even thousands of years to satisfactorily make. Who would have believed that a time would come when youth in a very short time could learn from competent instructors in universities, truths—some of them of great practical utility to the human race—which had required ages of observations and study by men, some of whom were as gifted and devoted in labor as were Copernicus, Galileo, Kepler and Herschel, to discover !

Millions upon millions of people have realized that they were surrounded by mysterious phenomena. Why, when the heavens would grow black with the approaching storm, would the darkness sometimes be for an instant dissipated by the flash of the zigzagging lightning, which would perhaps strike to the earth a human being or in an instant shatter a lofty tree? When the man of science discovered what was the mysterious agent which was employed in producing lightning he was enabled, to a certain extent and in a miniature degree, to artificially produce lightning. He was enabled to even devise a way by which he could summon lightning from the clouds and command it to do man no injury. Men of science in time asked themselves why the agent which produces lightning and manifests itself in various ways should not be employed in performing useful services for men. Reasoning thus a student of the science of electricity gives the world, with aid wisely extended to him by the State, the art of electrical telegraphy, by means of which a person in one part of the world can instantaneously hold intercourse with his fellows in many other parts of the world. It is true that no electric telegraph such as exists to-day was known in Jefferson's time, but the statesman's penetrating wisdom realized that electrical phenomena were deserving of careful investigation by man, and so he especially named, in a communication to the Legislature of his native State, electricity as one of the subjects respecting which instruction was to be given in the university which he and his colleagues were rearing for the youth of Virginia.

The atmosphere, as a vast areal sea, covers the earth. Man, whose condition on the earth is really that of a creature at the bottom of a vast ocean, feels the air as it fans the sad or joyous brow, or in fury bows the forest or ruffles into angry billows the bosom of the ocean. Of what is it composed? Has it peculiarities which an intelligent being can find out? Strange it is that although ages upon ages have passed since man first breathed air, yet until Jefferson's friend Priestley in 1774 discovered that air was composed principally of the gases which are now known as oxygen and nitrogen,—a discovery of inestimably great importance, even often being a means of saving life,—it was unknown to the human race. Yet such knowledge as this, and many other highly important facts growing out of it, can now be taught in a few lessons, and convincing illustrations of its value be made apparent, in every well-regulated seat of learning in the world. The branch of natural philosophy called pneumatics treats not only of the properties of the air, but also of those of other elastic fluids. Without pausing to speak of various sciences in detail or of the greatness of the dormant capabilities of man, suffice it here to notice that each branch of the natural and physical sciences has had given to it a name of its own. For example, the student who receives instruction relating to the pressure and equilibrium of such unelastic, or almost unelastic, fluids as water or mercury, is said to be studying hydrostatics. The youth who turns his attention to that part of mechanics which treats of forces in action as opposed to forces in equilibrium is said to be studying dynamics. It is hardly necessary to more than simply state that each science is intimately related to all the other sciences. It would be difficult to calculate exactly which one of many sciences is the most important to the human race. The mechanician may give a valuable contribution to the wealth of his country, but perhaps he will find that the geologist by a single discovery of metalliferous deposits has opened up a new industry and has been enabled to add more even than he has himself to the well-being of society. But undoubtedly some departments of learning may at times be worthy of especial encouragement. Imperfectly educated statesmen, it is to be feared, too often do not realize the value to the world of the abstract sciences. It was not so, however, with Jefferson. In his sixth Annual Message to Congress, when urging the founding of a great national university at Washington, he said : "A public institution can alone supply those sciences which, though rarely called for, are yet necessary to complete the circle, all the parts of which contribute to the improvement of the country, and some of them to its preservation."

The well-informed student of the natural and physical sciences knows that the world has been created and is governed in many respects by wise economic Divine ordainings which are commonly, but somewhat loosely, called laws of nature. Who will duly estimate the value to mankind of every new secret of nature which the scientist discovers? Who will say that the Almighty has not ordained physical laws of which the wisest natural philosophers of this age are as yet unacquainted,—laws which when discovered will be made to minister in new ways to human needs. The man who discovers that certain phenomena are the result of certain causes may so arrange matters as to prevent one of the ordinarily acting causes from producing its effect. He can then, not improbably, witness a new phenomenon. By varied experiments he may learn how to produce results which may be of practical utility to society. If he succeeds in making known to the world an hitherto unknown ordinance which the Almighty has established, he deserves the gratitude of his fellows. The newly discovered law, the natural philosopher knows, will hold good, under like circumstances, in the most distant parts of the illimitable universe. For example, if under certain circumstances electrical phenomena are produced in this world, the natural philosopher who has observed the unity of plan,— the economic system—adopted by the Creator of the universe, knows that under the same circumstances electrical phenomena must take place throughout the wide domains of the universe of which this world forms a part.

One of the sciences which as far back as the year 1779, especially attracted Jefferson's attention and which he aided in having introduced into the University of William and Mary, with whose management he was officially connected, was chemistry. The science of modern chemistry was in his day scarcely more than in its infancy. He naturally wished it to be duly cultivated in Virginia's State University. Who will estimate the wealth which the cultivation of this science in modern times has brought to the United States. With its aid metals of great value are economically obtained from ores which hitherto were so refractory as to be useless. With the aid of chemistry steel can be made far more cheaply than iron was made in Jefferson's day. It is perhaps not too much to say that the art of economically making steel rails—which will stand ten or even sometimes over thirty times more wear and tear than will iron rails,—and of making steel ships which are far stronger as well as lighter than are iron vessels, and therefore capable of carrying heavier cargoes, is worth to the world hundreds of millions of dollars. In innumerable ways many useful arts may be said to owe their existence to the cultivation of the science of chemistry.

Of course the great educational establishment which Jefferson planned was to be provided with fitting instruments and apparatus with which to make very many scientific experiments. In mediæval times it was far too common in educational institutions to make no adequate provision for making experiments with the aid of scientific apparatus and thus establishing or correcting current statements respecting mysteries of nature. A youth might even fancy that it was a sin to suspect that some authorities such as Aristotle or certain Romish ecclesiastics were sometimes very far from being infallible in many of their utterances. In modern times youth are, or should be, taught that truth has nothing to fear by subjecting it to examination. Youths are encouraged to examine for themselves phenomena. However interesting it may be to listen to a traveller gifted with descriptive talents as he tells of scenes in distant lands, it is often still more instructive—and the knowledge acquired in often exacter,—to see these scenes with one's own eyes. However interesting it may sometimes be to listen to a man who tells of the wonders of the starry heavens, it is still more interesting to see these wonders when aided with instruments which have the mystic power of bringing one a thousand and more times nearer than mortals with unaided vision can approach to their wondrous presence. Often as the student has looked for the first time through a telescope, at the glories of the heavens, he has uttered a cry of wonder! Often, within the last few years, as students have been aided in their examination of celestial phenomena by the marvellous spectroscope, which science has in recent times put into their hands, they have seen with their own eyes the demonstration of wonders which some of the most distinguished men of science in the bygone ages have never known! By being introduced to philosophical instruments the students are made to feel at home in a workshop of science and are qualified to intelligently examine, in any part of the world, many of the wonders of creation. Let a professor be imagined telling a student about electrical phenomena and not possessing instruments with which to exhibit any of the electrical mysteries with which man is surrounded ! A happy event it was in the life of Benjamin Franklin that at the same time that he listened for the first time to an English gentleman discoursing upon electricity he was shown an electrical apparatus and invited to aid in making experiments. He became interested in the phenomena which he saw and supplied himself with similar electrical apparatus and made one experiment after another until he made discoveries respecting electricity of deep interest to the world.

Suppose students at a university are told of minute life which is sometimes brought to the surface of the earth by even worms, where human beings or animals which have died of various diseases have been buried, and should be told that this minute life could be artificially bred and in time introduced into the blood of man or of beast— somewhat as vaccine is introduced into the human system to protect it against small-pox,—to protect man and beast against the ravages of cholera or of various other diseases, —suppose that many equally wonderful facts should be told students,—they might listen indeed with attention or, it might be, with incredulity. Should a professor, however, by means of a microscope enable students to see for themselves varieties of minute life, they would have profounder and more practical views of the wonders revealed by science than they could possibly have if their lesson was not illustrated by suitable instruments.

Often with deep interest would nations hear that men were making physical experiments, if they realized the vastness of the extent to which such experiments in time would be likely to affect the well-being of mankind. For example, with what interest would they have watched Dr. Black when making experiments with water and steam by which he was enabled to give to the world the theory of latent heat—a theory which he was enabled to explain to Watt and to thus help him to give to the world the modern steam-engine. The philosophical instruments with which Dr. Black and Watt experimented in the venerable University of Glasgow indeed cost that celebrated seat of learning money, but the money thus expended was returned many times to the world. Doubtless there were once people who criticised Yale College for spending a considerable part of a fund which it received from the State of Connecticut, for philosophical apparatus. But who would do so after one of its students, Prof. Morse, had given to the world a mystic and invaluable electric telegraph?

One of the branches of learning which Jefferson considered especially worthy of a place in an American university was what he called the science of government. Man is a social being. He cannot long live separated from his fellows. A large number of people to live happily together and to realize the greatest advantage from their association need to make wise regulations for their common welfare. The history of the human race has shown that to organize a government such as will best promote the happiness of all who are interested in its maintenance, is a task requiring much wisdom The art of government has received the attention of at least some thoughtful minds in every generation for thousands of years. In past ages there have quite often been framed wise laws which have been a blessing to humanity. In many respects, however, the condition of man for thousands of years has been far from being as happy as it might have been. Often has it happened that he has been obliged to obey, to a greater or less extent as a slave, some military chieftain or some tyrant who by monstrous wickedness has succeeded in holding thousands of the human family in subjection. Even superstitions, degrading as they are false, have been by various means employed to help to accomplish the enslavement of the populace. Christianity when she came to earth in unsullied purity from the Father of the human race had the inspiration of heaven in her lips, the nobility and love of Divinity in her eye, the loveliest gentleness in her mien, and was the bearer of the kindliest blessings to humanity. But in her name a certain class of misguided men, who, often without knowing the truth themselves have in reality been teachers of false religions to the ignorant, have joined hands with tyrants with the understanding that each was to help the other in maintaining their unholy power. To speak of all the ills which man has suffered from civil and religious tyranny would be to present a dark part of the picture of the history of the world—only exceeded, perhaps, by the wild scenes of anarchy which have sometimes taken place among an unlettered and oppressed people.

Jefferson believed that man was endowed by his Creator with certain rights which should be regarded as inalienable prerogatives. For example he believed that every human being should be allowed to worship his Creator without being tormented with such an institution as was the Spanish Inquisition, and that nations had a right to frame for themselves just Constitutional forms of government. Every one blessed with intelligence can readily realize that his happiness and welfare can be affected by the government under which he lives. Whether he lives in a community in which the freedom of the press is not secured to him;—whether he is, or is not, protected by some such wise law as that known as *habeas corpus*, so

6

that he may not be arrested and kept in prison without an opportunity of defending himself;—in short whether he lives in a land in which the will of an irresponsible despot is allowed to be supreme, or whether he lives in a land in which he enjoys such rights as the Virginian statesman regarded as inalienable, is of momentous consequence to him.   A large part of the world, Jefferson believed, was in his day incapable, on account of their lack of intellectual culture, of enjoying such a form of government as exists in the United States.   He believed, however, that even the most degraded people were entitled to enjoy certain rights which would soon fit them to enjoy the blessing of civil liberty.   To fully define civil liberty is not as easy a work as some might suppose. The learned Dr. Lieber in one of his valuable treatises on "Government" * has held that, "it chiefly consists in guaranties (and corresponding checks), of those rights which experience has proved to be most exposed to interference, and which men hold dearest and most important." It will readily be seen that even according to this limited definition, the work of the statesman of a republic is of high importance to the human family and cannot be performed without a certain amount of wisdom.

When an enslaved and unlettered people rise against a despot and hurl him from the seat in which he has intrenched himself, scenes of frightful anarchy are sadly often followed in their turn by new scenes of despotism. The world has been wofully slow to learn the lesson which Jefferson learned by observing the revolutions of his day —in which millions of people perished,—that statesmen who wish to meliorate the condition of the enslaved should feel it to be an indispensable part of their noble work to provide for the enlightenment of the intellects of

* Vol. i., p. 54,

their degraded countrymen. He had seen deeds of awful violence and bloodshed perpetrated by well-meaning patriots in different lands in their attempts to depose despotism and to secure to their countrymen the blessings of good government. He had known of many martyrs who had given their lives for, as they supposed, liberty, when they themselves were imperfectly qualified by education and knowledge to be reformers. He had thought upon the condition of the hundred and fifty or more millions of the people of Africa who live in wretchedness and amidst constant danger of strifes,—of wars in which hundreds of thousands of prisoners are yearly sold into hopeless slavery—and had even calmly considered the practicability of America's giving to Africa arts and sciences and the blessings of civil liberty and of self-government. He knew that in no land were highly learned statesmen born in a day. He had mingled with statesmen whom he had seen do a work for America which surpassed in beneficence the work of many of the greatest philanthropists whose deeds have been preserved in history. He felt that the statesman no less truly than the Christian minister could labor for the happiness and welfare of mankind.

The legislator is invested with power which may injure or benefit nations,—may sometimes be even so great that he may be enabled to bequeath ruin, or much happiness, to posterity. Wide indeed is the range of objects with which he should be conversant, and long and laboriously must he labor if he would wish to act the part of the noblest ideal of a statesman. He must visit libraries, he must at times collect statistics by which the better to understand social tendencies and phenomena as well as to have some knowledge of the resources of his own and of foreign nations. He may even have to travel in his own and in foreign lands to make observations of various kinds which may enlarge the range of his thoughts. He will at times have occasion to summon to his aid the facts brought to light by many sciences and to acquaint himself with many a lesson to the world recorded on the pages of history. Useful and noble should the science of legislation be esteemed to be by American citizens. Upon it one may almost say all other sciences depend to a great extent for their life and cherishment. In the statesman's hands are sometimes placed the safeguards of life, of liberty, of letters, as well as of the useful arts and sciences.

Jefferson believed that the best interests of the world especially demanded that America should be possessed of able statesmen. He believed that the golden age of American destiny was not in the past but in the future. He believed that European governments should not be allowed, under any pretence, to acquire territory on the American continent or to acquire any islands which lie off its coasts. He realized that a wise American policy should be carried out by which English, and not European languages, would spread over the American continent—a policy which would make it unnecessary for the people of America to maintain large standing armies and which would make the likelihood of war breaking out between the new and the old world very much less than would be the case if unwise artificial barriers between parts of America—some of them under the domination of European governments—were allowed to exist—barriers which would give rise to border-difficulties and mar the bright vision, which the people of the United States should cherish, of a continent consecrated to civil liberty and to a wise constitutional self-government. He looked upon permanent national debts with abhorrence. He felt that republics should rid themselves of national debts as soon as practicable,—indeed he believed that one generation should not fetter another with debt. He realized that if the citizens of a commonwealth wish to enjoy certain advantages they should raise money needed to successfully carry out their wishes and that every member of a community should cheerfully bear his share of necessary public expenses. A nation at times has its power, its wealth and happiness increased in the degree in which taxes are wisely imposed and justly collected. It often thus receives far more than an equivalent for its sacrifices. When a nation has a debt it not only has to pay a stated interest on its debt,—which of itself may be to a no inconsiderable extent a drain upon its resources even in ordinary times, to say nothing of critical periods in its history,—but it has to pay what may be called a second percentage by paying an army of officials to collect the revenues out of which to pay the interest,—which it cannot help sometimes doing in a way vexatious and costly to the people. There was a particular reason which made Jefferson hope that American statesmen would endeavor to protect the United States from being heavily burdened with debt. He had a cherished hope that the time would come when the United States Government would be enabled to afford to systematically raise a revenue to be collected by duties on imported luxuries, for the express purpose of promoting the interests of education throughout the length and breadth of the Republic. When he himself was President of the United States he had signed bills giving millions of acres of land to the cause of public schools and of colleges, but he keenly felt—as will be noticed in another division of this volume—that the national government should yearly and on a systematic and judicious

plan help every section of the Republic to provide for
the intellectual culture of youth. He would have no
American have any excuse for growing up illiterate,
and he would have no one allowed to vote who
could not read. He was wont to cherish a plan of government by which every community was, in a large measure, within a certain sphere, to govern itself. He justly
regarded, however, such a subject as that of education in
a great republic to be of national concern no less truly
than of local interest. Grand indeed were some of Jefferson's hopes for his country's future. No wonder that
he wished American youth blessed with opportunities to
do so to study the philosophy of government and to
qualify themselves to help to enable the Republic of the
Western Hemisphere to realize in times of peace and of
war its grandest and noblest possibilities!

That the American statesmen who were Jefferson's
contemporaries were remarkable for their wisdom respecting civil liberty will doubtless be conceded by even many
Europeans. They welcomed well-written books on the
philosophy of self-government. Thanks to the considerate and very valuable gifts of some Puritan friends in
England, the library of Harvard College was especially
rich in such a class of literature. The English Baptist-
Puritan, Thomas Hollis, who made many valuable gifts
to Harvard College, wrote feelingly to Mr. Mayhew, saying: " More books *especially on government* are going for
New England. Should these go safe it is hoped that no
principal books on that *first* subject will be wanting in
Harvard College, from the days of Moses to these times."
During the war of Independence it was customary for
the legislature of Massachusetts to annually invite one
of the clergymen of the Commonwealth to preach a discourse to them. These sermons have recently been

wisely published in book form and are a very valuable contribution to the interpretation of passages in the Bible on government. They point out the duty, and the limit to the obligation, of citizens of a commonwealth to obey rulers. One could wish that even in this day such a book could find its way into the hands of every thoughtful lover of liberty. Among the patriots of the Revolutionary period there was a widespread feeling that in a republic it was of high importance that youth should have broad and right views respecting the philosophy of government. As one especially likes to be enabled to hear such worthies express for themselves their views respecting such a subject, it may be proper to here pause for a moment to duly note some of them. Washington, who notwithstanding his many occupations found time to act for years as the Chancellor of the University of William and Mary, very earnestly urged upon the Republic the importance of teaching youth the science of government. In the last Annual Message which he, as President of the United States, delivered to Congress, after recommending the founding of a great national university in the city of Washington, he added : " A primary object of such a national institution should be, the education of our youth in the science of government. In a republic, what species of knowledge can be equally important, and what duty more pressing, on its legislature, than to patronize a plan for communicating it to those who are to be the future guardians of the liberties of the country." When Washington's will was opened it was found that after making provision for several institutions of learning, and pointing out how he wished a part of his estate to be devoted to aiding a national university, if Congress should decide to found such a centre of learning, he especially spoke of the valuable opportunity it would afford to youth to acquire, as he expressed it, "knowledge in the principles of politics and good government." This recommendation of Washington to provide for a great national university which would have a department in which to help to rear learned American statesmen was twice repeated by James Madison.

As early as Jan. 1st, 1769, the learned Benjamin Franklin had written to Lord Kames, saying: "I am glad to find you are turning your thoughts to political subjects, and particularly to those of money, taxes, manufacture and commerce. The world is yet much in the dark on these important points; and many mischievous mistakes are continually made in the management of them. Most of our acts of Parliament, for regulating them, are, in my opinion, little better than political blunders, owing to ignorance of the science, or to the designs of crafty men, who mislead the legislature, proposing something under the specious appearance of public good, while the real aim is to sacrifice that to their private interest. I hope a good deal of light may be thrown on these subjects by your sagacity and acuteness." Such reflections as these by Franklin were practical and earnest. In 1777, John Jay, who at that dark period of American history was Chief-Justice of the State of New York, at the first sitting of the court at Kingston after the adoption of the first Constitution of the United States or Colonies, in a charge to a grand-jury, said: "But let it be remembered that whatever marks of wisdom, experience, and patriotism there may be in your constitution, yet, like the beautiful symmetry, the just proportions, and elegant forms of our first parents before their Maker breathed into them the breath of life, it is yet to be animated, and till then, may indeed excite admiration, but will be of no use,—from the people it must receive its spirit, and by them be quickened. Let virtue, honor, the love of liberty and of science, be, and remain, the soul of this constitution ; and it will become the source of great and extensive happiness to this and future generations. Vice, ignorance, and want of vigilance, will be the only enemies able to destroy it. Against these provide, and, of these, be forever jealous. Every member of the State ought diligently to read and study the constitution of his country, and teach the rising generation to be free. By knowing their rights, they will sooner perceive when they are violated, and be the better prepared to defend and assert them." *

Very much in the same spirit as the learned Jay spoke to the people of New York the patriotic Dr. Ramsay spoke to the people of South Carolina. On the 4th of July, 1778, in an oration which he delivered in Charleston, he said : " The arts and sciences which languished under the low prospects of subjection, will now raise their drooping heads, and spread far and wide, till they have reached the remotest parts of this untutored continent. It is the happiness of our present constitution, that all offices be open to men of merit, of whatever rank or condition, and that even the reins of State may be held by the son of the poorest man, if possessed of abilities equal to the important station." In his oration he spoke of the time " when the single NO! of a king three thousand miles distant was sufficient to repeal any of our laws, however useful and salutary ; and when we were bound in all cases whatsoever by men, in whose election we had no vote, and who had an interest opposed to ours, and over whom we had no control." Dr. Ramsay also said : " We are

---

* See this eloquent charge of Jay's in " Principles of the Revolution," by Hezekiah Niles, p. 182.

no more to look up for the blessings of government to hungry courtiers, or the needy dependents of British nobility ; but must educate our children for these exalted purposes. When subjects, we had scarce any other share in government, but to obey the arbitrary mandates of a British Parliament. But honor, with her dazzling pomp, interest with her golden lure, and patriotism with her heartfelt satisfaction, jointly call upon us now to qualify ourselves and posterity for the bench, the army, the navy, the learned professions, and all the departments of civil government." He pointed out that, " in our present happy system, the poorest school-boy may prosecute his studies with increasing ardor, from the prospect, that in a few years he may, by his improved abilities, direct the determinations of public bodies on subjects of the most stupendous consequence." In this oration Dr. Ramsay declared that " A few years will now produce a much greater number of men of learning and abilities, than we could have expected for ages, in our boyish state of minority, guided by the leading-strings of a parent country."

He then added, " How trifling the objects of deliberation that came before our former legislative assemblies, compared with the great and important matters, on which they must now decide." Dr. Ramsay further ably pointed out that " the weight of each State, in the continental scale will ever be proportioned to the abilities of its representative in Congress. Hence an emulation will take place, each contending with the other, which shall produce the most accomplished statesmen. From the joint influence of all these combined causes, it may strongly be presumed, that literature will flourish in America, and that our independence will be an illustrious epoch, remarkable for the spreading and improvement of science.

"A zeal for the promoting of learning unknown in the days of our subjection, has already begun to overspread the United States. In the last session of our Assembly, three societies were incorporated for the laudable purpose of erecting seminaries of education. Nor is the noble spirit confined to us alone. Even now, amidst the tumults of war, literary institutions are forming all over the continent, which must light up such a blaze of knowledge, as cannot fail to burn, and catch, and spread, until it has finally illuminated with rays of science the remotest retreats of ignorance and barbarity." [*]

To the eloquent words of a past century which have just been quoted it may here be noticed that at the time when the Constitution of the United States was being framed there was a feeling among distinguished American statesmen that the literature on the science of government, worthy of a subject so important to the cause of liberty, was sadly meagre. Among Washington's papers, after his death were found what might be called a lengthy manuscript written in his own handwriting giving "An Abstract of the General Principles of Ancient and Modern Confederacies," with comments on the "vices" which history had shown had been by time developed in them. It is held by a biographer of James Madison that Madison was the author of this work and that it had been submitted to Washington who had copied it for his own benefit. The work showed an amount of research which would have been creditable to any scholar. John Adams who was a foreign minister when the Constitution of the United States was about being framed wrote—too hurriedly to give the attention to style which he would fain have ·given his work, but in time to enable

---

[*] Ibid., 375-383.

him to take part in the exchange of views respecting
a form of government suitable for the American continent,—his "History of the Principal Republics of the
World." In this valuable contribution to literature, he
collected, with, one might almost say marvellous industry
which indicated a wide range of reading, many historical
facts. He took occasion to draw attention to the importance to nations of studies respecting the art of government. He wrote: "The arts and sciences in general, during
the three or four last centuries, have had a regular course
of progressive improvement. The inventions in mechanic
arts, the discoveries in natural philosophy, navigation, and
commerce, and the advancement of civilization, and humanity, have occasioned changes in the condition of the
world, and the human character, which would have astonished the most refined nations of antiquity. A continua-
tion of similar exertions is every day rendering Europe
more and more like one community or single family.
Even in the theory and practice of government, in all the
simple monarchies, considerable improvements have been
made. The checks and balances of republican governments have been in some degree adopted by the courts of
princes." Adams, as he proceeded, after alluding briefly
to the improvements in government that had been made
in England and adopted in the United States, added:
"In so general a refinement, or more properly, reformation of manners and improvement in knowledge, is it not
unaccountable that the knowledge of the principles and
construction of free governments, in which the happiness
of life, and even the further progress of improvement in
education and society, in knowledge and virtue, are so
deeply interested, should have remained at a full stand
for two or three thousand years?" As he continued, he
alluded to his own work. He wrote: "If the publication

of these papers should contribute to turn the attention of the younger gentlemen of letters in America to this kind of inquiry, it will produce an effect of some importance to their country. The subject is the most interesting that can engage the understanding or the heart ; for whether the end of man, in this stage of his existence, be enjoyment or improvement, or both, it can never be attained so well in a bad government as in a good government."

Enough has now been said to illustrate how desirable it was believed to be by distinguished statesmen of a bygone generation, that American youth should study the comprehensive science of government. It is pleasant to be able to state that in modern times such branches of study are especially taught in Columbia College, in Cornell University, and in a number of institutions of learning in the United States and that the Constitution of the United States is studied in quite a thorough manner in a goodly number of the high schools of the land. Still it is to be feared that American youth are too often satisfied with simply manifesting their patriotism by thoughtlessly walking in some torch-light procession or in some other equally unintellectual manner. Too many young men are unable to intelligently speak upon affairs of national importance which are likely to influence for good or evil the history of the American continent and the destiny of coming generations. That civil and religious liberty will have, from time to time, battles to fight on the American continent may be considered almost certain. Jefferson felt that young men should be encouraged even in the courses of reading in which they should, for their own pleasure, be led to engage, to be duly influenced by patriotic and philanthropic considerations. Writing to Kosciuszko under date of Feb. 26th, 1810, he spoke of the young men to whom he had thrown open his large library. He wrote: " In advising the course of their reading, I endeavor to keep their attention fixed on the main objects of all science, the freedom and happiness of man. So that coming to bear a share in the councils and government of their country, they will keep ever in view the sole objects of all legitimate government."

There is one branch of useful literature which Jefferson regarded as of vital importance to citizens of a republic and which he believed should be taught in each of the divisions of the school system which he had draughted for Virginia. This branch of useful learning is history. He wished youth to be introduced to historical studies and to be thus helped to form a taste for elevating reading. One of the ways in which man differs from the brute creation is that he is able to record for his own welfare and for that of his posterity his own experience and observations. Every human heart has an unwritten history of its own ; a part of which is of a personal nature and is not to be revealed save to the Divine Searcher of all hearts, but much of a man's experience may be of great value to some fellow voyager through life. One can but feel at times a sense of sadness as he realizes how short in the eternity of time is a human life. What observations one can make in life respecting his fellow-mortals and of various scenes in the affairs of a great community are often, necessarily, incomplete and often superficial— indeed the truth in many instances may be entirely different from everything that had been suspected. Strictly speaking very much—if one may not indeed say mostly all—knowledge is derived from recorded observations made by men who have had exceptional opportunities for collecting reliable facts. Often a noble wish to be useful to at least some members of the great human family has impelled a considerate person to carefully record facts respecting some events about which he believes it to be important that others should be informed,—indeed upon some of which momentous events to nations have hinged. One might endeavor to imagine the feelings which have prompted various monumental piles to be erected and picture-writing and hieroglyphics to be engraved on rocks, but suffice it to say that the historian has, at times, been enabled to lift the veil which hides the past from the vision of the living, and to cause a panorama to pass before the statesman's eyes which has been instrumental in admonishing him respecting the course which he should take if he would avoid mistakes made by men in bygone times, and of showing him how to promote the best interests of his country.

The historian aims at presenting correctly many facts respecting human affairs with some degree of completeness and as a whole. He sometimes reveals secrets that the public had never suspected. He gives information, which he has perhaps spent much of his life in collecting, which enables one to sometimes view various important affairs from a vantage-ground of great value to them. If it be true that prejudices have their rise in false views of things, he helps to remove these wrong prepossessions in the kindest of ways.

If certain despotic governments by an artful policy prevent the great mass of the people from studying history, all the more important it is that American youth should be early helped to form a taste for historical reading. As a man looks into the "ghostly shadows of bygone ages" he sees how some men have made mistakes in life and how others have acted the part of heroes. As he reviews the records of the long struggle between despotism and liberty he may well have his heart glow with a warmer appreciation of such liberties as he enjoys. As he reviews such fascinating historical volumes as those of the eloquent Motley's " Rise of the Dutch Republic," he sees how baneful despots can be to a people's welfare, and gets some faint idea of how terrible has been the struggle between superstition and liberty, and instinctively is apt to feel how much he has to be thankful that Church and State are not united in his own land, and how dangerous to the best interests of a free people it would be to introduce sectarian despotism into American institutions.

Happily many historians have written in a style so interesting that one has but to be introduced to their volumes to be deeply interested in them. Thoughtful young men may well have it impressed upon their minds that the highest ideal of a noble youth forbids that history should be read merely for the pleasure of learning interesting events in the lives of men and women, and of nations. It should be read, at times, in a philosophic manner and various thoughtful deductions from the events of the past should be made and laid to heart. It was not merely in desultory reading of history that Jefferson would have American youth engage,—although even such reading might bring with it many a blessing and be probably vastly better than simply reading ordinary novels,—but he wished them to have a purpose in view. He wished them to read with the noble and patriotic object of the better qualifying themselves to promote the liberties and the happiness of their fellow-citizens. There are doubtless various ways of reading history with profit. One of many methods may here be mentioned. A student, after a proper preparatory course of studies by which some of the cardinal points and great epochs which have characterized the drama of history have passed somewhat briefly before him,—thus giving him some idea of the lives of leading nations as a whole,—could be advised when reading history by himself, to at times do so with well-defined and specific ends in view. Let him propose to himself a question to be solved, a doubt to be proved well founded or otherwise, a problem to be examined, the satisfying of his curiosity respecting some points upon which his mind should be well established. Let him be taught to philosophize as he reads;—to thoughtfully form his own inferences of the effects of certain forms of government and of various laws on the mechanism of society and upon the current of a nation's life. One might propound to himself such questions as: What is the influence exerted on civilization by different systems of religious belief? What form of religion is most friendly to liberty, to letters, and to the arts and sciences? Are there any facts in history which would justify an American or any friend of civil and religious liberty, dreading that the wiles of priestcraft in commonwealths may very injuriously affect the best interests of the people? What are the causes which have been instrumental in making any particular nation great or degraded? One who seeks light upon subjects such as these, and upon many others which might be named, and seeks for facts which will help him in forming right conclusions respecting them with something of the earnestness with which an excited Indian seeks his game, finds that one series after another of interesting and instructive events pass before his vision. Many a fond illusion will be dispelled while patriotism is enlightened. As when a man travels in the interior of the American continent to inform himself respecting mines from which mineral wealth is obtained, will, often in a peculiarly pleasant manner, incidently see much varied scenery,—

at one time travelling over thirsty plains, at another time finding himself surrounded by landscapes beautiful and grand beyond all that he could have imagined, will, it may be, have the pleasure of having his eyes attracted to some sections of country which he may discover are worthy of a special visit on some future occasion, so whoever will set out to historically examine any one of many subjects such as have been suggested, will incidently—sometimes in a very pleasant manner — learn much about varied scenes, and experiences, through which human beings have passed. His mind will be enriched with an experience which had he had to depend upon his own generally disconnected observations of society, he might not be enabled to learn, were his life prolonged a thousand years.

Should a person have his curiosity excited over such a question as, Why do arts flourish more in one land than in another? he would consult books and libraries in what might appear to a looker-on to be a somewhat random manner, but in reality in a way at once instructive and entertaining—and occasionally even highly fascinating. He would perhaps at the same time find that his studies were becoming more and more comprehensive and that he had been led insensibly into paths of historical research from which he could take, in a peculiarly pleasurable manner, a wide survey of the vast drama of human progress and be enabled to philosophically detect many of the causes which influence for good or evil the best interests of the human race. If he is honest in his desire to truly satisfy his own mind he will learn to examine the authorities upon which different historians base their statements respecting various important subjects and confirm or revise or even reverse the judgment of some of the narrators of history. By such exercise his mental faculties will often be strengthened. He will learn to appreciate at their proper value writers who instead of referring to their authorities for the truthfulness of some of their questionable statements, remark, in a loose manner, that their information has been collected from "too many sources to name them." A well-taught student may be taught to have a carefulness of thought which an uninstructed person sadly often does not possess.

Should the question be raised, What is the weightiest of all reasons for teaching history in public schools? perhaps it might justly be answered that independent of the historical facts learned by youth in their school days, are in many cases, to be especially prized the good results which flow from youths being introduced to such an elevating branch of learning and helped in forming a taste for such literature. Doubtless many a thoughtful person who has spent many a well-employed hour in looking over the records of the past, will testify that he might have remained a stranger to the pleasures and advantages flowing from such study, had he not happily been made acquainted with historical books in his school days. Jefferson felt that, even if youth should do no more than read some well-chosen selections from the histories of various countries, including that of their own, some of them would derive much benefit from doing so. In the volume which he published entitled, "Notes on Virginia," he spoke of the educational system which he had draughted for his native State. In words somewhat similar to those which he had addressed in 1779 to the Legislature of Virginia, he spoke of the great importance of a commonwealth's supporting a public-school system. Alluding to the proposed school system he said: "Of the views of this law none is more important, none more legitimate, than that of rendering the people the safe, as they are the ultimate guardians of their own liberty. For this purpose the reading in the first stage, where they [a certain class of the youth of Virginia] will receive their whole education, is proposed, as has been said, to be chiefly historical." He then added: "History by apprizing them of the past will enable them to judge of the future; it will avail them of the experience of other times and other nations; it will qualify them as judges of the actions and designs of men; it will enable them to know ambition under every disguise it may assume; and knowing it to defeat its views. In every government on earth is some trace of human weakness, some germ of corruption and degeneracy, which cunning will discover, and wickedness insensibly open, cultivate, and improve. Every government degenerates when trusted to the rulers of the people alone. The people themselves are its only safe depositories. And to render even them safe, their minds must be improved to a certain degree."

The views of Jefferson respecting the importance of history being taught in the public schools of a republic will be more and more seen to have great force the more one realizes the value of historical knowledge to the cause of liberty and of good government. In a republic such as the United States, in which all citizens may exert an influence in shaping the destiny of the American continent, and in influencing the measures of legislatures and of Executives, a knowledge of history should be widely diffused among the people. In the noblest days of the great Roman Republic, it was held to be a very important matter that the youth who wished to qualify themselves for stations of power in public life and to employ themselves usefully in the administration of public affairs, should at least be acquainted with the history of their own country. A time came, however, when Marius

could sarcastically intimate that the citizens of the great
Roman Republic had so far degenerated, that their distinguished men did not begin to read history until they
were already elevated to high offices of state. He declared that "they first obtained the employment, and
then bethought themselves of the qualifications for the
necessary discharge of it."

The evil in the Republic of Rome which Marius sadly
noticed, it is to be feared exists, to too great an extent, in
some parts of the United States. In the address which
Garfield delivered on June 16th, 1867,—to which allusion
has been made,—he criticised very earnestly the neglect
of the study of history by the rising generation in the
United States. He spoke earnestly of the lack of historical knowledge which was prevalent in the United
States at the breaking out of their great civil war. As he
continued, he said : " Seven years ago there was scarcely
an American college in which more than four weeks out
of the four years' course was devoted to studying the
government and history of the United States. For this
feature of our educational system I have neither respect
nor toleration. It is far inferior to that of Persia three
thousand years ago. The uncultivated tribes of Greece,
Rome, and Germany surpassed us in this respect. Grecian children were taught to reverence and emulate the
virtues of their ancestors. Our educational forces are so
wielded as to teach our children to admire most that
which is foreign, and fabulous, and dead. I have recently
examined the catalogue of a leading New England college, in which the geography and history of Greece and
Rome are required to be studied five terms ; but neither
the history nor the geography of the United States is
named in the college course, or required as a condition of
admission. The American child must know all the

classic rivers, from the Scamander to the yellow Tiber; must tell the length of the Appian Way, and of the canal over which Horace and Virgil sailed on their journey to Brundusium ; but he may be crowned with baccalaureate honors without having heard, since his first moment of Freshman life, one word concerning the one hundred and twenty-two thousand miles of coast and river navigation, the six thousand miles of canal, and the thirty-five thousand miles of railroad, which indicate both the prosperity and the possibilities of his own country.   It is well to know the history of those magnificent nations whose origin is lost in fable, and whose epitaphs were written a thousand years ago ; but if we cannot know both, it is far better to study the history of our own nation, whose origin we can trace to the freest and noblest aspirations of the human heart,—a nation that was formed from the hardiest, purest, and most enduring elements of European civilization,—a nation that, by its faith and courage, has dared and accomplished more for the human race in a single century than Europe accomplished the first thousand years of the Christian era."   Garfield, after pointing out how easy it would be to give invaluable instruction in history even in common schools, added : " After the bloody baptism from which the nation has arisen to a higher and nobler life, if this shameful defect in our system of education be not speedily remedied, we shall deserve the infinite contempt of future generations.   I insist," he continued, " that it should be made an indispensable condition of graduation in every American college, that the student must understand the history of this continent since its discovery by Europeans ; the origin and history of the United States, its constitution of government, the struggles through which it has passed, and the rights and duties of citizens who are to determine its

destiny and share its glory.". Long before Garfield spoke
these words, however, Jefferson had arranged that history
should be studied in the quiet shades of the University
of Virginia.

To arrange wise courses of study for youth having
different aims in life was a subject which might well
interest a parent, or a statesman, who believed that a
good system of education should be made the " keystone
of the arch of our government." How to most wisely
select and group together courses of study for the suitors
of knowledge in a State university for Virginia occupied,
at times, Jefferson's thoughts for at least well-nigh half a
century. Writing, under date of July 5th, 1814, to the
already venerable John Adams, he sought counsel respecting the subject of his patriotic contemplation.
" When sobered by experience," he wrote, " I hope our
successors will turn their attention to the advantages of
education. I mean of education on the broad scale, and
not that of the petty *academies*, as they call themselves,
which are starting up in every neighborhood, and where
one or two men, possessing Latin and sometimes Greek,
a knowledge of the globes, and the first six books of
Euclid, imagine and communicate this as the sum of
science. They commit their pupils to the theatre of the
world, with just taste enough of learning to be alienated
from industrial pursuits, and not enough to do service in
the ranks of science. We have some exceptions, indeed.
I presented one to you lately, and we have some others.
But the terms I use are general truths. I hope the necessity will, at length, be seen of establishing institutions
here, as in Europe, where every branch of science, useful
at this day, may be taught in its highest degree. Have
you ever turned your thoughts to the plan of such an
institution ? I mean of the specification of the particular

sciences of real use in human affairs, and how they might
be so grouped as to require so many professors only as
might bring them within the views of a just but enlightened economy. I should be happy in a communication
of your ideas on this problem, either loose or digested."
The question upon which Adams was requested to give
his counsel is one which deserves far more attention by intelligent and patriotic American heads of families than it
too generally receives. As the thoughtful Jefferson had
sought to surround himself by wise counsellors when engaging in momentous affairs of State, so he, as is revealed
by his letters, sought to compare the views of eminent
men of learning with his own respecting this highly important question. To the distinguished Thomas Cooper
—an English professor who was connected with Columbia College and with other seats of learning,—he wrote
under date of Jan. 16th, 1814: " I have long had under
contemplation and been collecting material, for the plan
of a university in Virginia which should comprehend all
the sciences useful to us and none others." To the learned
Cooper, Jefferson on the following 25th of August again
wrote: "To be prepared for this new establishment, I
have taken some pains to ascertain those branches which
men of sense, as well as of science, deem worthy of cultivation. To the statements which I have obtained from
other sources, I should value an addition of one from
yourself. You know our country, its pursuits, its faculties, its relations with others, its means of establishing and
maintaining an institution of science. * * * Will you then
so far contribute to our views as to consider this subject,
to make a statement of the branches of science which you
think worthy of being taught, as I have before said, at this
day, and in this country?"

Even when Jefferson was President of the United
States and weighed down with the many duties devolv-

ing upon one holding that high office, and having no inconsiderable part of his hours of rest taken up by his voluntary labors as Chairman of the Board of Education of Washington, his thoughts reverted to his cherished wish to see a worthy State Academic retreat secured to the youth of Virginia. Under date of Feb. 5th, 1803, he wrote asking counsel, to Prof. Pictet of the University of Geneva—an establishment which he years before, in a letter to Washington, had characterized as one of the "eyes of Europe." In this letter he said: "I have still had constantly in view to propose to the Legislature of Virginia the establishment of one [University] on as large a scale as our present circumstances would require or bear. But as yet no favorable moment has occurred. In the meanwhile I am endeavoring to procure materials for a good plan. With this view I am to ask the favor of you to give me a sketch of the branches of science taught in your college, how they are distributed among the professors, that is to say, how many professors there are, and what branches of science are allotted to each professor, and the days and hours assigned to each branch. Your successful experience in the distribution of business will be a valuable guide to us, who are without experience. I am sensible I am imposing on your goodness a troublesome task; but I believe every son of science feels a strong and disinterested desire of promoting it in every part of the earth, and it is the consciousness as well as confidence in this which emboldens me to make the present request."

The more one critically follows Jefferson's labors in founding a university in Virginia, the more he is apt to be surprised at the deep and long-continued thought which he gave to the cherished enterprise. In 1776, notwithstanding the excitement which attended the differences between Great Britain and her Colonies, he had been appointed by the Legislature of Virginia to take part with some distinguished associates in revising the code of the State. In a part of the revised code—a part which he himself draughted and presented to the Legislature during the war of the Revolution,—was an educational bill which carefully provided that a university should form a part of Virginia's school system. When Washington was President of the United States, Jefferson had submitted to him in a letter—which has happily been preserved and published among Washington's papers,—a plan by which Washington was to give a quite large sum of money, which he contemplated presenting to the cause of education, to an undertaking by which the University of Geneva, which had been closed by the French Revolution, was to be transplanted to the United States. He had also in a private correspondence with distinguished friends, proposed that the Legislature of Virginia should undertake to transplant in a body to Virginia all the professors of the University of Geneva. In the book which he had published he had written of the proposal of founding a State university in Virginia in a way which showed that he had the educational interests of his native State at heart. To the learned Joseph Priestley on Jan. 18th, 1800, he wrote a letter requesting the distinguished scientist to favor him with his views respecting the course of culture which it would be wise for a republic to provide for its youth. He said : " We wish to establish in the upper country, and more centrally for the State, an University on a plan so broad and liberal and *modern*, as to be worth patronizing with the public support, and to be a temptation to the youth of other States to come and drink of the cup of knowledge, and fraternize with us. The first step is to obtain a good plan ; that is, a judicious selection of the sciences, and a practicable grouping of some of them together, and ramifying of others, so as to adopt the professorships to our uses and our means." The Virginian statesman, after paying a high compliment to Priestley, continued : " To you therefore we address our solicitations, and to lessen to you as much as possible the ambiguities of our object, I will venture even to sketch the sciences which seem useful and practicable for us, as they occur to me while holding my pen. Botany, chemistry, zoölogy, anatomy, surgery, medicine, natural philosophy, agriculture, mathematics, astronomy, geography, politics, commerce, history, ethics, law, arts, fine arts. This list is imperfect because I make it hastily, and because I am unequal to the subject. * * * I do not propose to give you all this trouble merely of my own head, that would be arrogance. It has been the subject of consultation among the ablest and highest characters of our State, who only wait for a plan to make a joint and I hope a successful effort to get the thing carried into effect." Without pausing to speak of Priestley's views—some of which he had published in England,—it may here be incidentally stated, that this distinguished scientist was a friend of Prof. Small and of James Watt. Whatever may be thought of some writings of his on theological subjects, his services to the world as a scientist had been very great, and he had had a valuable experience as an instructor of youth. From many and varied-sources suggestions respecting useful courses of instruction for American youth were to be received.

In the year 1814 as Jefferson and others were engaged in founding, at their own expense, the college which ultimately became the University of Virginia, Jefferson under date of Sept. 7th, 1814, in a long letter to Peter Carr,*

---

* See " Early History of the University of Virginia," J. W. Randolph, Richmond, Virginia, 1856, pp. 384–390.

unfolded his views respecting public education in Virginia. He took occasion to speak of the various grades of schools which should be provided and went into details respecting the courses of studies for which provision should be made in the State College or University—courses which are too numerous to here present. Let it then suffice to note some unique features of the plan of education which he had at heart. Before doing so, however, the introductory part of this letter—a letter which was brought to the attention of the Legislature of Virginia and was so highly esteemed that it was published at the State's expense, and was widely distributed,—may here be given. The statesman wrote : " On the subject of the academy or college proposed to be established in our neighborhood, I promised the trustees that I would prepare for them a plan, adapted, in the first instance, to our slender funds, but susceptible of being enlarged, either by their own growth or by accession from other quarters.

" I have long entertained the hope that this, our native State, would take up the subject of education, and make an establishment, either with or without incorporation into that of William and Mary, where every branch of science, deemed useful at this day, should be taught in its highest degree. With this view, I have lost no occasion of making myself acquainted with the organization of the best seminaries in other countries, and with the opinions of the most enlightened individuals, on the subject of the sciences worthy of a place in such an institution. In order to prepare what I have promised our trustees, I have lately revised these several plans with attention ; and I am struck with the diversity of arrangement observable in them—no two alike. Yet, I have no doubt that these several arrangements have been the subject of mature reflection, by wise and learned men, who, contemplating local circumstances, have adapted them to the condition of the section of society for which they have been framed. I am strengthened in this conclusion by an examination of each separately, and a conviction that no one of them, if adopted without change, would be suited to the circumstances and pursuits of our country. The example they have set, then, is authority for us to select from their different institutions the materials which are good *for us*, and, with them, to erect a structure, whose arrangement shall correspond with our own social condition, and shall admit of enlargement in proportion to the encouragement it may merit and receive. As I may not be able to attend the meetings of the trustees, I will make you the depositary of my ideas on the subject, which may be corrected, as you proceed, by the better views of others, and adapted from time to time, to the prospects which open upon us, and which cannot be specifically seen and provided for.

" In the first place, we must ascertain with precision the object of our institution, by taking a survey of the general field of science, and marking out the portion we mean to occupy at first, and the ultimate extension of our views beyond that, should we be enabled to render it, in the end, as comprehensive as we would wish." Jefferson then sketched out a broad educational system, providing for each grade of learning up to the highest and providing for various studies—such as the physical sciences, including those of electricity and galvanism and magnetism and meteorology, agriculture, horticulture and veterinary, marine architecture and military sciences, and adding to the lengthy list of courses of study which he enumerated, remark, that to the list of studies which he had made, there should be added " an &c. not easily enumerated." While some young people were expected by Jefferson to fail to receive what would be called a highly literary education,

and some would leave the grammar school or college—
the intermediate schools which he had planned—" with,"
as he expressed it, " a sufficient stock of knowledge, to
improve themselves to any degree to which their views
may lead them," other youth were to enter what he
termed the " Professional Schools," and to pursue " each
science " " in the highest degree it has yet attained."
One department of the university, which was to be classed
in some respects with the professional schools was to be
so peculiar that it is proper to pause for a moment to give
it especial attention.   " The school of technical philosophy," the statesman wrote, " will differ essentially in its
functions from the other professional schools.   The others
are instituted to ramify and dilate the particular sciences
taught in the schools of the second grade on a general
scale only.   The technical school is to abridge those which
were taught there too much *in extenso* for the limited
wants of the artificer or practical man.   These artificers
must be grouped together, according to the particular
branch of science in which they need elementary and
practical instruction ; and a special lecture or lectures
should be prepared for each group—and these lectures
should be given in the evening, so as not to interrupt the
labors of the day.   The school, particularly, should be
maintained wholly at the public expense, on the same
principles with that of the ward schools."   After speaking
somewhat in detail of the classes of youth who would
attend the different professional schools, Jefferson added :
" To that of technical philosophy will come the mariner,
carpenter, ship-wright, pump maker, clock maker, machin-
ist, optician, metallurgist, founder, cutler, druggist * * *
dyer, painter, bleacher, soap maker, tanner, powder maker,
salt maker, glass maker, to learn as much as shall be necessary to pursue their art understandingly, of the sciences

of geometry, mechanics, statics, hydrostatics, hydraulics, hydrodynamics, navigation, astronomy, geography, optics, pneumatics, acoustics, physics, chemistry, natural history, botany, mineralogy and pharmacy."

Jefferson's idea of providing for courses of technical instruction was meant to meet a want which many thoughtful people have sometimes felt is worthy of very much more consideration in America than it has received. Perhaps there is no institution of modern times that more effectually accomplishes such an end as the statesman had in view than does the Cooper Institute of New York, where mechanical drawing is taught, and where evening courses of lectures, illustrated by experiments, especially interesting and valuable to mechanics, are delivered. There have been writers who have spoken with much approbation and pleasure of the good which is being accomplished in some European nations by making considerable provision for what is called technical instruction for youth. It is held that these departments of instruction have enabled many a youth to learn how to earn an honorable support and have raised the taste and skill of workingmen to a degree which has sensibly added to national wealth and honor, and that this sagacious improvement in the courses of public instruction has been especially apparent at great International exhibitions which have been held in England and in France. There have been thoughtful people who have felt that American youth too often grow to manhood destitute of any knowledge of mechanics or of useful trades and are thereby in danger of leaving profitable and honorable manual employment to foreigners who have enjoyed in European schools advantages of a kind which should be widely introduced into America. While all intelligent people will agree with much that has been

said by these thoughtful writers, yet, to arrange the details of an industrial department of any educational establishment will require much wisdom. There are people
who shrink from contemplating a question which, if of
very great importance to a republic, is at the same time
very difficult to solve in a practical and satisfactory manner. There are some general propositions with which
every one may be expected to agree. For example, a
knowledge of letters is of such importance to all classes
of citizens that it may be said to be the basis of almost
all studies—scientific and industrial not less truly than of
literary acquirements. A very large number of artisans—
indeed of all classes of people—would find a knowledge
of mechanical drawing—by which the eye can be addressed sometimes far more satisfactorily than the ear—
highly useful to them in many departments of work.
Such instruction might well be given in all public day
and night schools. A knowledge of commercial arithmetic would be valuable to every class of society and
might be taught sometimes in very practical ways—such,
for example, as by commercial book-keeping. Almost
every section of a land so vast as that of the United States
has some special industry that in some cases it would be
of a great advantage to youth to understand. In some
parts of the United States there are mines of the precious
metals or of coal or of some other useful products of
the earth, respecting which much that would be interesting and useful could be taught even in common schools,
as well as to evening classes of people particularly interested
in such industries. In other sections of the United States
there are other industries such as manufactures, or fisheries,
about which information might be very interesting to
a certain class of citizens. While the number of lec-
turers who are capable of interesting and instructing

classes of artisans—especially on some important branches of industry—are not as numerous as could be desired, yet wisely arranged courses of lectures will have an elevating tendency in a community. Doubtless, however, as far as many industries are concerned, money could probably be laid out even to better advantage than by providing courses of lectures respecting them. For instance arrangements could be made by which whoever chose to do so could consult books respecting these useful employments. Jefferson held that the establishment of libraries which would be accessible to mechanics of every community would be instrumental in doing a vast amount of good. Books which would render friendly services to scientists, and to men engaged in various useful handicrafts, he would have welcomed into the United States free of duty.

Almost every industry is dependent more or less on one or more of the sciences. Scientific schools such as have been established in recent times in connection with some of the leading colleges in the United States give much of the kind of instruction needed by youth who are to engage in industries in which chemical and various kinds of other knowledge is required. Jefferson proposed in a paper which he wrote and submitted to the Legislature of Virginia—a paper which was signed by Madison and by Caleb and by other of his distinguished colleagues who were associated with him in founding the University of Virginia—that students should be helped in gaining an acquaintance with some of the useful industrial arts by being enabled to visit, in a way just to every one, different factories. He wrote * : " The use of tools too is worthy of encouragement, by facilitating, to such as chose it, an

---

* "Early History of the University of Virginia," J. W. Randolph, 1856, p. 442.

7

admission into the neighboring workshops." A plan
similar to the one suggested by Jefferson has been recommended by an able writer on technical education, who has
further advised that students should write essays respecting the industries which they examine, and thus be encouraged to see what is written on these arts in encyclo-
pedias and in other works of information. By such a
plan they would be introduced to a variety of industries
some of which might be esteemed especially worthy of
cultivation.

Many an American youth who has grown to manhood
without having acquired a knowledge of any useful
handicraft, or business, has felt that his education had
been imperfect, and has, perhaps, even died of a broken
heart, feeling that however useful he might hope to be in
a general way to society, his life was a failure because he
was unable to earn his own support. Jefferson was far
too wise not to recognize that while a certain class of youth
might be so happily situated in life that he could
conscientiously advise them to devote their time to
studies by which they might be enabled to promote the
general well-being of society, yet that there were vast
numbers of youth who should be skilled in manual arts
or in professions. In the University of Virginia some
young men were to be prepared to become engineers,
others physicians, others lawyers or members of some
other useful professions. It is hardly necessary to here
dwell upon the time which he gave to the establishment
of the departments of law and of medicine. It may,
however, be here stated that Jefferson felt that the science
of medicine was in his day in a very unsatisfactory state.
While of surgery he had a high opinion he felt that physicians often did more harm to their patients than good.
He felt that in his day the custom of bleeding patients

and of giving them strong purgatives and pills of various kinds was wofully often a cause of deadly injury to the sick. A time was to come when he himself was, while lying on his death-bed, to spend some of his waning strength in resisting the efforts of a well-meaning physician who, in a way far too common with some physicians with their patients, put to his lips a spirituous liquor. If, however, the art of medicine was in a deplorable condition, all the more need there was that efforts should be made to provide the means of a high medical education to students of medicine in Virginia. There was one industry which the distinguished statesman wished to receive especial encouragement. In the university, to the founding of which he was giving his best talents, the art of agriculture was to be studied as a science.

One of the ways in which civilized people differ from savages is that they are better acquainted with the art of making the earth yield treasures of food for mankind, than are their uncultured brethren. Doubtless, for thousands of years in some parts of the world, there have been people who have been skilled in cultivating the earth. For many centuries the emperors of China have been wont, with much pomp and ceremony, at stated times to set an example to the people of the Empire of China of preparing the soil to yield them food. Many a Roman aristocrat loved to be considered learned in the dignified art of husbandry. When the clenched hand of many a mummy which has lain in its silent resting-place for thousands of years has been opened, it has been found to contain grains of wheat or of some other useful plant. The noble works for irrigating the soil, built by people who lived in bygone ages, attest the industry and skill with which agriculture has been pursued by at least a part of the great human family. The Grecians were possessed of the art of cultivating the apple, the luscious pear, the cherry, the plum, the quince, as well as the peach and the nectarine, and with some other fruits,—including the fig and the lemon. Strange, however, one may well feel it to be that for thousands of years a large part of the human race has been ignorant of the existence of many useful plants which are invaluable to man. Some of these plants are instrumental in protecting vast numbers of the present generation from some dreadful scourges which for ages were wont to shorten and often render miserable human life—scourges such as never fail to sooner or later make their appearance where man is not supplied with food containing certain elements needed for his healthful sustenance. The extent to which the dreadful disease scurvy existed in the world before the potato, and some other antiscorbutics, came into common use is well calculated to amaze a thoughtful student of history. Although the English people have been probably for centuries little, if at all, behind in intelligence hundreds of millions of the human race, yet they did not even know for many ages of such fruits of the earth as Indian corn, squashes, carrots, cabbages, or turnips, or potatoes. It has been stated by some Portuguese writers,[*] that the progenitor of all the European and American oranges was an Oriental tree still living in the last century, which had been introduced into Lisbon. Even the common weeping willow-tree and very many flowers and plants, have been imported into the United States in very recent times—indeed the vegetable immigration into America has been amazingly large and important. Other plants—such as sorghum, which may prove to be of far more value to America than even the cotton plant or wheat,—

---

[*] See " The Earth as Modified by Human Action," by George P. Marsh, p. 66.

are probably to further illustrate the inestimable wealth which the art of agriculture has it sometimes in its power to evoke from the earth.

The importance of agricultural knowledge might well claim the consideration of a statesman. The amount of land on the North and South American continent which will return a profitable harvest to the husbandman is probably as large as is all the fertile land of all other continents united in the world. Owing to the form of the American continent which enables the fructifying exhalations of the oceans, and of its great lakes—which alone contain one third of all the fresh water of the world, —and of its great rivers—nowhere else equalled,—there is, compared to Africa and Asia, but a small amount of desert land. It has been estimated that, at a low calculation, the American continent can supply subsistence for about two and a half times as many people as are at present on the surface of the earth. Moreover, the American continent is happily free, to a great extent, from the scorching rays of the sun which enervate the body and mind of man on some of the great continents of the world. Even much, if not almost all, of what has been called the deserts of America are suitable for pasturage for domestic animals. Millions upon millions of husbandmen are to have honorable, healthful, dignified and profitable employment in summoning to their call the treasures of the earth.

The United States, by its invaluable Agricultural Department and by its wise legislation, has greatly aided the interests of agriculture. Plants have been introduced to American soil whose value are so great to the Republic that one may well hesitate to make calculations which must aggregate sums which might be deemed, by any one who has not given attention to the subject, to be incredi-

ble. The United States, by its wise homestead laws, has
done more than one can easily describe to lift a worthy
class of citizens above the curse of poverty and to kindle
in their breasts the fire of patriotism, while at the same
time lands are redeemed which for ages have lain waste,
and useless, and are made to minister to the wealth of the
human family. The vast public domain has been partly
surveyed and every citizen—indeed every one who even
states his intention of becoming a citizen,—may, by complying with some simple and wise laws which have been
enacted, become owners of a quite large tract of land and
of a home. Well would it be if many a man in the
crowded cities of the Republic who perhaps is tempted to
adopt lawless views respecting industry and wealth, could
have unfolded to him the reward which a knowledge of
the art of agriculture in America can be made to yield
to the well-meaning American citizen!

The more one considers the wealth and comfort which
the art of agriculture brings to the people of the United
States, the more it will be held in honor. The value of
forest products by the census of 1880 was $700,000,000.
Estimating the value of wheat at prices which would
probably be judged strangely low by many Europeans, the
amount raised in the United States by the census of
1880, was $474,291,850. Of hay there was raised an
amount which was estimated at $371,811,085. The oat
crop was valued at $150,243,565. The cotton crop at
$280,266,242. The yield of potatoes was estimated at
$81,000,000. Not to speak of many other crops of vari-
ous kinds the amount of corn raised was estimated—
perhaps indeed too largely—to be worth $679,714,499.
In short, the agricultural produce including the yield of
wool and of domestic animals—and probably a billion of
dollars would be a low estimate for the cattle which were

to be found on farms and plains,—amounted to billions of dollars. The vast yearly yield of coal, of iron, of gold and silver, and of copper, and of several other highly important minerals, were, altogether only estimated by the census of 1880, at a valuation of $218,385,452. Surely the citizens of a republic possessing such a magnificent domain as that of a large part of the continent of America, should make a wise provision for the enlightenment of at least some of its youth respecting such an important industry as that of agriculture.

Even as an amusement Jefferson felt that the study of botany had claims upon the attention of many Americans. Writing to the learned Dr. Thomas Cooper, under date of Oct. 7th, 1814, he said: "Botany I rank with the most valuable sciences, whether we consider its subjects as furnishing the principal subsistence of life to man and beast, delicious varieties for our tables, refreshments from our orchards, the adornments of our flower-borders, shade and perfume of our groves, materials for our buildings, or medicaments for our bodies. * * * To a country family it constitutes a great portion of their social entertainment. No country gentleman should be without what amuses every step he takes into his fields." Even when President of the United States Jefferson had found time to express his views respecting the importance of turning the attention of a large class of youth to the claims of agricultural pursuits. To the learned David Williams who had sent him a volume which he had written on the claims of literature, he, under date of Nov. 14th, 1803, wrote: "The greatest evils of populous society have ever appeared to me to spring from the vicious distribution of its members among the occupations called for. I have no doubt that those nations are essentially right, which leave this to individual choice, as a better guide to an advantageous distribution than any other which could be devised. But when, by a blind concourse, particular occupations are ruinously overcharged, and others left in want of hands, the national authorities can do much towards restoring the equilibrium. * * * The evil cannot be suddenly, nor perhaps ever entirely, cured: nor should I presume to say by what means it may be cured. Doubtless there are many engines which the nation might bring to bear on this object. Public opinion and public encouragement are among these. The class principally defective is that of agriculture. It is the first in utility, and ought to be the first in respect. The same artificial means which have been used to produce a competition in learning, may be equally successful in restoring agriculture to its primary dignity in the eyes of men. It is a science of the very first order. It counts among its handmaids the most respectable sciences; such as Chemistry, Natural Philosophy, Mechanics, Mathematics generally, Natural History, Botany. In every College and University, a professorship of agriculture, and the class of its students, might be honored as the first. Young men closing their academical education with this, as the crown of all other sciences, fascinated with its solid charms, and at a time when they are to choose an occupation, instead of crowding the other classes, would return to the farms of their fathers, their own, or those of others, and replenish and invigorate a calling, now languishing under contempt and oppression." *

In a valuable report which the aged Jefferson, when he had been appointed a commissioner to select a site for a State University,—a report which was signed by James Madison and by his other distinguished associates,—sub-

---

* By oppression Jefferson perhaps had in mind African slavery which he abhorred.

mitted to the Legislature in the year 1818,—he unfolded at considerable length his views respecting the branches of knowledge which could be wisely provided for American youth. In the courses of study which he draughted he did not forget to speak of the wisdom of providing for the teaching to American youth of foreign languages. With a very large part of the human race one who can only speak a single language cannot commune. Only a fraction of the human race can speak the English language. This state of affairs is probably a much sadder evil than it is generally realized to be by the unlearned. Who can picture all the wealth of knowledge which nations could place at each others' disposal, or the vastness of the blessings which could be enjoyed in common, if all the members of the human family could intelligently communicate with each other! There have been men who have loved to dream of a plan by which learned men should be brought together to invent a common language for all nations. There have been statesmen who have pictured the blessings which will be enjoyed by posterity if by wise American statesmanship the whole of the continent of America shall be secured to the Republic of the United States,—a continent which is to be inhabited by many hundreds of millions of people,—and if by means of public schools and wise laws a common language shall be spoken from the far north to the sunny south and from the Atlantic Ocean to the Pacific main. Jefferson and Monroe had such visions. At the present time, however, if Americans are to enjoy the innumerable advantages which flow from being enabled to speak some of the important languages which are at this day found upon the earth, they must be favored with opportunities to acquire these strange tongues. Jefferson, in the paper to which allusion has just been made, said : " The considerations which have governed the specification of languages to be taught by the professor of modern languages were, that the French is the language of general intercourse among nations, and as a depositary of human science, is unsurpassed by any other language, living or dead; that the Spanish is highly interesting to us, as the language spoken by so great a portion of the inhabitants of our continents, with whom we shall probably have great intercourse ere long, and is that also in which is written the greater part of the earlier history of America.   The Italian abounds with works of very superior order, valuable for their matter, and still more distinguished as models of the finest taste in style and composition.   And the German now stands in a line with that of the most learned nations in richness of erudition and advance in the sciences.   It is too of common descent with the language of our own country, a branch of the same original Gothic stock, and furnishes valuable illustrations for us."

It has sometimes been stated, and it is to be feared with a lamentable degree of truth, that in some distinguished seats of learning in Great Britian and America, the study of the English language does not receive the consideration which it deserves.   Jefferson did not propose that such a fault should exist in the State University which he and his colleagues were planning for Virginia.   Among the studies which he urged should receive especial consideration was that of the English language. He urged at considerable length the wisdom of American youth studying Anglo-Saxon.   " It," he said, "will form the first link in the chain of an historical review of our language through all its successive changes to the present day, will constitute the foundation of that critical instruction in it which ought to be found in a seminary of general learning; * * * a language already fraught with all the eminent science of our parent country, the future vehicle of whatever we may ourselves achieve, and destined to occupy so much space on the globe, claims distinguished attention in American education."

In the report of 1818—to which attention has just been drawn—it was pointed out that a gymnasium, for the physical training of students was "a proper object of attention for every institution of youth." Learned remarks were also made respecting the difference which it was deemed proper to make between the exercises practised by youth in "ancient nations" and the physical culture suitable for American youth. One could wish to dwell upon the priceless value to youth of wise physical culture. But time forbids. It may here be briefly stated that Jefferson had a favorite plan by which all the young men of the United States would have to learn how to go through military evolutions. In the learned letter on education to Peter Carr which Jefferson wrote on Sept. 7th, 1814, he said, "Through the whole of the collegiate course, at the hours of recreation on certain days, all the students should be taught the manual exercise, military evolutions and manœuvres, and should be under a standing organization as a military corps, and with proper officers to train and command them." He felt that at some time such training might be especially useful to citizens of a republic.

It might be interesting to especially notice the efforts of Jefferson to get able English professors for the university. He proposed that the most attractive of all of the features of the university which he was helping to found should be the high character of its instructors. In his letters he quite often dwelt upon his desire to secure to the University of Virginia the ablest of professors. Without here pausing to quote from these letters suffice it to

notice that to be a good instructor of youth requires
sometimes the greatest of talents—indeed, to teach youth
in a worthy manner may be called one of the highest and
noblest of arts. A professor, who is what he should be,
may sometimes be an unspeakable blessing to youth. He
needs to be possessed of many gifts. He should possess
at once a certain gentleness and firmness of character.
He should instinctively cause youth to realize that he is
their friend and that he possesses treasures of knowledge
worthy of their respect. He should be prepared by a
noble heart, and true wisdom, and sometimes by indescribable characteristics, to kindle in youth elevating, and in
various ways noble, aspirations, and to sometimes, in a
most delicate manner, introduce them to sciences. A
worthy professor will often be enabled to make his instruction fascinatingly interesting, and at the same time
teach students in one hour more than an inferior instructor could teach them in a day. Youth are thus
not only saved valuable time but are taught the art of
studying and of making various researches themselves;
they catch a certain kind of enthusiasm and love for
their studies, when under a less gifted instructor they
would become disgusted with their work. What a good
minister, a judicious lawyer, a competent physician is
to a community so is a worthy professor to the youth
who come under his influence. He may even intuitively
and in the happiest manner instil the truest and noblest
greatness into the character of his students. By holding
intercourse with such a preceptor the minds of students
may be elevated for life. Such a professor should be well-
poised in character, wise in the exercise of authority,
sympathetic and noble-hearted in bearing, of exact and
truthful habits of observation, and should be possessed of
tact and of good sense. He should teach with good

taste, and should be wisely considerate and patient. After spending years of life in qualifying himself for one of the noblest of employments, he may have to spend many an hour of toil in preparing in a way most suitable to the mind of young suitors of useful knowledge some of the profoundest of the truths to which they can turn their attention.

It has been realized in Prussia that the schoolmaster or the professor is worthy of peculiar regard by the State. He is often furnished with a house and a garden and is enabled to collect around him many comforts of life. When the humble schoolmaster retires from his honorable employment, he is given a pension. But to return to Jefferson's labors in the cause of education. Writing to his English friend Mr. Roscoe, under date of Dec. 27th, 1820, after declaring that his remaining days and faculties would be devoted to the University of Virginia, he continued: "When ready for its Professors we shall apply for them chiefly to your Island. Were we content to remain stationary in science, we should take them from among ourselves; but, desirous of advancing, we must seek them in countries already in advance; and identity of language points to our best resource. To furnish inducements, we provide for the Professors separate buildings, in which themselves and their families may be handsomely and comfortably lodged, and to liberal salaries will be added lucrative perquisites." Jefferson when bowed with the weight of four-score years wrote to his distinguished colleagues in organizing the institution of learning to which he was giving his best talents, under date of Oct. 7th, 1822, that the university should only have "Professors of the first eminence in their respective lines of science." He added that "The Visitors consider the procuring of such characters * * * as the peculiar

feature which is to give reputation and value to the institution and constitute its desirable attractions." *

Without dwelling on the details of the great work of
founding the University of Virginia, suffice it to say that
when eighty-three years of life pressed heavily on its
Rector he drew up a long list of books and arranged for
the purchase of thousands of useful volumes. It has
been held by some learned Europeans that amongst the
essentials of a university, a good library should be ranked
first in importance; good instructors second; and third,
suitable buildings. It is to be feared that too many
founders of collegiate institutions have not realized that
a good library is a very essential part of a university.
Much of education in its preliminary stages, and even into
the meridian of life, is the training of the mind to use
books wisely, rather than to overload the memory with
the knowledge contained in many volumes. The nobler
a man's aims the more extensive should be the facilities
placed within his reach. The world of thought, at times,
advances. If professors have no means of supplying
their minds with new stores of knowledge, they labor at a
great disadvantage, and their instruction does not keep
pace with the times. The intellectual hermit is not the
man to teach in a worthy institution of learning. If a
student is troubled with doubts respecting some historical statement, or some fact in regard to science or religion, by means of a library rich with the treasures of
wisdom of the learned his distressing doubts are removed
and the truth flings its rays upon his mind as does the
sun, when it shines upon one with refreshing splendor.
He is thus, in some respects, made mentally strong, and
enjoys blessings of which he must ever have remained a

* "Early History of the University of Virginia," J. W. Randolph, 1856,
p. 473.

stranger had he not been enabled to consult the shelves of a worthy library. The suitor for knowledge understands how great a blessing it is to him to be enabled at times to understand both sides of a question; and to be enabled to form broad and intelligent views respecting important subjects—drawing even inspiration from the works of great authors. Even in Jefferson's day the University of Oxford contained four or five hundred thousand volumes besides many thousands of manuscripts. Some of the great centres of learning are especially to be praised for their great libraries. There are few ways sometimes in which a friend of education can do more good to a college than by presenting it with useful books.

Happily the University of Virginia was blessed with an English friend. On Nov. 9th, 1825, the aged Jefferson wrote a long letter to Evelyn Denizon, a member of Parliament, who had been his guest and had presented some books to the university library. After gracefully thanking the English friend of education, Jefferson alluded to the infant Virginian seat of learning. He said: " It is going on as successfully as we could have expected; and I have no reason to regret the measure taken of procuring Professors from abroad, where science is so much ahead of us. You witnessed some of the puny squibs of which I was the butt on that account. * * * The measure has been generally approved in the South and in the West; and by all liberal minds in the North. It has been peculiarly fortunate, too, that the Professors brought from abroad were as happy selections as could have been hoped, as well for their qualifications in science as correctness and amiableness of character. I think the example will be followed, and that it cannot fail to be one of the efficacious means of promoting that cordial good will which it is so much the interest of both nations to cherish. These teachers can never utter an unfriendly sentiment towards their native country; and those into whom their instructions will be infused are not of ordinary significance only: they are exactly the persons who are to succeed to the government of our country, and to rule its future enmities, its friendships and fortunes. As it is our interest to receive instruction through this channel, so I think it is yours to furnish it; for these two nations holding cordially together have nothing to fear from the united world. They will be the models for regenerating the condition of man, the sources from which representative government is to flow over the whole earth." As Jefferson proceeded he made some remarks on the study of Anglo-Saxon, which was to receive attention in the university, and which was of mutual interest to Americans and to Englishmen.

One characteristic of the university which was being moulded by Jefferson, upon which it would be highly interesting and instructive to dwell, will here be but briefly pointed out in the statesman's own words. In his letter to his English friend, Mr. Roscoe, under date of December 27th, 1820, just after speaking of the efforts which were to be made to procure worthy professors for the university, he added: " This institution will be based on the illimitable freedom of the human mind. For here we are not afraid to follow truth wherever it may lead, nor to tolerate any error, so long as reason is left free to combat it."

Years after Jefferson had been laid in his grave, one of the English professors, Dr. Robley Dunglison, who had been welcomed to the University of Virginia, and who became especially celebrated because of his valuable medical works,—works which are to this day standard authorities in American Medical Colleges,—wrote of the aged statesman thus : " His philanthropy was actual and active. It embraced, I believe, the whole globe. His desire was to see all people prosperous and happy—all *peoples* I may say. * * * He was kind, courteous; hospitable to all; sincerely attached to the excellent family that were clustered around him; sympathizing with them in their pleasures, deeply distressed in their afflictions. * * * He was of commanding aspect, dignified, and would have been striking to any one not knowing in whose presence and company he was. * * * His expression—as I recollect it—was pleasing, intellectual, contemplative. He was tall and thin * * * As a university officer, he was always pleasant to transact business with, was invariably kind and respectful, but had generally formed his own opinion on questions and did not abandon them easily. * * * To sum up, I had the most exalted opinion of him. I believed him essentially a philanthropist, anxious for the greatest good to the greatest number; a distinguished patriot, whose love of country was not limited by any consideration of self; who was eminently virtuous, with fixed and honorable principles of action not to be trammelled by any unworthy considerations; and whose reputation must shine brighter and brighter, as he is more and more justly judged and estimated."

At last the university was duly opened. To Edward Livingston, Jefferson wrote on March 25th, 1825 : " The institution is at length happily advanced to completion, and has commenced under auspices as favorable as I could expect. I hope it will prove a blessing to my own State, and not unuseful, perhaps, to some others. At all hazards, and secured by the aid of my able coadjutors, I shall continue, while I am in being, to contribute to it whatever my weakened and weakening powers can. But assuredly it is the last object for which I shall obtrude myself on the public observation." To William B. Giles, on December 26th, 1825, the venerable Jefferson wrote: "A finer set of youths I never saw assembled for instruction. * * * A great proportion of them are severely devoted to study, and I fear not to say, that within twelve or fifteen years from this time, a majority of the rulers of our State will have been educated here. * * * You may account assuredly that they will exalt their country in a degree of sound respectability it has never known, either in our days, or those of our forefathers. I cannot live to see it. My joy must be only in anticipation."

Jefferson, it may here be briefly stated, although he believed that the University of Virginia should be unsectarian, labored in various ways to throw around the students who should reside in the university town, good influences. He gave more money than his fortune justified him in giving to the support of Christian churches. His labors of this nature, however, will perhaps be noticed at some length at some future time.

It of course required a great deal of money to found a State university such as Jefferson believed should form a part of the school system of Virginia. A rich planter might say that he could send his sons to a private school, or to a private university, and, that however desirable a public-school system of education was for the common people, that as for him he got nothing for the money which he was obliged to pay in taxes to support the schools, and colleges or high schools, and the university which such men as Jefferson wished States to establish. Jefferson, living as he did in a State in which was the institution of slavery, very probably heard of some such case. To Joseph C. Cabell, under date of January 14th, 1818, he wrote * : "And

---

* See letter in full in "Early History of the University of Virginia," J. W. Randolph, 1856, pp. 102–6.

will the wealthy individual have no retribution ? and what will this be ? 1. The peopling his neighborhood with honest, useful, and enlightened citizens, understanding their own rights and firm in their perpetuation. 2. When his own descendants become poor, which they generally do within three generations, (no law of primogeniture now perpetuating wealth in the same families) the children will be educated by the then rich ; and the little advance he now makes to poverty, while rich himself, will be repaid by the then rich, to his descendants when become poor, and thus give them a chance of rising again. This is a solid consideration and should go home to the bosom of every parent. This will be seed sown in fertile ground. It is a provision for his family looking to distant times, and far in duration beyond that he has now in hand for them. Let every man count backward in his own family, and see how many generations he can go before he comes to the ancestor who made the fortune he now holds. Most will be stopped at the first generation, many at the second, few will reach the third, and not one in the State can go beyond the fifth."

In the year 1825 Jefferson was visited by Lafayette. By cruel confinement in an Austrian prison Lafayette had been made lame. Although Jefferson was ill and weak he walked to the porch of his house to meet him and to embrace him with tears. To Lafayette a grand banquet was given in the imposing university buildings. Some of the most distinguished citizens of the United States took their places at the feast. Amidst many gay and pleasant remarks a sentiment was proposed in Jefferson's honor. All eyes were turned toward the venerable patriot. He handed a written speech to a friend to read. In the course of his speech he said : " My friends, I am old, long in the disuse of making speeches, and without voice to

utter them.   In this feeble state, the exhausted powers of
life leave little within my competence for your service. If
with the aid of my younger and abler coadjutors, I can
still contribute anything to advance the institution within
whose walls we are mingling manifestations to this our
guest, it will be, as it ever has been, cheerfully and zeal-
ously bestowed.   And could I live to see it once enjoy the
patronage and cherishment of our public authorities with
undivided voice, I should die without a doubt of the future
fortunes of my native State, and in the consoling contemplation of the happy influence of this institution on its
character, its virtue, its prosperity and safety.

"* * * I add, for our nation at large, the aspirations of a heart warm with the love of country; whose
invocations to Heaven for its indissoluble union, will be
fervent and unremitting while the pulse of life continues
to beat, and, when that ceases, it will expire in prayers for
the eternal duration of its freedom and prosperity."*

At last Jefferson could feel that one of his great life
works was completed.   Indeed, a noble dream of a great
statesman was in a good degree realized.   He had by his
labors in behalf of true learning set an example worthy
of the admiration of every intelligent lover of civil liberty
in every land! He had by his actions proved, in a manner
eloquent even to being pathetic, the sincerity of his convictions of the importance to a republic of universities.

---

* "Life of Thomas Jefferson."   By Henry S. Randall, LL.D., vol. iii.,
p. 504.

IV.

"OUR COLORED BRETHREN."

IT is well, sometimes, for students of the science of government to notice how great statesmen have viewed certain questions of great national importance, and to ask themselves how some of the greatest and wisest of these men would act were they to-day the custodians of all the best interests of the American continent.

A subject of inexpressibly vast importance to the people of the United States, to which Jefferson gave deep, heart-felt, and prayerful consideration, was one respecting the well-being of those whom he called "our colored brethren." He formed some far-reaching conclusions which are worthy of the most serious consideration of the statesmen of modern times.

Upon the system of negro slavery which prevailed in his day in the United States—especially in the Southern States—he looked with abhorrence, and with feelings of the gravest apprehension as he considered the effect which it would some day have upon the welfare of his country. In the year 1775, having been taken ill while on his way to the Continental Congress, he forwarded to his fellow statesmen, for the inspection of such of them as cared to look at his written opinion respecting America's controversy with England, an essay, entitled "The Rights of Englishmen in America." Some members of Congress, less cautious than others, published the essay, and the

eloquent Edmund Burke, with some alterations, repub-
lished it in England. The English Government in
impotent displeasure placed Jefferson's name on a proscribed list. In this pamphlet, or book, Jefferson indignantly declared that, " The abolition of domestic slavery
is the great object of desire in those colonies, where it was,
unhappily, introduced in their infant state. But previous
to the enfranchisement of the slaves we have, it is necessary to exclude all further importations from Africa. Yet
our repeated attempts to effect this, by prohibitions, and
by imposing duties which might amount to a prohibition,
have been hitherto defeated by his Majesty's negative;
thus preferring the immediate advantages of a few British
corsairs, to the lasting interests of the American States,
and to the rights of human nature deeply wounded by the
infamous practice."

At the Congress of 1776, Jefferson draughted the
Declaration of American Independence, which was slight-
ly revised by his colleagues John Adams and Benjamin
Franklin. As I write I have a *fac-simile* copy of the
original document before me. The handwriting of the
Declaration may be said to betray especially deep feeling
when allusion is made to the last of a series of enumerated
wrongs committed by Great Britain against the people of
America. The only words that were underscored in the
whole document were on this last paragraph. The words
are so feelingly marked that it is perhaps impossible in print
to give the force of the emphasis which the writer evidently intended them to have. Jefferson, of the King of
Great Britain, thus wrote : " He has waged cruel war
against human nature itself, violating its most sacred
rights of life and liberty in the persons of a distant people
who never offended him ; captivating and carrying them
into slavery in another hemisphere, or to incur mis-

erable death on their transportation thither. This piratical warfare, the opprobrium of *infidel* powers, is the warfare of the CHRISTIAN king of Great Britain. Determined to keep open a market where MEN should be bought and sold, he has prostituted his negative for suppressing every legislative attempt to prohibit or to restrain this execrable commerce. * * * " In the Continental Congress there were found two men who objected to this part of the Declaration of Independence. One of them was a delegate from Georgia, the other was a delegate from South Carolina. The Congress felt that it was of great importance that union should be preserved among the colonies, and rather than run the risk of separating any colonies from the Union it was decided that the whole paragraph should be stricken out. The first Continental Congress, on October 20th, 1774, had signed and promulgated "Articles of Association." These "Articles" formed a bond of union among the colonies who were pledged by them to " neither import nor purchase any slave," and to " wholly discontinue the slave-trade." In this bond of union it was declared that any one who violated the Articles should be pronounced "foes to the rights of British America," should be " universally contemned as the foes of American liberty," and should be regarded as unworthy of the rights of freemen." These pledges of the Continental Congress were adopted by colonial conventions, county meetings, and by other assemblies throughout the colonies. It may indeed have been in part for another reason than that of hatred to negro slavery that the people thus acted, but it is certain that there were American statesmen who hated slavery and were not afraid to avow, in burning language, their convictions. Hatred to slavery was not confined to descendants of the Puritans. The Assembly of Virginia, after discussing the evil of slavery, had voted to tax every cargo of slaves, but the King of England had negatived the bill. To an address from the Legislature of Virginia to the King of Great Britain in 1772,—an address in which the inhumanity of holding human beings in bondage was dwelt upon, and in which the conviction was expressed that it was opposed to the security and happiness of the people and would even in time endanger their existence,—his Majesty replied that "upon pain of his highest displeasure the importation of slaves should not be in any respect obstructed." South Carolina had decided in its Legislature that the slave trade should be discouraged by taxing the slaves brought to the colony, but the Crown had in 1761, negatived the bill. Two years after the Declaration of Independence Jefferson successfully moved in the Assembly of Virginia that the slave trade should be prohibited in every port over which Virginia had control. In the book entitled "Notes on Virginia," which Jefferson wrote during the Revolutionary War—he estimated the number of free inhabitants of Virginia at 296,852 and the number of slaves at 270,762, or, as he expressed it "nearly as 11 to 10." He feelingly wrote that, "Under the mild treatment our slaves experience, and their wholesome, though coarse food, this blot in our country increases as fast, or faster than the whites. During the regal government we had at one time [in Virginia] obtained a law which imposed such a duty on the importation of slaves as amounted nearly to a prohibition, when one inconsiderate Assembly, placed under a peculiarity of circumstance, repealed the law. This repeal met a joyful sanction from the then reigning sovereign, and no devices, no expedients, which could ever be attempted by subsequent Assemblies, and they seldom met without attempting them, could succeed in getting the royal assent to the renewal of the duty. In the very first session held under the republican government, the Assembly passed a law for the perpetual prohibition of the importation of slaves. This will in some measure stop the increase of this great political and moral evil, while the minds of our citizens may be ripening for a complete emancipation of human nature." Jefferson was to have a far more influential part in the sad drama with which the abolition of slavery was to take place in the United States than is generally known!

In Massachusetts, during the war for Independence a State Constitution was adopted by the people, whose " Bill of Rights " was so worded that slavery could not lawfully exist in the State. It has been falsely said if I mistake not, by some uninformed speakers, that the Northern States in a very cheap way to themselves got rid of slavery,—that they sold their slaves to the Southern States. Doubtless for years before the Civil War the legislation of the State of New York, and to a greater or less extent the legislation of other States, was sadly tainted with indifference to the turpitude of slavery; and yet it may be doubted whether in the history of the great State of New York there are many more illustrious incidents than the way it got rid of slavery. The State of New York decreed liberty to the enslaved at a specified period, and made it an offence to which a severe penalty was attached for any one to convey away or in any manner whatever to sell out of the State, any one held as a slave. If any citizen of New York, in view of the day of emancipation, wished to visit the South with his slaves, he was obliged to give bonds for their return before he was allowed to go, and he had to give an account of them if he returned without them. What is true of the humane emancipation laws of New York is, in general, true of the laws of all the Northern States. Governor

John Jay, who, with Alexander Hamilton, was an out and out Abolitionist—the one being President and the other Secretary of an Abolitionist society in New York,—used his influence as Governor with good effect in behalf of his colored friends.

More horrible than the most dreadful tales ever told of pirates, were the scenes of sickening wickedness enacted in the prosecution of the slave-trade. To give even a faint idea of the traffic in human flesh and blood, an account would have to be given of the way in which wars were fomented in Africa so that slaves could be obtained for the slave-ship;—of how villages were fired in the night and the fleeing women and children captured, loaded with irons, and compelled to walk sometimes many hundreds of miles to reach the vessel which was to bear them into hopeless bondage;—of the innumerable treacheries and piratical attacks upon the people by heartless ruffians;—and of how even venal African princes for intoxicating beverages would sell their own subjects. Once on board the slaver the wretched men and women and children were often obliged to occupy as little room as possible. They were chained to each other and to their respective places. In thousands of cases the slaves were given as little room as is allowed to the dead when placed in coffins. Lying, in many cases naked on bare boards, the motion of the vessel would sometimes cause their flesh to be scraped to the bones. At times the steam from their bodies would come up from the openings in the decks of the vessel as from a horrid furnace. The slaves would often be seized with delirium or with despair, or would lie in a swoon until death, as an angel of mercy, would deliver them from their tyrants. Did a slave disturb the vessel by sobbing, gags of a peculiar construction were brought into use. If water gave

out on the passage, or, if a storm overtook the slave-ship
loaded down with its cargo, moans of unutterable anguish
could not be prevented, or, if, as might happen, a peculiar
pestilence broke out among the suffering and the dying
chained in their places, and in some cases to the dead in
whom dissolution had already commenced, the scene
would become too woful to describe. For one reason
and another hundreds of thousands of slaves found a
grave in the waters of the ocean. One eighth to one
fourth of the cargoes of slaves may be said, on the average, to have perished on the vessels. When the enslaved
arrived in port they would sometimes be filled with
agony and terror as they realized that they were to be
sold into life-long bondage. The horrors of the scene
would only be exceeded by its wickedness! No wonder
that Madison should speak of the slave-trade as an " infer-
nal traffic ";—that Jefferson should feel indignant with the
British Crown for its responsibility for man-stealing and
the trade in human flesh and blood!

It may here be incidentally remarked that African
slavery was first introduced into South America at the
instance of Las Casas, a Roman Catholic ecclesiastic, who
possibly hoped that negro slavery would at least take the
place of the well-nigh indescribable,—the appalling,—enslavement by the Spaniards of the vast hordes of Indians
who were dying in numbers which might seem incredible
if they were here stated. Las Casas, before his death became to some degree enlightened respecting the unutterable horrors of the slave-trade and sadly repented of the
error which he had committed in taking part in the work
of introducing a new system of human bondage into South
America. It is hardly historically correct to say that he
was the only one responsible for the infamous business.
The monarchs of Spain at different periods, had at least

to some extent encouraged the introduction of negroes into the part of the new world scourged by their tyranny. In 1518, the Jeronimite Order of the Roman Catholic Church had recommended that licenses should be given to the people of Hispaniola or to other persons, to bring negroes to Hispaniola. From a letter of theirs one may infer that even before the year 1518 they had sent to Spain a similar recommendation. Fray Bernardino de Manzanedo, sent to Spain by his Order, not only recommended that negro slavery should be introduced, but added especially that as many negro women should be sent as negro men.* Although it has been said that at least one distinguished ecclesiastic,—a man connected with the Inquisition—disapproved of the business, and although a time was to come when from the Papal throne denunciations in Latin were to be uttered against the sin of man's enslaving his fellow-man,—yet Las Casas' project respecting introducing African slaves was approved by powerful ecclesiastics. Pope Martin V. gave his approval to the traffic—a traffic which, in justice it should be said, was probably but little understood by the Roman Pontiff. The Spanish Crown gave to a man named De Brasa a license to carry on the slave business, who in his turn sold the license to some Genoese merchants, who were soon unable to supply the large demand in Cuba, Jamaica, San Juan and Hispaniola and on the South American coast. The trade being found to be very profitable, some Dutchmen entered the business. On May 22d, 1620, a Dutch vessel landed twenty slaves on Virginian soil. In time slavery was introduced into all the colonies which were to sever themselves from the

---

* See "The Conquerors of the New World and their Bondsmen," by Arthur Helps, 1848, p. 272-3, and "Coleccion de Muñoz," tomo 76, from which ancient letters are quoted.

British Crown. Queen Elizabeth was a partner in the second voyage of the first English captain of a slave vessel. James I. and Charles II. chartered companies to deal in slaves. Of the first company chartered by Charles II., the Duke of York was President. To the second African company which he chartered he as well as the Duke subscribed. After the Stuarts were expelled from Great Britain the nefarious business was still continued. In 1713, at the peace of Utrecht, England insisted that she should have the monopoly of the slave-trade with the Spanish West Indies. The English government agreed by treaty with the King of Spain * to bring into the West Indies of America belonging to his Catholic Majesty, in the space of thirty years, 144,000 negroes at the rate of 4,800 a year, at a fixed rate of duty, with the right to import any further number at a lower rate. As nearly all the coast watered by the Gulf of Mexico was claimed by the Spanish throne, England soon undertook to stock with slaves what was one day to be the southern part of the United States. It is calculated that the English ships transported between the year 1700 and 1750, 1,500,000 colored people, of whom, however, a good many met with a premature death. In 1763, it has been calculated that in North America there were about 300,000 people of color. The slave dealer's profits were very large. At the commencement of the nineteenth century a slave could be captured with often little cost to the slave-dealer, or bought on the coast of Africa for about ten dollars. A schooner of even ninety tons could carry two hundred and twenty colored people in her hold—and of course a bigger vessel a larger number. Each negro that survived the voyage could be sold in Cuba, or in certain harbors of North or South America

* " The War of American Independence, 1775-1783," by J. M. Ludlow.

for five hundred dollars. To make a round trip from America to Africa might take about four months' time. After deducting all expenses the slaver could make an enormous profit.

In the colonies of North America there were found men who boldly denounced slavery from the pulpit, and through the press, and for doing so were, by a certain class of people, stigmatized "Abolitionists." One of these men was Anthony Benezet, whose ancestors had been driven from France by the persecution of the Romish Church. This noble Huguenot, becoming a citizen of the United States, was filled with horror at the wickedness of the slave-trade and of slavery. He wrote a book which was destined to have an astonishing influence for good. The book fell into the hands of a young Englishman named Thomas Clarkson, who, being deeply affected by the facts which it made public, became one of the most distinguished philanthropists of his age. His life may even be said to have been heroic and romantic. He had had his attention especially called to the slave traffic as he was about finishing his collegiate course by some one having thoughtfully offered a prize for a dissertation on that subject. He was instrumental in influencing Wilberforce to take a stand in Parliament against the accursed traffic. After years of labor Wilberforce was enabled to induce England —especially as the United States government had commenced to take effective measures against the further importation of slaves into the Republic—to give up the execrable business and to appropriate about 100,000,000 dollars for the purchase and freedom of the 750,000 or more slaves in the British West Indies ;—an act which in its turn was to have a far-reaching influence for good on what was sometimes called Spanish America, where people had

freed their slaves when they, at a cost of perhaps not less
than a million of lives, cast off the horrid yoke of the
Spanish Crown.   The Revolutions in Mexico and in
Central and South America were in their turn the means
of causing, during the Administration of President John
Quincy Adams, many a debate in the United States Congress on questions respecting slavery—debates which were
constantly to be reopened until the abolition of slavery
in the United States was accomplished.   The Christian
sentiment against holding human beings in bondage was
in time to be felt even in the large, wondrously fertile,
and beautiful island of Cuba—an island whose history is a
sad tale of oppression by a despotic European monarchy.
Even to the vast and sunny land of Brazil was to be borne
a sentiment—which in time was to have its effect—opposed to men owning as beasts of burden their brethren.
In future from America, instead of the slave-dealer, are to
go to the dark continent many colored missionaries, who
have been Americanized in the best sense of the word,—
missionaries bearing the wondrous light of Christianity
and its accompanying blessings.

> " Thy chains are broken, Africa, be free !
> Oh ! ye winds and waves,
> Waft the glad tidings to the land of slaves."

Jefferson believed that it was not only the duty of
American statesmanship to stop the slave-trade, but it
may here be somewhat incidentally stated that, in a
plan which he drew up for the abolition of slavery in the
United States, he provided that the federal government
should, at its own expense, educate the colored people.

When Secretary of State, under Washington's administration, Jefferson in various ways endeavored to exert an
influence against the slave-trade.   When President of the
United States,—at a time when the slave-trade was still

held to be a legitimate business by the English government,—he addressed Congress in a forcible manner on the
importance of providing, just as soon as it could constitutionally be done, measures to stop the slave traffic. When
in France he had been invited to become a member of a
society which had for its object the abolition of the slave-
trade. Although for prudential reasons he did not join
the association—fearing that it would not be proper for
an American Minister in a foreign land to take such a
step, and that if he did so he would excite prejudices
against himself which might some time be a means of de-
feating projects in which he might engage in the interests
of the colored people,—yet under date of Feb. 12th, 1788,
to a member of this society, a Mr. Warville, he wrote:
" I am very sensible of the honor you propose to me, of
becoming a member of the society for the abolition of the
slave-trade. You know that nobody wishes more ardently
to see an abolition, not only of the trade, but of the
condition of slavery; and certainly, nobody will be more
willing to encounter every sacrifice for that purpose."

One day, in the year 1815, a stranger called at Monticello—the beautiful home of Jefferson. The visitor was
a Mr. Julius Melbourn. Greatly admiring the venerable
statesman, he had sought from a friend a letter of introduction to him. A book in the New York State Library,
at Albany, can be seen by the careful student of history,
in which there is an account of this visit and the testimony of Mr. Melbourn to some remarks on colored
people which Jefferson made to him,—remarks which in
due time will be seen to be worthy, to some extent, of
the consideration of a class of citizens found even to this
day in the United States. The book is entitled " Life
and Opinions of Julius Melbourn, with Sketches of the
Lives and Characters of Thomas Jefferson, J. Q. Adams,

John Randolph and Several Other Eminent American Statesmen "—" Edited by a Late Member of Congress [Jabas Hammond], Syracuse." Published in 1847.* Mr. Melbourn thus describes his visit:

" I was conducted to his study, or reading-room, where I found him at a table covered with books and papers. He rose when I entered and received me with great politeness and apparent cordiality. I instantly found myself at perfect ease in his presence. * * * There was such strong evidence of high intellectual power in his high forehead, and in the form of his face and head, that I could not fail of admiring him. A philosophic calmness and a glow of benevolence, so distinctly marked every feature of his face, that while he was reading Mr. Pendleton's letter, and before he had uttered a word, I was charmed with him, and loved him as an old and familiar friend. I suppose that part of Mr. Pendleton's letter, which stated that I was born a slave, and was of African descent, excited his curiosity, for he immediately commenced a conversation, evidently with a view to ascertain the strength of my mind, and to what degree it had been cultivated. He inquired of me whether I had seen the building, then lately erected for the University of Virginia, and said he intended it should be free for the instruction of all sects and *colors*. He expressed his deep anxiety for the improvement of the minds, and the elevation of the character of, as he was pleased to call them, ' our colored brethren.' * * * I remained in the neighborhood of Monticello nearly a week, and spent a portion of every day in Mr. Jefferson's library, at his pressing invitation. On Tuesday before I left these quiet philosophic shades, I received a card from Mr. Jefferson, inviting me to dine with him in company with a few

* The publishers of the " Life and Opinions of Julius Melbourn," etc., were Hall and Dickson, Syracuse, N. Y. and A. S. Barnes & Co. of New York.

8

friends the next day at four o'clock.   I went to his house
and found there Chief-Justice Marshall, Mr. Wirt, Mr.
Samuel Dexter of Boston, and Dr. Samuel L. Mitchell of
New York. The Chief-Justice had come into the neighborhood on some business pertaining to the University, Mr.
Wirt was on his annual visit to Mr. Jefferson, and Mr.
Dexter and Mr. Mitchell being on a tour to South Carolina, so arranged their journey as on their way to call on
the old sage of Monticello.   I was announced as a young
gentleman from North Carolina,—introduced by Mr. Pendleton, who was well known to most of the persons present.

   " It will be recollected that in the year 1798, Judge
Marshall was a Virginian Federalist, that he was the
favorite of the then President, Mr. John Adams, who
appointed him ambassador to France, Secretary of State,
and afterwards Chief-Justice of the United States. * * *
Mr. Dexter was, during the presidency of the elder Adams,
an ardent Federalist and Secretary of the War Department. * * * Dr. Mitchell was a very learned man, pas-
sionately devoted to the natural sciences.   He had been
a Democratic senator of the United States, when Mr.
Jefferson was President. * * * Of Mr. Wirt, I need not
speak otherwise than to say he was one of the most
amiable of men.   His talents are universally known and
acknowledged. * * * There was also there one other
remarkable man from the North.   It was Elder John Leland. * * * He was a Baptist minister, who then lived in
the western part of Massachusetts.   He was very zealous,
both as a politician and sectarian, and was a man of some
wit.   He was the author of a pamphlet entitled ' *Jack
Nips* on Infant Baptism.' "

   It was certainly kind in Jefferson to invite Mr. Melbourn to his table.   Little did his distinguished guests
suspect that their fellow-guest had been born a slave in

North Carolina. Mr. Melbourn had told his host his history in the earnest, friendly conversations which they had had together in the library at Monticello. The talented company made a pleasant social circle. One of the subjects into which the conversation finally drifted was slavery. Mr. Dexter expressed the opinion that slavery, and only slavery, could break up the United States, and alluded to the strange arrangement by which the States in which slavery existed were allowed a much larger representation in the federal government than were the free States.

" 'Oh,' said Mr. Jefferson, 'dismiss your fears on that subject, slavery will soon be abolished in all the States.'

" 'Never,' said Judge Marshall, 'never by the voluntary consent of the slaveholding States.'

" 'I regret,' replied Mr. Jefferson, 'that so attentive an observer as you are, Chief-Justice, should entertain such an opinion. I well know that at the time American Independence was declared, no member, either north or south, expected that slavery would continue as long as it has.'

" 'I can well believe that,' said Mr. Wirt, 'for they must have felt that the continuance of slavery was directly adverse to their declaration, that all men are born free and equal, &c.'

" 'But,' said Dr. Mitchell, 'I very much doubt whether, according to the laws of nature, the Africans are not formed to be subject to the Caucasian race. From my own observations I am satisfied that nature has formed an essential difference between the two races, and much to the disadvantage of the negro race.' The learned gentleman then dwelt upon the brain of a negro and of his white brother and ended by saying, 'If your position, that all men are born equal is politically true, it is physically false.'

"'As regards personal rights,' said Mr. Jefferson, 'it seems to me most palpably absurd, that the individual rights of volition and locomotion should depend on the degree of intellectual power possessed by the individual. I should hardly be willing to subscribe to the doctrine, that because the Chief-Justice has a stronger mind or a more capacious and better formed brain than I, that therefore he has a right to make me his slave. But, Doctor,' continued Mr. Jefferson, 'may not the diet and exercise, bodily and mentally, of a child produce some effect on the size, shape, and quality of the brain? I will suppose that my friend, Mr. Dexter, has two sons, the oldest of whom shall be six years old, as nearly alike as brothers of the age of five and six years generally are. Suppose the younger to be transferred to a rice plantation in South Carolina, placed in a negro cabin, and brought up with the field-slaves, associating with them; and that the elder should be continued in Mr. Dexter's family, associate with none but highly intellectual people; then let his education be completed by four years residence and tuition at Cambridge. Look at the heads and faces of these boys when they shall respectively arrive at mature age. * * * Do you not all know that the difference would be immense? But to do justice to the negro race, and in order to carry out the experiment fairly, we ought to suppose that the younger has married a Caucasian slave, and let Dr. Mitchell dissect and compare the heads of the great-grandchildren of the issue of the elder brother. I ask what would be the result of that experiment?'

"'I do not mean to advocate slavery,' said the Chief-Justice,—'I wish, from my soul I wish, it was abolished.'"*

The learned judge then with judicial eloquence spoke

---

* See " Life and opinions of Julius Melbourn," p. 75.

of the difficulties in the way of enacting laws abolishing slavery, and alluded to how Jefferson and Wythe
had been prevented from even presenting such a bill when
they had been members of the Assembly of Virginia.

Mr. Leland, the minister, held that slavery ought not
to be abolished, and had considerable to say on the theory
that the colored people were descended from Ham, and
that it was decreed in the Bible that they should not be
emancipated from slavery.

Mr. Jefferson requested the minister to look at Mr.
Melbourn, who it may be incidentally remarked, was
three quarters white. The guests were astonished when
told that Mr. Melbourn had been born a slave and freed
by a pious lady. Jefferson paid him high compliments,
adding: " He is now a man of wealth. He has by his
own efforts and industry cultivated and well-improved his
mind—a mind which I religiously believe, your missionary observations, friend Leland, and Doctor Mitchell's
dissections to the contrary notwithstanding, is of the first
order of human intellects." The gaze of the entire dinner party was turned upon Mr. Melbourn—the piercing
eye of the Chief-Justice in particular rested upon him.
Jefferson then related to his guests some parts of Mr.
Melbourn's history.

Julius Melbourn had been born a slave on a small
plantation, owned by a Major Johnson, situated about ten
miles from Raleigh, North Carolina. His mother, who
was half-white, was but seventeen years old when he was
born. His young mother was too delicate to do as much
work as was required of her, so she was sold by a negro
buyer to be driven to Georgia. The separation from her
child was deeply affecting. As she shrieked and in madness tore her hair and bathed her son's face with scalding
tears, she was manacled. Her son, in after years, tried to

solace himself with the sad hope that his loving mother had probably *perished* in the damp and chilly rice-fields of Georgia. The boy lived on Johnson's plantation until he was about five years of age, when the noble widow of Lieutenant Melbourn of the British Navy bought him and gave him an education, and his liberty, and every thing which he valued in life. Mrs. Melbourn had heard in England much about "liberty" in the United States. Fascinated with what she had heard of the liberty which prevailed in the United States, she had come to the "land of the free," there to be filled with horror and indignation against the slavery which existed in the Southern States. She had a considerable fortune, and had brought to America a valuable collection of books left her by her husband. She had a son of her own on whom was centred her affections.

Although the little slave boy whom she had bought was three quarters white and had blue eyes, yet race prejudice was so great in the neighborhood in which Mrs. Melbourn resided that she could not send him to school. She therefore employed a Methodist minister to teach the more than orphan boy. Mrs. Melbourn sent her own son to Princeton College, where he graduated with the highest honors of his class. There was a noble and beautiful young lady, who belonged to a wealthy family near to where Mrs. Melbourn lived, to whom her son became engaged in marriage. One day when the young lady was visiting the mother of her affianced, a stranger rode in haste to the house and as gently as possible broke the sad news that young Mr. Melbourn had been betrayed into a duel and that he had been killed. The widow, learning that her only son was dead, fainted. The young lady also swooned. This is not the place to speak of a noble mother's love for a son. Suffice it to say that Mrs. Melbourn never recovered from her sorrow, but erelong was lying on a death-bed. The young lady, in a measure, recovered from the desolating blow which had fallen upon her, but she was to go through life with a broken heart, and also to sink into an untimely grave. The young lady had a maid, or companion, who although seven eighths white was a slave. She was, however, but a slave in name, as she was educated and allowed every liberty, and it was her happiness to do acts of kindness to her mistress, Miss Laura, to whom she was very much of a companion, almost a sister. As Julius—the name given to the youth rescued from slavery—approached manhood he fell in love with the refined and beautiful young maid, who was called Maria. It was arranged that Maria should be given her freedom as soon as the lovers were old enough to marry. As Mrs. Melbourn lay on her dying bed she called Julius to her side and told him that she had left in her will money to be appropriated for the buying of the freedom of Maria should any unforeseen event happen by which the girl's kind owners should be unable to free her. Mrs. Melbourn also, after providing for some benefactions, left the bulk of her fortune to Julius.

> " The death-bed of the just is yet undrawn
> By mortal hand : it merits a divine."

In time a young Virginian named St. John paid attentions to the young lady to whom Mrs. Melbourn's son had been engaged. The young lady, however, did not reciprocate his professed regard. Her father earnestly used his influence with her to induce the young heiress to accept Mr. St. John's hand. At last she yielded to her father's wishes and was married. Before long it became evident that she had married a gambler and, what was worse, a drunkard. Her father, realizing that his daugh-

ter had married her dissipated husband through his influence, had an affecting interview with her in the course of
which he bitterly upbraided himself for being responsible
for his daughter's misery. Suddenly he fell to the ground
struck with apoplexy. As soon as the old man was buried
a great change took place in the position of the slaves on
the plantation. The old man had died without making a
will. His fortune passed to St. John as the husband of
his only daughter. Maria's position was especially terrible, as her dissipated new master had designs upon her
honor which must not here be even mentioned. He refused to permit her to be sold. He forbade her marriage
to Julius. Her former mistress, however, caused Julius
to be sent for in Mr. St. John's absence, and sent for a
minister, and expressed her wish that the marriage should
at once take place. While the wedding ceremony was
being performed, Mr. St. John returned to the house and
was infuriated at learning that Julius and Maria were
about being married. His wife, however, who had always
been meek and submissive, became uncontrollably indignant with her immoral husband, and insisted that the
marriage should proceed. In Julius' hand a dagger
gleamed, but, happily, the ceremony was allowed to proceed. Maria, however, was still a slave. Any children
born to her would be slaves.

Mr. St. John mortgaged his wife's property and visited
Saratoga, New York. He there fell in with some professional gamblers, who won from him all his fortune.
Mr. St. John, hoping to retrieve his losses in a last desperate move, risked at the gaming table even his horses
and carriage. He lost; and was not even in a position to
pay his way back to his wife's plantation. In the meanwhile Maria had borne to Julius a son. Julius had been
called to Princeton College for a short time to settle an

account which the college had forgotten to forward to Mrs. Melbourn for the tuition of her dead son. The creditors of Mr. St. John at once took possession of his wife's estate and sold the slaves and everything belonging to the estate. The son of the man who had owned Julius cast covetous eyes on Maria. A kind minister in Julius' absence did everything that he could to buy her freedom. It was arranged that Maria's infant should be hidden in the cellar of the minister's house, but it was feared that it would be impossible to there secrete Maria. While Maria was thinking how she could hide herself until her husband's return, she was seized, manacled, and secreted from her friend the minister, and surreptitiously sold, and borne off in the direction of New Orleans. Mrs. St. John had in the meantime sunk into an untimely grave. When Julius Melbourn returned he was frenzied with grief. He at once bought the freedom of his son, who had been left behind the gang of slaves in which walked his forlorn wife. He started in pursuit of his wife, with the object of effecting her freedom, if that were possible. At last, after travelling a great distance, he caught up with Johnson, who had bought his wife. Johnson, on learning that Julius Melbourn was in the neighborhood, went at once, as the law allowed him to do, before a magistrate and declared that Julius was born a slave on his father's plantation; he did not add, however, that he had since been freed by Mrs. Melbourn. Julius was forthwith loaded with chains and cast into a dungeon. He was detained until, with the aid and by the kindness of the jailer, he could send to his far-distant, desecrated home and get written evidence of his emancipation. Before the days of railroads travelling was slow work, and three months were consumed before Julius Melbourn could again go in pursuit of the slave driver. In the meantime Johnson had made haste to ship Maria to New Orleans. On arriving in New Orleans horror entered the soul of the broken-hearted husband as he learned that his wife had been sold and resold until she had been bought for a certain plantation by its overseer. On going to the negro overseer he learned to his anguish that his wife had been afflicted with melancholy, and that about a month before he arrived she one evening had escaped and drowned herself in the river. Her body had not been recovered. Some of her clothes, however, had been found on the river's bank, which a negro kindly showed to the wretched husband. He found pinned in the frock bosom, in the handwriting of his young wife, a quotation which ran thus:

> " Shall they bury me in the deep,
> Where wind-forgetting waters sleep ?
> Shall they dig a grave for me
> Under the green-wood tree ?
> Or on the wild heath
> Where the wilder breath
> Of the storm doth blow ?
> Oh, no ! oh, no !"

There was nothing that attached the broken-hearted husband to life save his infant son. Full of despair young Melbourn returned to his far-off, former home. In time he came into possession of the fortune left him by his benefactress. He made suitable provision for the nurture and education of his child, whom he named Edward, after the son of Mrs. Melbourn who had been killed in the duel. He made good investments, and, restless, he might be called a wanderer on the earth.

As Mr. Jefferson related this story, he denounced, with great severity, laws which legalized the outrages to which Mr. Melbourn had been subjected. Mr. Wirt's countenance several times reddened with apparent indignation.

The dinner and conversation had been prolonged to a late hour. As Mr. Melbourn retired, Mr. Wirt, who at a later period became a member of the Cabinet of John Quincy Adams, followed him into the hall and took him by the hand and expressed a desire to continue the acquaintance. "I am mortified and ashamed," said Mr. Wirt, "that this glorious country sustains such laws as those under which you have suffered."

It may here be incidentally stated that however sorrowful was Mr. Melbourn's after-history it was not as sad as was the history of a vast number of slaves. As his son approached manhood he sent him to Princeton College within whose noble walls he was welcomed, although he had been born a slave. In time Edward graduated, and was seized with a longing to visit New Orleans and to look upon the sad spot where his mother in her loneliness and melancholy had preferred death to a life of cruellest outrage. Mr. Melbourn not only consented to his son's making the proposed pilgrimage, but agreed to accompany him. In New Orleans the desolate father and orphan youth traced the history of Maria. They visited the scenes of her sufferings. Her last purchaser had been a Mr. De Lisle, who had an overseer, into whose possession, practically, Maria had fallen. De Lisle proved himself to be a kind old man. The overseer had been killed in a broil with a Spaniard. From an old female slave, they learned that Maria had wept a great deal after being brought to the plantation, not because of the hard tasks allotted to her, but because of certain infamous designs, which must not here be mentioned, planned by her brutal overseer. "She was very handsome, and spoke with a kind, sweet voice," added the aged slave. As the poor old slave showed the father and son where the young slave-wife and mother had laid some clothes before meeting death, the son's eyes filled with tears, and the father stood like a statue, unable to move or speak. Many years had passed since he had for the last time seen his wife. His infant son had in the meanwhile grown to manhood. But the same love which he had ever felt for his wife burned within his bosom. He realized, however, the hopelessness of his ever meeting her again, until that great day when the grave shall give up its dead.

A part of Mr. Melbourn's sad history may be told in his own words. "We lingered some time around that fatal spot, that last trace of my ill-fated Maria. At length entering the carriage we rode about twenty miles, and stopped at a small village on the road to New Orleans, where we designed to remain until the next day. The evening being very pleasant, after tea I walked through the village, which was beautifully situated on the bank of the river. In returning to my lodgings I passed a small brick building, having the appearance of a Methodist chapel. A religious assembly were gathered there, and were then singing a hymn. To see what kind of people were collected on this occasion, and to wear away a part of the evening, I stepped into the house. It being quite full I took a seat near the door. Among the singers was a woman in the dress of a Quaker, with a hymn-book in her hand, on which her eyes were intently fixed, whose features forcibly brought Maria to my remembrance. I looked again; the resemblance was so perfect, that, forgetting for a moment the impossibility of her being alive, a faintness came over me. It soon occurred to my mind that it was an illusion of fancy, produced by the scenes so recently visited. I involuntarily groaned audibly. The woman looked up and saw me. She instantly turned pale, gave a piercing shriek, and fell to the floor. ' Mighty God ! ' I exclaimed, ' *it is* —*it is my Maria !* " Regardless of the proceedings of the meeting and every one around me, I sprang towards her and raised her in my arms. The congregation was in confusion : some ran for water, others seized hold of me, until I recovered sufficient recollection to say that this was my wife, whom I had for years believed dead. I caressed her and called her by name. At the sound of my voice, so long unheard, she revived and uttered a few incoherent words; every effort was made to restore her —but for some time her mind was much bewildered. She would cry out, ' Take care ! take care ! there they come to take me away ! where is my dagger ? I will never go alive ! ' I will not continue a description of this scene. She at length became calm ; her first inquiry after the return of her reason, was for her child. I told her he was alive and well, but dare not tell her he was so near. Maria fell on her knees and poured forth a prayer of thanksgiving and praise. It was eloquent, because it was the overflowing of her heart. The whole audience joined her, and responded audibly ' Amen.' Maria was conveyed to her home near by the chapel, and I hastened to seek Edward with the joyful intelligence that his mother lived. He could not be restrained from seeing her that night, and I returned to prepare her for the interview. I will not attempt to describe the affecting scene that followed. Maria was constantly distressed by the fear of being discovered ; and so long had she endured life without hope, that it was with difficulty she could be made to believe that I had abundant means to procure her ransom and that no possible danger could be apprehended. The reader can imagine how happily and quiet that night was the sleep of this long-persecuted being, this victim of slavery."

Maria's strange appearance at the religious meeting, where her practically long-dead husband met her, was thus briefly explained. On the plantation near New Orleans to which she had many years before been taken, she had been subjected by her brutal overseer to scourgings and innumerable insults. He had taken steps to accomplish by force her deepest dishonor. Rather than live a life of infamy and disgrace so dreadful that it must not be dwelt upon here, she, filled with despair, determined to seek relief in death. Wishing that it might be known that she had sought death rather than lead a life of deepest shame as well as slavery, she left evident indications of what she was about to do. She had laid some clothes on the banks of the Mississippi, whose turbid waters had received many a forlorn slave who had been driven by despair and woe to committing suicide. Mr. Melbourn in his account of his wife's history thus continues: " The road at that place approaches near the river; and at that point is a bluff of land which rises suddenly, so that a person travelling the road cannot be seen many yards from the place where Maria stood. It was a calm moonlight night. She had taken as she believed a last look upon the earth and sky, and ejaculated a prayer for her husband and son. At the moment she was about to take the fatal plunge, a gig, in which was a lady and servant, came in sight. ' Stop,' said the lady in a firm voice, ' what is thee doing?' Maria instantly recognized the language of a Quaker, having been acquainted with some members of a society of Friends in North Carolina, and she knew that they were not only friends to each other, but friends of man and of the slave. She instantly ran to the carriage and cried, ' Save me! O save me! I am a wretched creature who cannot live, and ought not thus to die.' In a few words she related to the lady her situation. Mrs. Benson, (for that was the name of the lady,) with great presence of mind, told her to get into the carriage, gave her a cloak to cover herself, and advised her to leave the dress hanging on a tree, as that might prevent pursuit. * * * She charged the boy, a negro, who scrupulously obeyed her injunctions, on pain of her displeasure, never to mention to any person where they had found Maria, and before morning this long-oppressed but unoffending woman was lodged in a neat secluded room in the cottage of Mrs. Benson."

Mr. Melbourn in a sketch of his life tells how the kind Quakeress had given it to be understood that Maria, whom she caused to be dressed as a Quakeress, was a niece of hers just come from Cuba. Maria was not supposed to speak English, so that she should not be betrayed by her voice. The overseer had traced Maria to the river's banks, but it will be readily understood that even with the help of bloodhounds he could not trace her any farther. The poor woman supposed that her husband, who had been cast into prison when he had caught up with the slaves with whom she had been driven to New Orleans, was, as well as was her child, hopelessly lost to her, or, more probably, they were both dead. Mr. Melbourn continuing his narrative said: "I rendered my thanks to Mrs. Benson with deep feelings of reverence and gratitude. I begged her to accept of some reward, which she refused, but I quite forced upon her a sum of money. In order that my long-lost wife might become *my own property*, and that no chances hereafter might be left for her last owner or his heirs to claim her, I returned with Maria to the house of Mr. De Lisle, and informed him of her existence, and in a brief manner made him acquainted with her history and my own. He listened attentively during the recital, and showed evidence of much feeling and kindness of heart. I proposed to restore him the money paid for Maria, with the interest from that time, and requested him to make a conveyance of her to me. 'No,' said the generous Frenchman, 'you have both had trouble enough—I will take nothing.' I remonstrated with him without effect; he sent for a scrivener, and executed a bill of sale of Maria to me. On receiving it I could not refrain from taking Maria in my arms, saying, 'Now, indeed, you are mine by the laws of God and man!' She could not utter a word, but her countenance was lighted up with a smile, and her eyes swam with tears.'" Mr. Melbourn does not fail to record how Mrs. Benson, the kind Quakeress, gave Maria motherly admonition. She told Maria that she had done wrong when she had determined to take her own life;—that, at the moment when she was about taking the fatal plunge, God was sending her deliverance; and that if any trouble should ever again overtake her, not to so far forget her heavenly Father's goodness as to think of taking her own life. Mr. Melbourn and his family, after witnessing some scenes of slavery as dreadful as were some of the horrors of the Inquisition, went to England, where he was treated with kindness and respect. As strange as it may seem, Mr. Melbourn, once being asked an alms, by a wretched intemperate creature, who turned out to be Mr. St. John, gave the degraded being a dollar. Johnson, who had done him cruel wrong, in time became an inmate of a prison. He had the boldness or effrontery to beg Mr. Melbourn to help him in his wretchedness. Remembering the lessons taught him by his benefactress, Mrs. Melbourn, he returned him good for evil, and sent the prisoner, whose penitence was doubtful, fifty dollars. A slave who had been kind to his wife, Mr. Melbourn ransomed and gave her employment in his family.

Mrs. Melbourn ever dressed as a Quakeress. Edward Melbourn was furnished with quite a large capital and engaged in business in England. Mr. Melbourn will doubtless be pardoned for having published some remarks contrasting unfavorably the boasted liberty—the race prejudices—which prevailed in the United States and the nobler spirit which, as a rule he felt, prevailed in England.

It may here be incidentally remarked that Mrs. Melbourn's kindness to Julius is not the only instance in which the heart of woman has beat with kindness for the orphan. In Greenwood Cemetery the visitor, on looking at one of the most beautiful monuments of that lovely, picturesque resting-place of the dead, can see writing which in substance reads thus: " Erected to the Memory of —— by the poor orphan boy whom she educated and to whom he owes every thing dear to him in life." It was to the kindness of a woman that Martin Luther owed his education.

It has been seen, and let the fact be especially noticed, that in the account which Mr. Melbourn has recorded of his first visit to Monticello, Jefferson stated that he intended the University of Virginia to "be free for the instruction of all sects and *colors*"; and that he expressed his deep anxiety for the improvement of the minds, and the elevation of the character of, as he was pleased to call them, "our colored brethren." In many parts of the United States colored youth are welcomed in public halls of learning and hold scholarly fellowship with their white brethren. People of all colors worship together in the house of God and love to look upon each other as brethren. But even to this day, in too many parts of the Republic, race prejudice—which may be called a relic of the vile institution of slavery,—is sadly

evident.   Many weighty reasons may justly be urged in
favor of opening the fane of knowledge to youth of all
colors.

It may here be asked : " Did not Jefferson himself own
slaves?"   Alas, it must be answered that he did.   Such
an excuse as he made when he said, " The laws do not
permit us to turn them loose,   *   *   *   and to commute
them for other property, is to commit them to those
whose usage of them we cannot control," could not be
accepted by some friends of civil liberty.   Prof. Wythe,
who was one of Jefferson's old instructors and a signer of
the Declaration of Independence and one of the framers
of the Constitution of the United States, found a way to
liberate his slaves, as did General Gates, into whose hand
the British General Burgoyne had surrendered his sword
and army.   John Quincy Adams even criticised Jefferson for
not having, while entertaining the convictions which he
did respecting slavery, taken a bolder stand than he did
in the struggle of his day in behalf of the abolition of
slavery.   Adams himself indeed at times acted an heroic
part in that struggle.   He saw it affect in many ways the
policy of the United States government.   He had reason
to even feel that the fear of new free States being formed
out of the splendid territory, at present under the English
flag, stretching as far north as what is now known as
Alaska, led President Polk, who was too partial to the
peculiar institution of the South, to surrender the claims
of the United States to that territory, and that in various
ways the so-called slave power was the greatest enemy
with which what is known as the " Monroe Doctrine " had
to contend.   Probably John Quincy Adams would not
have criticised Jefferson, if he had known how wonderfully great was to be the service which he was to have a
mysterious part in rendering his country by his quiet

efforts to educate and to encourage youth to view intelligently the evils of slavery and to war in the most effective
manner against the institution. One cannot perhaps help
feeling, however, that when Franklin was acting as president of an abolition society in Pennsylvania and nobly
petitioning Congress to exert its influence against slavery,
and when John Jay was acting as president of an abolition society in New York,—the gifted Hamilton being
associated with him,—and when men were abolishing
slavery in Northern States—Jefferson might have acted a
bolder part than he did. It is, however, but fair to state
that Jefferson, as far as is known, never bought a slave.
His slaves came to him by inheritance. His wife also
owned slaves, having inherited one hundred and thirty-five
of them. When, in the year 1767, Jefferson entered the
House of Burgesses of Virginia he introduced a bill into
the House—and that, it would seem, inside of five days
after taking his seat—empowering slave-owners to free their
slaves. When he became a member of the Assembly of
Virginia during the war of the Revolution he seconded a
bill to abolish slavery in Virginia. Although the bill was
not passed, yet he did succeed in carrying successfully
through the Assembly a bill abolishing the slave-trade as
far as Virginia was concerned. In a sketch of "Life at
Monticello"—Jefferson's home,—written by the overseer
of Jefferson's plantation and published by the Rev.
Hamilton W. Pearson, it is stated that one of his slaves
made his escape. It is also stated that on the plantation at
which Jefferson generally lived, a slave-girl, almost white,
was born. The overseer states that some people said that
Jefferson's honor was compromised in the birth of this
child. He added, however, that to his own positive
knowledge such was not the case, as he himself knew who
was the father of the child. Jefferson treated the girl

kindly, gave her her liberty and fifty dollars, and had her taken to Philadelphia to live. He also provided for the freedom and support of other slaves—"humbly and earnestly," as he wrote in his will, praying the Legislature of Virginia to add to the favors which it had in past times conferred upon him, by permitting, notwithstanding the laws of Virginia, these slaves to be free.

Before the death of Jefferson's wife—as early as 1778,—Washington had earnestly, in a letter, urged Jefferson and some other patriots not to be satisfied with "places in their own State * * * but to attend to the momentous concerns of an empire." After Jefferson had emerged from the long and dreadful stupor caused by the death of his wife, he had for some time before going to Europe served in the Continental Congress. He and a Mr. Chase of Maryland, and a Mr. Howell of Rhode Island, acted as a committee to prepare a plan of government for the Western territory of the United States. The bill, which Jefferson himself reported to Congress, contained a clause which provided : " That after the year 1800 of the Christian era there shall be neither slavery nor involuntary servitude in any of the said States, otherwise than in punishment of crimes, whereof the party shall have been personally guilty." In Congress, on the 19th of April, 1784, Mr. Spaight of North Carolina, moved, and Mr. Read of South Carolina seconded the motion, that the clause prohibiting slavery in the vast territory be stricken out of the bill. Eleven States were at the time represented in Congress. All the Representatives of the Northern States voted in favor of the prohibition of slavery, while all the Representatives of the Southern States voted in favor of slavery—except Jefferson, and Hugh Williamson of North Carolina. Mr. Williamson was at a later day held in such honor in

North Carolina that he was elected to the convention which framed the Constitution of the United States. Sixteen members voted against allowing slavery to be introduced into the great Western territory, and seven members voted against the proposed prohibition. In accordance with a rule of procedure at the time in force in Congress, the vote against slavery was not large enough by one vote to carry the day. What were Jefferson's feelings on the announcement of this vote? The answer to this question may be inferred from sad lines which he wrote when making some written criticisms on an article on the "United States" which a French author submitted to him in manuscript before inserting it in the "Encyclopédie Méthodique." He thus wrote: "There were ten States present; six voted unanimously for it [that is for the prohibition of slavery in the territory], three against it, and one was divided; and seven votes being requisite to decide the proposition affirmatively, it was lost. The voice of a single individual of the State which was divided, or of one of those which were of the negative, would have prevented this abominable crime from spreading itself over the new country. Thus we see the fate of millions unborn hanging on the tongue of one man, and heaven was silent in that awful moment! But it is to be hoped it will not always be silent, and that the friends to the rights of human nature will in the end prevail." * Jefferson as he proceeded drew attention to the fact that Congress had again taken the matter up.

About the same period that Jefferson wrote the lines which have just been quoted, he wrote to M. de Meusnier, who was connected with the "Encyclopédie Méthodique," quite an account of the efforts which he, and his justly distinguished friend Wythe, and others had made to abolish

---

* "Jefferson's Works," vol. ix., p. 276.

slavery in Virginia. In his remarks he said: "What a stupendous, what an incomprehensible machine is man! who can endure toil, famine, stripes, imprisonment, and death itself, in vindication of his own liberty, the next moment be deaf to all those motives whose power supported him through his trial, and inflict on his fellowmen a bondage, one hour of which is fraught with more misery than ages of that he rose in rebellion to oppose. But we must await, with patience, the workings of an overruling Providence, and hope that that is preparing the deliverance of these, our suffering brethren. When the measures of their tears shall be full, when their groans shall have involved heaven itself in darkness, doubtless, a God of justice will awaken to their distress, and by diffusing light and liberality among their oppressors, or, at length, by his exterminating thunder, manifest his attention to the things of this world, and that they are not left to the guidance of a blind fatality."*

However sadly Jefferson felt on account of the failure of the bill to prohibit slavery in the Western territory, the policy which he had helped to inaugurate was soon in part, and ultimately altogether, to prevail. On March 8th, 1785, Timothy Pickering wrote to Rufus King, drawing attention to the importance of making provision for the founding of schools and academies, etc., in the Western territory. In the course of his letter he said: "Congress once made this important declaration, 'that all men are created equal; that they are endowed by their Creator with certain inalienable rights; that among these are life, liberty, and the pursuit of happiness; and these truths were held to be self-evident. To suffer the continuance of slaves till they can gradually be emancipated, in States already overrun with them, may be pardonable,

* Ibid., vol. ix., p. 279.

because unavoidable without hazarding greater evils; but to introduce them into countries where none now exist can never be forgiven. For God's sake, then, let one more effort be made to prevent so terrible a calamity! The fundamental constitutions for those States are yet liable to alterations, and this is probably the only time when the evil can certainly be prevented. It will be infinitely easier to prevent the evil at first than to eradicate it, or check it, in any future time." *

In the last Continental Congress, the question of establishing a government for a large part of the territory which Jefferson had striven to save from being cursed with slavery, came up for settlement. On this occasion Southern statesmen acted in a right noble manner. They were in the majority in Congress and could do as they pleased. They unanimously voted to adopt the measure which Jefferson had recommended, prohibiting slavery in the territory. Thus an immense territory was saved from the intellectual, economic, and moral blight which ever accompanies slavery, and a policy opposed to the extension of human bondage was inaugurated which was destined to exert a vast influence on the future destiny of the world. Provision had been made in 1785, by the Continental Congress, for the instruction in letters of the future citizens of this territory. On May 20th, 1785, Congress enacted that "there shall be reserved the lot No. 16 of every township for the maintenance of public schools within the said township." Thus about one thirty-sixth of the territory was at once consecrated to the support of its future schools. On July 13th, 1787, the last Continental Congress added, without a dissenting voice, to the

---

* " Pickering's Pickering," v. i., pp. 509, 510. See Bancroft's " History of the Constitution," v. i., p. 178—a work worthy of being in every statesman's hands.

first enactment providing for the intellectual culture of the States which were one day to be formed out of the vast territory, the following provision : " And for extending the fundamental principles of civil and religious liberty, which form the basis whereon these republics, their laws and constitutions, are erected ; to fix and establish these principles as the basis of all laws, constitutions, and governments which forever after shall be formed in the said territory ; * * * religion, morality, and knowledge being necessary to good government and the happiness of mankind—schools and the means of education shall be forever encouraged." This Congress also, when selling a large tract of land to John Cleves Symmes, provided for the establishment of a university in what was at the time a wilderness. When selling another immense tract of land, a similar wise provision was made. Washington in a letter dated 19th June, 1788, speaking of a colony which was about to settle on one of the tracts of land which had been sold, wrote : " No colony in America was ever settled under such favorable auspices, as that which has just commenced at the Muskingum. Information, property and strength will be its characteristics. * * * If I was a young man, just preparing to begin the world, or if advanced in life, and had a family to make provision for, I know of no country where I should rather fix my habitation than in some part of that region." When Washington was President of the United States he officially, with the concurrence of both Houses of Congress, confirmed the great land grant which the old Continental Congress had made for educational purposes in the Western territory. Out of this territory consecrated to enlightened liberty—of which Washington spoke so highly —were to be raised many men who were to take a conspicuous part in redeeming the nation from the woes caused by slavery. The bill excluding slavery from the vast Western territory, which Jefferson as chairman of a committee introduced into the Continental Congress, embraced in many respects a policy which Hamilton urged when a member of the Continental Congress. It suggested a policy which was in time to be championed by such great statesmen as John Quincy Adams, William H. Seward, and Abraham Lincoln. The policy which it embraced was to lead to a civil war in the United States, and to the tragic termination of slavery on the North American continent. The bill by which slavery was to be unknown in the territories, which Jefferson reported to Congress, is still preserved in his own handwriting in the archives of the national Capitol. Many highly exciting scenes were to take place in Congress, and in other parts of the Republic, whenever the question of not permitting slavery in new territories was to be discussed. When the great and angry debate known as "the Missouri Compromise" was in progress, even Jefferson, once speaking of the discussion in one of his letters, sadly faltered. With plausible but fallacious reasoning he suggested that it would be better for the slaves not to be confined within narrow limits, and that at best not allowing slaves to go into new territory would not eradicate slavery from the United States, which he held should be the aim of good statesmanship.

But to return to the noble labors of Jefferson in behalf of the enslaved. In a book which he published when in France, entitled "Notes on Virginia,"—a book made up largely, if not altogether, of letters to the French government, which he had written before his wife's death,—he sadly said: "There must doubtless be an unhappy influence on the manners of our people, produced by the influence of slavery among us. The whole commerce

between master and slave is a perpetual exercise of the
most boisterous passions, the most unremitting despotism
on the one part, and degrading submission on the other.
Our children see this, and learn to imitate it ; for man is
an imitative animal.   This quality is the germ of all education in him.   From his cradle to his grave he is learning
to do what he sees others do.   If a parent could find no
motive either in his philanthropy or his self-love, for re-
straining the intemperance of passion towards his slave, it
should always be a sufficient one that his child is present.
But generally it is not sufficient.   The parent storms, the
child looks on, catches the lineaments of wrath, puts on
the same airs in the circle of smaller slaves, gives a loose
to the worst of passions, and thus nursed, educated, and
daily exercised in tyranny, cannot but be stamped by it
with odious peculiarities.   The man must be a prodigy
who can retain his manners and morals undepraved, by
such circumstances.   And with what execration should
the statesman be loaded, who, permitting one-half the
citizens thus to trample on the rights of the other, trans-
forms those into despots, and these into enemies,
destroys the morals of the one part, and the *amor patriæ*
of the other.   For if a slave can have a country in this
world, it must be any other in preference to that in
which he is born to live and labor for another ; in which
he must lock up the faculties of his nature, contribute as
far as depends on his individual endeavors to the evan-
ishment of the human race, or entail his own miserable
condition on the endless generations proceeding from
him.   With the morals of the people, their industry is
also destroyed.   For in a warm climate, no man will
labor for himself, who can make another labor for him.
This is so true, that of the proprietors of slaves a very
small proportion indeed are ever seen to labor.   And can

the liberties of a nation be thought secure when we have removed their only firm basis, a conviction in the minds of the people that these liberties are the gift of God? That they are not to be violated but with his wrath? Indeed I tremble for my country when I reflect that God is just; that his justice cannot sleep forever; that considering numbers, nature and natural means only, a revolution of the wheel of fortune, an exchange of situation, is among possible events; that it may become probable by supernatural interference! The Almighty has no attribute which can take sides with us in such a contest. But it is impossible to be temperate, and to pursue this subject through the various considerations of policy, of morals, of history natural and civil. We must be contented to hope they will force their way into every one's mind. I think a change already perceptible, since the origin of the present revolution. The spirit of the master is abating, that of the slave is rising from the dust, his condition mollifying, the way I hope preparing, under the auspices of heaven, for a total emancipation, and that this is disposed, in the order of events, to be with the consent of the masters, rather than by their extirpation."*

Jefferson issued a private edition of the volume in which he expressed his views on negro slavery. In a way costly to himself he endeavored to create a right feeling in Virginia respecting this iniquitous institution. In a letter to General Chastellux, dated June 7th, 1785, alluding to his observations on slavery, he said: "It is possible that in my own country these strictures might produce an irritation which would indispose the people towards the two great objects I have in view; that is, the emancipation of their slaves, and the settlement of their constitution on a firmer and more permanent basis. If I

---

* "Notes on Virginia," chap. xviii.

learn from thence, that they will not produce that effect, I have printed and reserved just copies enough to be able to give one to every young man at the College. It is to them I look, to the rising generation, and not to the one now in power, for these great reformations." In a letter to James Madison and in another to Monroe, Jefferson expressed similar intentions. Madison and Monroe wrote to Jefferson encouraging him to give to the students the book. Before he went to France—indeed, as early as 1779—Jefferson had been elected a member of the Board of Visitors of the University of William and Mary, and had given much attention to the course of study of the students.

Under date of August 7th, 1785, Jefferson wrote a letter to Dr. Price, of England, who had sent him a pamphlet on slavery. In the course of this letter, he said : " In Maryland I do not find such a disposition to begin the redress of this enormity as in Virginia. This is the next State to which we may turn our eyes for the interesting spectacle of justice, in conflict with avarice and oppression ; a conflict wherein the sacred side is gaining daily recruits, from the influx into office of young men grown, and growing up. These have sucked in the principles of liberty, as it were, with their mother's milk ; and it is to them I look with anxiety to turn the fate of this question. Be not therefore discouraged. What you have written will do a great deal of good : and could you still trouble yourself with our welfare, no man is more able to give aid to the laboring side. The College of William and Mary, in Williamsburg, since the re-modelling of its plan, is the place where are collected together all the young men of Virginia, under preparation for public life. They are there under the direction (most of them) of a Mr. Wythe, one of the most virtuous of characters, and whose sentiments on the subject of slavery, are unequivocal. I am satisfied, if you could resolve to address an exhortation to those young men, with all that eloquence of which you are master, that its influence on the future decision of this important question, would be great, perhaps, decisive."

From the halls of the University of William and Mary were indeed to go forth influences in opposition to slavery which were to have a singularly important bearing on American history. It is not given to mortals to trace all the mysterious workings of Divine providence ; but the thoughtful historian may well sometimes pause to notice how one event has led to another, until a grand result has surprised a nation. Could the world always see the grandeur of even an humble effort to direct aright the thoughts of youth, or the ultimate effects which sometimes follow a noble act, it would see some of the secret springs of the greatest and most praiseworthy events of history. Among the youth who attended the celebrated University of William and Mary—a university whose Chancellor for years was George Washington — was a youth named Edward Coles. This young man was born on Dec. 15th, 1786, in the same county in which Jefferson was born and in which he lived. Edward Coles' father had been a colonel in the Revolutionary war and at his house some of the most distinguished statesmen of Virginia were wont to visit. Young Coles, after studying at Hampden Sidney College, which was under Presbyterian control, repaired to the University of Virginia. Among his classmates were young men who were to rise to the highest stations in life. When the time had nearly come for him to graduate he severely fractured his leg and came near losing his limb. After leaving college he devoted two years to reading and study,—going over a wide range of history and of politics. At college and in his private reading he earnestly considered the subject of slavery. A time was to come when he was himself at his own expense to publish Jefferson's views respecting the holding of human beings in bondage, and to exert an influence which was to be felt for many a year—if not, indeed, forever—against the spread of slavery in America.

In the year 1809 Edward Coles was twenty-three years of age. He was the proprietor of a plantation and slaves which had recently by his father been bequeathed to him. He was a young man of high education, of good manners, and was handsome. His friend President Madison invited him to accept the appointment of private secretary to the President, a position of much dignity and importance. Peculiar reasons bade young Coles accept this position. He had formed convictions respecting slavery which called upon a generous nature to make costly sacrifices. He had determined that as for himself he would not hold human beings in bondage, nor would he live in a part of the country in which the laws were as unjust to a large part of the human family as they were in the slave States,—even though he should have to give up home and friends and comparative wealth. By accepting the position to which President Madison invited him, he felt that he could, while earning an honorable subsistence in the service of his country, lay plans by which he could free all of his slaves and provide for their future welfare.

Amidst the varied duties of public office young Coles unbosomed his heart to Jefferson, at the same time earnestly and eloquently exhorting him to undertake even in his old age to marshal every force at his command against slavery, and to inaugurate measures which would begin the great work of removing from the Republic a feature which was a weakness and a disgrace to a liberty-loving people. With great delicacy and ingeni-

ousness on July 31st, 1814, he wrote to Jefferson *: " I
never," he said, " took up my pen with more hesitation,
or felt more embarrassment than I now do in addressing
you on the subject of this letter. The fear of appearing
presumptuous distresses me, and would deter me from
venturing thus to call your attention to a subject of such
magnitude, and so beset with difficulties as that of a general emancipation of the slaves of Virginia, had I not the
highest opinion of your goodness and liberality, in not
only excusing me for the liberty I take, but in justly
appreciating my motive in doing so. * * * My object is to entreat and beseech you to exert your knowledge and influence in devising and getting into operation
some plan for the gradual emancipation of slavery. This
difficult task could be less exceptionally and more successfully performed by the revered fathers of all our
political and social blessings than by any succeeding
statesmen ; and would seem to come with peculiar propriety and force from those whose valor, wisdom and
virtue have done so much in ameliorating the condition
of mankind. And it is a duty, as I conceive, that devolves
particularly upon you, from your known philosophical and
enlarged view of subjects, and from the principles you
have professed and practised through a long and useful
life, preëminently distinguished as well by being foremost
in establishing on the broadest basis the rights of man,
and the liberty and independence of your country, as
being throughout honored with the most important trusts
by your fellow-citizens, whose confidence and love you
have carried with you into the shades of old age and
retirement. * * *

" I hope that the fear of failing at this time, will have
no influence in preventing you from employing your pen

* See " Sketch of Edward Coles," by E. B. Washburne, pp. 21–24.

to eradicate this most degrading feature of British Colonial policy, which is still permitted to exist, notwithstanding its repugnance as well to the principles of our revolution as to our free institutions. For however prized and influential your opinions may now be, they will still be much more so when you shall have been taken from us by the course of nature. If therefore your attempt should now fail to rectify this unfortunate evil—an evil most injurious both to the oppressed and to the oppressor—at some future day when your memory will be consecrated by a grateful posterity, what influence, irresistible influence, will the opinions and writings of Thomas Jefferson have in all questions connected with the rights of man, and of that policy which will be the creed of your disciples. * * *

" I will only add as an excuse for the liberty I take in addressing you on this subject which is so particularly interesting to me, that from the time I was capable of reflecting on the nature of political society, and of the rights appertaining to man, I have not only been principled against slavery, but have had feelings so repugnant to it as to decide me not to hold them ; which decision has forced me to leave my native State, and with it all my relations and friends."

To this letter of Coles, Jefferson replied on Aug. 25th, 1814: "Your favor of July 31st was duly received, and was read with peculiar pleasure. The sentiments breathed through the whole, do honor both to the head and heart of the writer. Mine, on the subject of the slavery of negroes, have long since been in possession of the public, and time has only served to give them stronger root. The love of justice and the love of country plead equally the cause of these people, and it is a mortal reproach to us that they should have pleaded it so long in vain, and should have produced not a single effort, nay, I fear, not much serious willingness, to relieve them and ourselves from our present condition of moral and political reprobation.

"From those of the former generation, who were in the fulness of age when I came into public life, which was while our controversy with England was on paper only, I soon saw that nothing was to be hoped. Nursed and educated in the daily habit of seeing the degraded condition, both bodily and mental, of those unfortunate beings, not reflecting that that degradation was very much the work of themselves and their fathers, few minds had yet doubted but that they were as legitimate subjects of property as their horses or cattle. The quiet and monotonous course of colonial life had been disturbed by no alarm, and little reflection on the value of liberty ; and when alarm was taken at an enterprise of their own, it was not easy to carry them the whole length of the principles which they invoked for themselves.

"In the first or second session of the legislature, after I became a member, I drew to this subject the attention of Colonel Bland, one of the oldest, ablest, and most respected members, and he undertook to move for certain moderate extensions of the protection of the laws to these people. I seconded his motion, and, as a younger member, was more spared in the debate ; but he was denounced as an enemy to his country, and was treated with the greatest indecorum. From an early stage of our Revolution, other and more distant duties were assigned to me, so that from that time till my return from Europe, in 1789, and I may say, till I returned to reside at home in 1809, I had little opportunity of knowing the progress of public sentiment here on this subject.

"I had always hoped that the younger generation, receiving their early impressions after the flame of liberty

9

had been kindled in every breast, and had become, as it were, the vital spirit of every American, that the generous temperament of youth, analogous to the motion of their blood, and above the suggestions of avarice, would have sympathized with oppression wherever found, and proved their love of liberty beyond their own share of it. But my intercourse with them, since my return, has not been sufficient to ascertain that they had made towards this point the progress I had hoped.

"Your solitary but welcome voice is the first which has brought this sound to my ear; and I have considered the general silence which prevails on this subject, as indicating an apathy unfavorable to every hope. Yet the hour of emancipation is advancing in the march of time. It will come; and whether brought on by the generous energy of our own minds, or by the bloody process of St. Domingo, * * * is a leaf in our history not yet turned over.

"As to the method by which this difficult work is to be effected, if permitted to be done by ourselves, I have seen no proposition so expedient, on the whole, as that of emancipation of those born after a given day, and of their education and expatriation at a proper age. * * *

"I am sensible of the partiality with which you have looked towards me as the person who should undertake this salutary but arduous work. But this, my dear sir, is like bidding old Priam to buckle on the armor of Hector —'*trementibus ævo humeris et inutile ferrum cingi.*' No, I have outlived the generation with which mutual labors and perils begat mutual confidence and influence. This enterprise is for the young—for those who can follow it up, and bear it through to its consummation.

"It shall have all my prayers, and these are the only weapons of an old man. But in the meantime are you right in abandoning this property and your country with it ? I think not. My opinion has ever been that, until more can be done for them, we should endeavor, with those whom fortune has thrown on our hands, to feed and clothe them well, protect them from ill-usage, require such reasonable labor only as is performed voluntarily by freemen, and be led by no repugnancies to abdicate them, and our duties to them. The laws do not permit us to turn them loose, if that were for their good ; and to commute them for other property, is to commit them to those whose usage of them we cannot control.

" I hope then, my dear sir, you will reconcile yourself to your country and its unfortunate condition ; that you will not lessen its stock of sound disposition, by withdrawing your portion from the mass. That, on the contrary, you will come forward in the public councils, become the missionary of this doctrine, truly Christian, insinuate and inculcate it, softly but steadily, through the medium of writing and conversation, associate others in your labors, and, when the phalanx is formed, bring on and press the proposition perseveringly until its accomplishment.

" It is an encouraging observation that no good measure was ever proposed which, if duly pursued, failed to prevail in the end. We have a proof of this in the history of the endeavors, in the British Parliament, to suppress that very trade which brought this evil on us. And you will be supported by the religious precept : ' Be not wearied in well doing.' That your success may be as speedy and as complete as it will be honorable and immortal consolation to yourself, I shall as fervently and sincerely pray, as I assure you of my great friendship and respect." *

---

* This letter is published in full and for the first time in Randall's " Life of Jefferson," vol. iii., pp. 643–5. A fac-simile of Jefferson's letter is published in " Sketch of Edward Coles," by Washburne, p. 28.

Young Coles was not altogether satisfied with the sentiments of this letter of Jefferson's. He wrote to him a second letter, in which he, in a manner as noble as it was respectful and gentlemanly, controverted some of the aged statesman's views. He told him that he felt justified in deciding to free his slaves, and that he had determined to move them to the territory northwest of the Ohio. He stated that he trusted that Jefferson's prayers would be heard in heaven and that their influence would be felt on earth. " But," he continued, " I cannot agree with you that they are the only weapons of one of your age ; nor that the work of cleansing the escutcheon of Virginia of the foul stain of slavery can best be done by the young." He then eloquently reasoned that aged, wise, and influential statesmen could do far more in influencing public opinion in favor of abolishing human slavery than could men of less worth of character and young in years. He pointed out to him how Benjamin Franklin—to whom he stated that Pennsylvania was indebted for its deliverance from laws permitting negroes to be held in bondage —had performed grand services for his country when he was more advanced in years than was Jefferson. In short Coles spoke with the earnestness of a true reformer.

In the way of carrying out far-reaching plans Coles met with difficulties which detained him six years in the household of President Madison. He then visited the Western territory and made arrangements to settle in Illinois, which young State had been formed out of the territory in which slavery had been, thanks in part to Jefferson, excluded. But business which was deemed to be even more important than that of securing to his slaves immediate freedom demanded his attention. Madison, who was still President of the United States, earnestly requested him to perform a work for his country of high

and far-reaching importance. Coles was requested to go
on a very delicate and momentous mission to the Emperor of Russia. The Government of the United States
is so different in some respects to that of European nations that foreign ministers have been sometimes tempted
to think that they can take liberties in America. They
have awakened sometimes suddenly to the fact that in
some respects there are few governments which insist more
decidedly on certain observances of propriety than does
the government of the Republic. The Russian minister
had made some serious mistakes which had been resented
by the United States government. The Emperor of
Russia, not understanding why the United States had
been displeased with his minister, threatened to expel or
imprison the representative of America at St. Peters-
burg. The United States and Russia have always been
on exceptionally good terms. To America Russia has
always manifested kindness, and it was on many accounts
highly desirable that both nations should cherish kindly
feelings to each other.

Coles sailed on an American man-of-war to Russia. On
the Emperor of Russia he made a very favorable impres-
sion. The Tzar offered to punish the offending minister
in any way which the President of the United States
would suggest. After completing his diplomatic labors
in Russia Coles paid a short visit to Berlin, and before returning to America he met some of the most distinguished men of Europe. He also hastily visited Scotland
and Wales. The humane mission which he had to
perform in America, however, would not allow him to
linger in Europe, so he hastened back to Virginia. Once,
speaking of his feelings, he said: "I could not reconcile it
to my conscience and sense of propriety to participate in
slavery ; and being unable to screen myself under such a

shelter, from the peltings and upbraidings of my own conscience, and the just censure, as I conceived, of earth and
heaven, I could not consent to hold as property what I
had no right to, and which was not and could not be
property according to my understanding of the rights and
duties of man—and therefore I determined that I would
not and could not hold my fellow-man as a slave."

At last Coles succeeded in completing arrangements to
carry out his cherished plans. His property in Virginia
was sold and land was bought in Illinois. By acting
promptly and complying with certain provisions of law he
could take his slaves out of Virginia. On the 1st of
April, 1819, he started from his plantation with all his
slaves and their offspring—excepting two who were too
old to make the journey. For these two colored people
he decided to provide for the rest of their lives. Coles
possessed to a marked degree the rare virtue of not
divulging unwisely his plans. The slaves knew not where
they were being led, but they instinctively felt that they
were following one who was very kind to them. A part
of their journey was on flat-boats on the beautiful Ohio
River. On these boats, which Mr. Coles had bought for
the purpose, his followers slowly travelled six hundred
miles.

Alluding to this journey Coles once wrote: "The
morning after we left Pittsburg, a mild, calm and lovely
April day, the sun shining bright, and the heavens without a cloud, our boats floating gently down the beautiful
Ohio, the verdant foliage of Spring just budding out on
its picturesque banks, all around presenting a scene both
conducive to and in harmony with the finest feelings of
our nature, was selected as one well suited to make
known to my negroes the glad tidings of their freedom.
Being curious to see the effect of an instantaneous sever-

ing of the manacles of bondage, and letting loose on the buoyant wings of liberty the long pent up spirit of man, I called on the deck of the boats, which were lashed together, all the negroes, and made them a short address, in which I commenced by saying it was time for me to make known to them what I intended to do with them, and concluded my remarks by so expressing myself, that by a turn of a sentence, I proclaimed in the shortest and fullest manner possible, that they were no longer slaves, but free—free as I was, and were at liberty to proceed with me, or to go ashore at their pleasure.

"The effect on them was electrical. They stared at me and at each other, as if doubting the accuracy or reality of what they heard. In breathless silence they stood before me, unable to utter a word, but with countenances beaming with expression which no words could convey, and which no language can now describe. As they began to see the truth of what they had heard, and to realize their situation, there came on a kind of hysterical, giggling laugh. After a pause of intense, an unutterable, emotion, bathed in tears, and with tremulous voices, they gave vent to their gratitude, and implored the blessing of God on me. When they had in some degree recovered the command of themselves, Ralph said he had long known I was opposed to holding black people as slaves, and thought it probable I would some time or other give my people their freedom, but that he did not expect me to do it so soon; and moreover, he thought I ought not to do it till they had repaid me the expense I had been at in removing them from Virginia, and had improved my farm and ' gotten me well fixed in that new country.' To this, all simultaneously expressed their concurrence, and their desire to remain with me, as my servants, until they had comfortably fixed me at my new home.

"I told them, no. I had made up my mind to give to them immediate and unconditional freedom ; that I had long been anxious to do it, but had been prevented by the delays, first in selling my property in Virginia, and then in collecting the money, and by other circumstances. That in consideration of this delay, and as a reward for their past services, as well as a stimulant to their future exertions, and with a hope it would add to their self-esteem and their standing in the estimation of others, I should give to each head of a family a quarter section, containing one hundred and sixty acres of land. To this all objected, saying I had done enough for them in giving them their freedom ; and insisted on my keeping the land to supply my own wants, and added, in the kindest manner, the expression of their solicitude that I would not have the means of doing so after I had freed them. I told them that I had thought much of my duty and of their rights, and that it was due alike to both that I should do what I had said I should do ; and accordingly, soon after reaching Edwardsville, I executed and delivered to them deeds to the lands promised them.

"I stated to them that the lands I intended to give them were unimproved lands, and as they would not have the means of making the necessary improvements, of stocking their farms, and procuring the materials for at once living on them, they would have to hire themselves out till they could acquire by their labor the necessary means to commence cultivating and residing on their own lands. That I was willing to hire and employ on my farm a certain number of them (designating the individuals) ; the others I advised to seek employment in St. Louis, Edwardsville, and other places, where smart, active young men and women could obtain much higher wages than they could on farms. At this some of them mur-

mured, as it indicated a partiality they said, on my part to those designated to live with me ; and contended that they should all be equally dear to me." As Coles proceeded he related how he assured them of his determination to befriend them should they ever get in trouble or need his help, and of the very considerate advice on various subjects which he gave them.

In Illinois Coles received a kind request from his friend President Monroe to take the position of Register of the Land Office. While occupying this position he was always so polite and just to all with whom he had business, that he became very popular, and was elected in 1822 governor of Illinois. Distinguished men had striven to obtain the high station to which Coles was elected. One of these men was the chief-justice of the State, and the other was the associate justice of the Supreme Court. Both these men were in favor of repealing the provisions by which slavery was prohibited in Illinois. Another candidate for the position was the major-general of the militia of the State. Coles was known to be heart and soul opposed to slavery. He was elected by only a small majority over one of the candidates in favor of slavery. One of the reasons why the election was of extraordinary importance was that it was proposed by the friends of slavery to call a convention in Illinois, so that all laws preventing the introduction of slavery into the young State should be abrogated. Coles and his friends were called upon to fight probably as momentous a battle for liberty as was ever fought on the American continent.

Governor Coles made an admirable public officer. He impressed upon the attention of the Legislature of Illinois the importance of free schools to a State, and the wisdom of promoting agriculture and of constructing a great system of canals, by which not only the great lakes of North America would be united with the waters of the harbor of New York, but by which vessels could go by means of canals and lakes and rivers from the Atlantic ocean to New Orleans. His action on the slavery question in Illinois was indeed momentous. He drew the attention of the Legislature, among other subjects respecting human bondage, to the ordinance of 1787 by which slavery had been excluded from the great Territory, out of a part of which Illinois had been formed. He pointed out how slave-holders were ignoring this provision, and recommended the adoption of wise and effective laws in the interests of the oppressed. He also proposed that measures should be taken to prevent the kidnapping of free colored people in Illinois. As a majority of the Legislature was in favor of slavery, a dreadful storm was at once aroused. It was determined by the majority of the State Legislature that every barrier in the way of Illinois becoming a slave State should be swept away. They had on their side the lieutenant-governor of the State, but Coles was a host in himself.

Long and most deeply interesting was the conflict respecting the changing of the Constitution of Illinois in the interest of slave-owners. By many and costly sacrifices, Coles, as the leader of the cause of freedom, strove to save Illinois from becoming a slave State. Friends rallied round him. Even the Quakers of Philadelphia, hearing echoes from the strife which was being carried on in Illinois, in ways which were deeply interesting but upon which space will not allow one to here dwell, came to his assistance. By the press, by tracts on slavery, by the voice of itinerant clergymen, and in many highly interesting ways, at last, at an election upon which the destiny of liberty in America may be said to have been determined, a majority of the people of Illinois were induced to decide by their votes that there should be no abrogation of the laws forbidding the introduction of slavery into Illinois.

How an attempt was made to ruin Coles in fortune by charging him with having violated a cruel law respecting colored people when he freed his slaves, and how he was saved from paying thousands of dollars' fine—how he was prevented from becoming a Senator of the United States —how he was defeated when a candidate for Congress,— need not here be dwelt upon. Before he retired from Illinois and married in Philadelphia he had won a great victory for freedom, and had helped to arouse a feeling of opposition to slavery in the young and enterprising State of Illinois which was destined to find a lodgment in the heart of another young man—to whom attention will presently be called,—who was to carry forward the great work which Coles had so nobly inaugurated in Illinois, on a scale which was to be national in its dimensions.

And now to glance again for a moment at Jefferson's views respecting slavery. In a letter to Mr. Barrow, under date of May 1st, 1815, Jefferson, after stating that the subject of slavery had been to him one of early and tender consideration, added: "Had I continued in the councils of my own State it should never have been out of sight." He continued: "We are not in a world ungoverned by the laws and the power of a Superior Agent. Our efforts are in his hand, and directed by it ; and he will give them their effect in his own time." He in this letter declared that it would be his "last and fondest prayer," that slavery would be abolished in all parts of his country.

Not long after returning from Europe, Jefferson received a letter dated August 19th, 1791, from a negro, a Mr. Benjamin Banneker, who spoke feelingly to the statesman about slavery, and may even be said to have severely criticised him for not taking a nobler stand on the slavery question than he was taking. He also presented him with a book which he had published—a kind of almanac. Under date of August 30th, 1791, Jefferson replied to him, thanking him for his letter and his scientific work. " Nobody wishes more than I do," he wrote, " to see such proofs as you exhibit, that nature has given to our black brethren talents equal to those of the other colors of men, and that the appearance of a want of them is owing merely to the degraded condition of their existence, both in Africa and America. I can add with truth, that nobody wishes more ardently to see a good system commenced for raising the condition both of their body and mind to what it ought to be, as fast as the imbecility of their present existence, and other circumstances which cannot be neglected, will admit. I have taken the liberty of sending your Almanac to Monsieur de Condorcet, Secretary of the Academy of Sciences in Paris, and member of the Philanthropic Society, because I considered it a document to which your whole colour had a right for their justification against the doubts which have been entertained of them." The statesman signed this letter thus: " I am with greet esteem, Sir, Your most obedient humble servant, Tho. Jefferson."

Writing to John Holmes on the slavery question on April 22d, 1820—a time of high excitement in Congress, —Jefferson said: " I can say with conscious truth, that there is not a man on earth who would sacrifice more than I would to relieve us from this heavy reproach, in any practicable way." In a letter to Jared Sparks, the distinguished author, under date of Feb. 4th, 1824, the aged Jefferson drew attention to a plan for the abolition of slavery in the United States which he had forty years ‑before published in his " Notes on Virginia." The plan which he had sketched in his book it would be hardly

just to criticise in these days, save to notice that the
colored youth born after the passing of the act were to be
free, but they were to "continue"—to use Jefferson's
words—"with their parents to a certain age, then to be
brought up, at the public expense, to tillage, arts, or
sciences, according to their genuises, till the female
should be eighteen and the males twenty-one years of
age." Jefferson further proposed that the United States
government should go to other expense in their behalf in
certain ways to which attention may again be incidentally
drawn. In his letter to Sparks he enlarged upon some of
the features of the bill which he had prepared, and then
continuing added: "I do not go into all details of the
burthens and benefits of this operation. And who could
estimate its blessed results? I leave this to those who
will live to see their accomplishment, and to enjoy a
beatitude forbidden to my age. But I leave it with this
admonition, to rise and be doing. * * * I am aware
that this subject involves some constitutional scruples.
But a liberal construction, justified by the object, may
go far, and an amendment of the Constitution, the whole
length necessary."

To Miss Wright, who was what was called an Abolitionist, and who bought quite a large number of slaves
especially to free them—some slave-owners parting with
their slaves at a low price because they sympathized with
her work,—Jefferson wrote on Aug. 7th, 1825: "My
own health is very low, not having been able to leave the
house for three months, and suffering much at times.
* * * At the age of eighty-two, with one foot in the
grave, and the other uplifted to follow it, I do not permit
myself to take part in any new enterprises, even for bet-
tering the condition of men, not even in the great one
which is the subject of your letter, and which has been

through life one of my greatest anxieties. The march of
events has not been such as to render its completion
practicable within the limits of time allotted to me; and I
leave its accomplishment as the work of another generation.
And I am cheered when I see that on which it is devolved,
taking it up with so much good will, and such minds engaged in its encouragement. The abolition of the evil is
not impossible; it ought never therefore to be despaired
of. Every plan should be adopted, every expedient tried,
which may do something towards the ultimate object.
That which you propose is well worthy of trial. It has
succeeded with certain portions of our white brethren,
under the care of a Rapp and an Owen; and why may it
not succeed with the man of color? An opinion is haz-
arded by some, but proved by none, that moral urgencies
are not sufficient to induce him to labor; that nothing
can do this but coercion. But this is a problem which the
present age alone is prepared to solve by experiment. It
would be a solecism to suppose a race of animals created,
without sufficient foresight and energy to preserve their
own existence. It is disproved, too, by the fact that they
exist, and have existed through all the ages of history.
We are not sufficiently acquainted with all the nations of
Africa to say that there may not be some in which habits
of industry are established, and the arts practiced which
are necessary to render life comfortable. The experiment
now in progress in St. Domingo, those of Sierra Leone
and Cape Mesurado, are but beginning. Your proposition has its aspects of promise also; and should it not
answer fully to calculations in figures, it may yet, in its
developments, lead to happy results. These, however,
I must leave to another generation. The enterprise of
different, but yet important character, [of founding the
University of Virginia] in which I have embarked too

late in life, I find more than sufficient to occupy the en-
feebled energies remaining to me, and that to divert them
to other objects would be a desertion of these. You are
young, dear Madam, and have powers of mind which may
do much in exciting others in this arduous task. I am
confident they will be so exerted, and I pray to heaven
for their success, and that you may be rewarded with the
blessings which such efforts merit."

Jefferson at times pictured to himself with horror
scenes of bloodshed and dire evils which would take
place in Virginia if slavery were permitted to continue.
In a letter to St. George Tucker, who had written a
pamphlet advocating the abolition of slavery, Jefferson,
under date of Aug. 28th, 1797, alluding to the pamphlet,
wrote: "You know my subscription to its doctrines."
He then, continuing to dwell on the abolition of slavery,
wrote: "The sooner we put some plan under way, the
greater hope there is that it may be permitted to proceed
peaceably to its ultimate effect. But if something is not
done, and soon done, we shall be the murderers of our
own children. The ' murmura venturos nautis prudentia
ventos ' has already reached us; the revolutionary storm,
now sweeping the globe, will be upon us, and happy if we
make timely provision to give it an easy passage over our
land."

In Jefferson's day it was dangerous for any one—
especially in a Southern State—to be known as opposed
to slavery. It would be difficult, if not impossible, for any
one at the present day to realize what an excitement
might be enkindled in Congress should any one criticise
the moral right of slave-owners to hold human beings in
bondage—indeed a time was hastening on when sentiments such as Jefferson often uttered respecting slavery
were not even to be allowed to be carried by the United

States mail into Southern States. But the influence which Jefferson had helped to exert against slavery was not to be lost upon the history of the Republic, as will be, to at least some extent, in due time seen.

At the close of the war with Mexico the United States came into possession of an immense territory, much, if not indeed all, of which was at the time free from slavery. There were men in Congress who claimed that "the peculiar institution of the South" should be introduced into all the Territories of the Republic. Happily, however, there were statesmen who did not agree with such views and could not be frightened into adopting them. Some statesmen did not care whether slavery was introduced into new Territories and States or not. Some would make compromises of one kind or another. Others would save, in every way that they rightly and constitutionally could, virgin territory from being dishonored by the institution of slavery. Jefferson had sometimes thought of dreadful evils which he feared slavery would bring upon the Republic, and he had thanked God that his eyes would be closed in death before the arrival of those days of ruin. Some of his worst fears were to be sadly nearly realized and for many years new and peculiar evils were to hang as a dark cloud over the Republic—evils which, if not removed, as will soon be pointed out, are likely to yet cause immeasurable injury to the United States.

Doubtless there were people of noble and lovely characters who owned, through no fault of their own, slaves. Everything that was kind and noble, that they possibly could do for the colored people, they gladly did. But Jefferson believed that the effect of holding in bondage human beings was fearfully injurious, as a rule, to the character of a master. The proprietors of slaves were

never a large part of the population of the Southern
States. They, however, formed a privileged class, and
were—speaking in general terms—bound together by a
common interest in preserving and in extending their
"peculiar institution." They at times exercised an appalling influence on the national government. By the
census of 1850, the number of slave-holders in the United
States was 347,525. Quite a large percentage of this
number did not own slaves, but merely hired them from
slave-owners. The number of slave-holders who had each
but one slave was 68,820. The number who held less
than five slaves was 105,683. The total number of slaves
in 1850 was 3,200,324. The free colored population was
228,138. The population of the whites in the slave States
was 6,184,477. The slave-owners, supported by the labor
of millions of enslaved people, ruled, to no inconsiderable
degree, millions of whites. They were a homogeneous,
compact body, having one great interest to promote and
one policy to pursue. Probably in no Southern State was
the influence of what has been called "the slave power"
more marked than it was in South Carolina at the time it
inaugurated civil war in the United States. The Sixth
Section of Article First of the Constitution of South Carolina provided that no one should be allowed to be a member of the House of Representatives of the State, unless
he possessed a certain, quite large, amount of wealth, clear
of encumbrance, or owned, to use the words of the instrument, "a settled freehold estate of five hundred acres of
land and ten negroes." The representatives of the slave
interests were not only powerful in their respective States,
but could do much towards controlling the government
of the United States. The slave States were not only
represented in the national Capitol according to the
number of their white inhabitants, but also in proportion

to the number of slaves they contained—each slave being
counted as three fifths of a human being. Thus the
slave-owner who owned five hundred slaves had a power
in Congress and in electing the President of the United
States, equal to three hundred and one people in the free
States. In South Carolina—if I mistake not—the Representatives to Congress were not elected directly by the
people, but by the vote of the Legislature—in the same
way as were the members of the United States Senate.
The slave States naturally sent slave-holders to the national Capitol. Thus the strange anomaly in a republican government was seen of the legislative representation
of people by their masters. Slave-holders, once getting
the political affairs in their States under their own control
could so manage them that sometimes, if not indeed
often, the majority of the whites, even though made up
largely of tax-payers and of men capable of bearing arms
in the slave States, would be unrepresented in legislative
councils. The slave-holders were able to elect more men
than the non-slave-owners, and thus the States could be
virtually ruled, not by the people through their elected
representatives, but by a combination of slave-holders.
Any statesman who opposed the wishes of the slave
power was liable to be stricken down. It is related of
Lincoln that, in a conversation with a Mr. Gillespie on
some events which had attracted his attention, he said:
" There were about six hundred thousand non-slaveholding whites in Kentucky to about thirty-three thousand
slave-holders; in the convention then recently held, it
was expected that the delegates would represent these
classes about in proportion to their respective numbers;
but, when the convention assembled, there was not a
single representative of the non-slaveholding class: every
one was in the interest of the slave-holders." These

remarks by Abraham Lincoln are not here introduced to re-open wounds which were once cruel indeed, but to draw due attention to the fact that the cause of public education was sacrificed to a great extent—as were many other interests of the whites who were poor—to the interests of slavery. The rich planter could send his children to private schools. There were indeed some public schools in the Southern States—thanks to the wise measures which Jefferson, when President of the United States, had been led to take, by which an immense amount of land was consecrated to the cause of public education. But under the upas tree of slavery such beneficent institutions did not flourish as they did on soil uncursed by the demoralizing spectacle of human beings living in a state of hopeless bondage. Among the slave population were sometimes individuals of Anglo-Saxon blood who had, when children, been kidnapped in Northern cities, or had been sold to the domestic slave-trader by indigent and depraved whites. In the veins of a considerable percentage of slaves, owing to one feature of the demoralization often caused by the relation of slave and master, there flowed Anglo-Saxon blood.* In a letter to Francis C. Gray, under date of March 4th, 1815, Jefferson drew attention to the fact that if a human being was fifteen sixteenths of Anglo-Saxon blood, having only one sixteenth of African blood, he or she was virtually white; but that, nevertheless, if the mother was a slave, by the laws of Virginia, her children were also slaves, unless emancipated.

The slave codes of the Southern States could do much towards utterly crushing the spirit of the slave. Who will fully describe the wickedness which could be committed under the authority of some of the slave codes!

---

* See "John Jay on Slavery," p. 144.

Extracts from these codes could be given, which would amaze and fill with sorrow and indignation a true friend of liberty. The pious John Wesley could not forbear characterizing the "peculiar institution" as "the sum of all villainies."

It is strange how people under various circumstances view moral questions. Many a one, who has perhaps known only kind and considerate owners of slaves, has naturally felt otherwise than did Jefferson or Wesley respecting slavery. The Legislature of South Carolina sent as her champion John C. Calhoun to the national Capitol. This able man, in 1849, draughted a very inflammatory address to the people of the slave States. The address was signed by himself and by Jefferson Davis, and by forty-six Congressmen and Senators from the slave States. In the course of this singular and very violent address on the slavery question, it was declared that there were people in the Northern States who were opposed "to the peculiar institution of the South," and that the owners of slaves were in danger of not being allowed to take their slaves into the Territories of the United States, and that, if such a policy were allowed by the slave States, it would come about in course of time that free States would be formed out of the territories, until three fourths of all the States in the Union would be free States;—that then the Abolitionists would vote for a constitutional amendment abolishing slavery, and that "the social and political superiority of the white race" was in danger of being destroyed, so that the whites would have to exchange places with the blacks. In this address it was claimed that England had made a mistake when she paid one hundred millions of dollars for the liberation of slaves in the West Indies, and the citizens of the slave States were exhorted, "without looking to consequences," to resort "to all means necessary" to repel "a blow so dangerous." In this address Abolitionists were bitterly and in very heated language stigmatized as "fanatics."

This is not the place to dwell upon the stern boldness with which John Quincy Adams and Joshua R. Giddings and others in Congress opposed the slave power, or how William H. Seward, a United States Senator, contended that the struggle between slavery and liberty was an "irrepressible conflict," inasmuch as slavery was a local, a sectional institution, while liberty was national. Nor is this the place to dwell at length upon how it came about that Abraham Lincoln was elected to the Presidency of the United States by citizens who believed that in all constitutional ways the National Government should prevent the introduction of slavery into new and vast territories.

When the Southern leaders decided to make the Southern States secede from the United States, they formed for the slave States a Constitution. In the Constitution of the United States the word "slave" had not been allowed a place, as the name was odious to such men as Hamilton and Franklin. In the Constitution which the leaders in the slave States formed for themselves they inserted the word "slaves." They provided that in all territory which the new Confederacy should ever acquire —and there were vast territories which it might conquer —slavery should exist. They provided, to use the words of their Constitution, that "in all such territories, the institution of negro slavery, as it now exists in the Confederate States, shall be recognized and protected by Congress and by the territorial government; and the inhabitants of the several Confederate States and Territories shall have the right to take to such territory any slaves lawfully held by them in any of the States or Territories of the Confederate States."

It may here be incidentally noticed that while the advocates of the extension of slavery were in many respects controlling the government of the United States, the opponents of slavery were often timid, and easily frightened by the excitement which followed debate on the slavery question. Already a statesman, destined to become a central figure in history, had attracted much public attention. Abraham Lincoln was born in Kentucky, a slave State, on February 12th, 1809,—in the same State and in the same year as was Jefferson Davis. He was of Southern birth, both of his parents having been born in Virginia. This is not the place to dwell upon his early history. In the year 1818, Lincoln was living in Indiana, a State which adjoins Illinois, and was formed out of the rich territory which Jefferson had labored to save from the evil of slavery, and in which large provision had been made for the intellectual culture of its future citizens. It will be remembered that in Illinois, from time to time, a certain class of people had striven to have the prohibition of slavery removed, and had endeavored to elect public officers in sympathy with their plans. The echoes of the conflict when slavery was about to be introduced into Illinois would naturally be heard in Indiana. In 1830 Lincoln settled in Illinois. The excitement incident to such a strife as Edward Coles had waged in Illinois was not soon to be forgotten. It would be difficult to think of any nobler leader, or more praiseworthy example for youth, than was Jefferson's friend, the cultured Edward Coles. By an interesting providence Abraham Lincoln's father settled with his family in a county named after Coles and known to this day as Coles County. The noble impetus which Coles and the men whom he had rallied around him had given the cause of freedom in Illinois had made its very air inspiriting. A degree of culture had been diffused by the wise educational provisions which had been made for it when it was but a part of the Western territory,—provisions which Jefferson had helped to secure it and which had been fostered by Gov. Coles and other friends of education,—which were to exert a happy influence upon many a young man. Upon a youth twenty-two years of age, open to generous influences, as was Lincoln, such influences were not to be wholly lost. Deprived in his youth of many educational advantages, he when a man earnestly endeavored to avail himself of such opportunities as he had for acquiring useful knowledge. When the capital of Illinois was at Vandalia, he was often to be seen in the State library. The Hon. Elihu B. Washburne, Lincoln's cherished friend, in an eloquent paper on Abraham Lincoln published in the *North American Review* for October, 1885, speaking of this interesting feature of his education, states that "he always read understandingly, and there was no principle of law but that he mastered, and such was the way in which he always impressed his miscellaneous readings on his mind, that in later life people were amazed at his wonderful familiarity with books—even those so little known to the great mass of readers." The use which Lincoln made of the State library when the capital of Illinois was at Vandalia, and after the capital, largely through his instrumentality, was moved to Springfield, is naturally pointed out in the "Life of Lincoln" published by his warm friend, the late Mr. Isaac N. Arnold. This able writer states that Lincoln, when living at Vandalia and at Springfield, "had access to all the books he could read, and the world of English literature, history and science lay open before him." Mr. Arnold adds: "He became and continued through life a student, always seeking and constantly acquiring knowledge."

It would be interesting to dwell upon Lincoln's career as a statesman,—how wisely and boldly he acted respecting the rights of the colored people and the interests of education during the eight years that he was a member of the Legislature of Illinois; how, as a member of Congress, he endeavored, in a way by which the slave-owner would be paid for his so-called property, to effect the abolition of slavery in the District of Columbia; how he regarded a decision respecting what is known as the "Dred Scott case," rendered by certain judges of the Supreme Court of the United States whose hearts and minds had been, he believed, sadly corrupted by the influence exerted upon them by the system of human bondage in the presence of which they had been educated; and how he was the means of having a platform drafted for a political party, which was to be known as the Republican party, in which a part of the Declaration of Independence was adopted as a living principle, and by which the extension of slavery into territory as yet unpolluted by its introduction was to be prevented. It would be inspiring indeed to dwell upon how, when the representatives of the young Republican party were gathered together at a great convention in 1860, and many of them wavered for a moment in adopting the principles of the platform which Lincoln cherished, they were gloriously rallied under appeals of wonderful eloquence addressed to them by the then young George William Curtis, and how Lincoln was nominated for the Presidency of the United States. Much of this instructive history has been given to the world in the highly valuable and interesting "Life of Lincoln" given to the public in the year 1885 by the late Hon. Isaac N. Arnold, whose kindly bearing as President of the Chicago Historical Society will long be remembered by his friends. His book is well worthy of a place in every American home. Suffice it here to merely notice that the public debates which Lincoln had with Stephen A. Douglas, who in time became the leader of the Democratic party in the Northern States, attracted wide attention. One or the other of them was to be elected a United States Senator. In all these debates Lincoln argued that in all constitutional and honorable ways the people should prevent the introduction of slavery into new Territories and States. With singular ability, yet with a mildness the more noticeable because of his iron firmness, he revealed to the people a conspiracy to spread slavery over the Territories, and even to introduce it into the free States.

On April 6th, 1859, Lincoln declined to attend a festival in honor of Jefferson's birthday, tendered to him by some gentlemen known to belong to "the Democratic party." In this letter he pointed out some of the differences between the views entertained by Democrats and the party to which he belonged on the slavery question. He declared that, "Soberly, it is now no child's play to save the principles of Jefferson from total overthrow in this nation. * * * This is a world of compensations; and he who would be no slave, must consent to *have* no slave. Those who deny freedom to others, deserve it not for themselves; and under a just God cannot long retain it." Lincoln added: "All honor to Jefferson; to a man who, in the concrete pressure of a struggle for a national independence by a single people, had the coolness, forecast, and capacity to introduce into a merely revolutionary document an abstract of truth, applicable to all men and all times, and so to embalm it there, that to-day and in all coming days it shall be a rebuke and a stumbling-block to the harbingers of reappearing tyranny and oppression."

On the 27th of February, 1860, Lincoln, in a speech

delivered in New York, examined critically the history of the framers of the Constitution of the United States in relation to slavery, and showed that Washington and an astonishing number of his colleagues, whose history could be traced, acted on the principle that slavery should not be introduced into new Territories.   Lincoln submitted to the calm reflection of the people whether much that was said about the party to which he belonged was just.   He alluded to the celebrated decision rendered by a majority of the judges of the Supreme Court of the United States, known as the Dred Scott case, by which slavery was to be permitted, however offensive to some of the States, in all the States and Territories of the national Republic, and explained some of his own views respecting the decision.   On July 17th, 1858, he had startled Stephen A. Douglas by reading a letter which Jefferson had written on September 28th, 1820, in which sentiments respecting the authority of the Supreme Court of the United States were enunciated somewhat similar to certain views which Douglas affected to condemn.   Indeed, in a celebrated speech delivered in New York, Lincoln betrayed a very praiseworthy acquaintance with American history.

At the election for President of the United States in 1860, Douglas, the candidate of the Democrats of the Northern States, received in the Electoral College 12 votes; Breckenridge, the slavery candidate, 72 votes; Mr. Bell, who was supposed to be in favor of the States remaining united whether slavery was extended or not, received 39 votes; Lincoln received 180 votes,—more votes in the Electoral College than was given to all the other candidates united.

Shortly after his election to the Presidency Lincoln made a speech in Cincinnati, a part of which was especially addressed to the slave State in which he had been born

He said: "We mean to treat, as near as we possibly can, as Washington, Jefferson, and Madison treated you. We mean to leave you alone and in no wise to interfere with your institutions, to abide by all and every compromise of the Constitution; and in a word, coming back to the original proposition, to treat you as far as degenerate men, if we have degenerated, may, according to the examples of those noble fathers Washington, Jefferson, and Madison." As he continued, Lincoln spoke in the most generous manner of the people of the slave States, reared under different circumstances than were the people of the free States, but possessed, he declared, of as much goodness of heart as he claimed for himself. It would perhaps be impossible to find a more generous-hearted statesman than Lincoln, by his speeches, showed himself to be.

In his inaugural address Lincoln said: "One section of our country believes slavery is right, and ought to be extended, while the other believes it is wrong, and ought not to be extended; and this is the only substantial dispute; and the fugitive-slave clause of the Constituticn and the law for the suppression of the foreign slave-trade, are each as well enforced, perhaps, as any law can be in a community where the moral sense of the people imperfectly supports the law itself."

It might be interesting to here turn for a moment from Abraham Lincoln to the leaders in the slave States who had formed a Confederacy among themselves. In this Confederacy Jefferson Davis was elected President and Alexander H. Stephens Vice-President. Shortly after his election Mr. Stephens made a speech in Savannah in which he said:

"The new Constitution has put at rest forever all agitating questions relating to our peculiar institution—

African slavery, as it exists among us—the proper *status* of the negro in our form of civilization. This was the immediate cause of the late rupture and present revolution. Jefferson, in his forecast, had anticipated this, as the 'rock upon which the old Union would split.' He was right. What was conjecture with him, is now a realized fact. But whether he fully comprehended the great truth upon which that rock stood and stands, may be doubted. The prevailing ideas entertained by him, and most of the leading statesmen at the time of the formation of the old Constitution,.were, that the enslavement of the African was in violation of the laws of nature; that it was wrong in principle, socially, morally, and politically. It was an evil they knew not well how to deal with; but the general opinion of the men of that day was, that, somehow or other, in the order of Providence, the institution would be evanescent and pass away. This idea, though not incorporated in the Constitution, was the prevailing idea at the time. The Constitution, it is true, secured every essential guarantee to the institution while it should last, and hence no argument can be justly used against the constitutional guarantees thus secured, because of the common sentiment of the day. Those ideas, however, were fundamentally wrong. They rested upon the assumption of the equality of races. This was an error. It was a sandy foundation, and the idea of a government built upon it was wrong—when the 'storm came and the wind blew, it fell.'

"Our new government is founded upon exactly the opposite ideas; its foundations are laid, its corner-stone rests, upon the great truth that the negro is not equal to the white man; that slavery, subordination to the superior race, is his natural and normal condition. This, our new government, is the first in the history of the world, based upon this great physical, philosophical, and moral truth. This truth has been slow in the process of its development, like all other truths in the various departments of science. It is even so amongst us. Many who hear me, perhaps, can recollect well that this truth was not generally admitted even within their day. The errors of the past generations still clung to many as late as twenty years ago. Those at the North who still cling to these errors with a zeal above knowledge, we justly denominate fanatics."

Mr. Stephens, after calling for some time people who he confessed looked upon slavery as did Jefferson fanatics, stated that he could not allow himself to doubt the ultimate recognition of the view taken of slavery by the Confederate government, " throughout the civilized and enlightened world." In January, 1863, Jefferson Davis, in a message to the Congress of the Confederate States, spoke with bitterness of the United States. Alluding to Lincoln's proclamation emancipating the slaves of all States in arms against the United States Government, he said : " We may well leave it to the instinct of that common humanity which a beneficent Creator has implanted in the breasts of our fellow-men of all countries, to pass judgment on a measure by which several millions of human beings of an inferior race—peaceful, contented laborers in their sphere—are doomed to extermination, while at the same time they are encouraged to a general assassination of their masters by the insidious recommendation ' to abstain from violence, unless in necessary self-defence.' "

Turning from advocates of slavery to Lincoln, it may here be noticed that at his second election, which took place when men's feelings were naturally somewhat heated by the Civil War, he received 3,604,474 more votes than was received by his distinguished opponent, General George B. McClellan. In his second inaugural address Abraham Lincoln sadly said :

" One-eighth of the whole population were colored slaves, not distributed generally over the Union, but localized in the Southern part of it. These slaves constituted a peculiar and powerful interest. All knew that this interest was somehow the cause of the war. To strengthen, perpetuate, and extend this interest was the object for which the insurgents would rend the Union by war, while the Government claimed no right to do more than to restrict the territorial enlargement of it.

" Neither party expected for the war the magnitude or the duration which it has already attained. Neither anticipated that the cause of the conflict might cease even before the conflict itself should cease. Each looked for an easier triumph, and a result less fundamental and astounding.

" Both read the same Bible and pray to the same God, and each invokes His aid against the other. It may seem strange that any men should dare to ask God's assistance in wringing their bread from the sweat of other men's faces, but let us judge not, that we be not judged. The prayer of both could not be answered. That of neither has been answered fully. The Almighty has his own purposes. Woe unto the world because of offences, for it must needs be that offences come, but woe to that man by whom the offence cometh ! If we shall suppose that African slavery is one of these offences which, in the providence of God, must needs come, but which having continued through His appointed time, He now wills to remove, and that He gives to both North and South this terrible war as the woe due to those by whom the offence came, shall we discern there any departures from those

Divine attributes which the believers in a living God always ascribe to him? Fondly do we hope, fervently do we pray, that this mighty scourge of war may speedily pass away. Yet if God wills that it continue until all the wealth piled by the bondsman's two hundred and fifty years of unrequited toil shall be sunk, and until every drop of blood drawn with the lash shall be paid by another drawn with the sword, as was said three thousand years ago, so, still it must be said that the judgments of the Lord are true and righteous altogether.

"With malice towards none, with charity for all, with firmness in the right as God gives us to see the right, let us finish the work we are in, to bind up the nation's wounds, to care for him who shall have borne the battle, and for his widow and his orphans, to do all which may achieve and cherish a just and lasting peace among ourselves and with all nations."

Lincoln, if lacking in some respects the education which could justly be desired for a President of the great Republic of the New World, yet was learned to no ordinary degree in certain parts of American history. He had for years been a member of the Legislature of Illinois. By a very wise arrangement worthy of the highest praise every State has a library at its capital. Often might Lincoln have been seen with noble industry earnestly consulting the Illinois State library, and thus, unconsciously perhaps, fitting himself to act a grand part in the drama of history. He possessed many virtues, not the least of which was his firm devotion to his country. He possessed, one may almost say, a giant's strength, physically and mentally. Many, if not indeed all, of his State papers breathe a spirit which may well fill one with wonder when the circumstances under which they were written are borne in mind. He surrounded himself with singularly able counsellors.

With Jefferson and Madison and Clay and many other distinguished statesmen, Lincoln at one time entertained the idea that one way to abolish slavery was to colonize the colored people somewhere where they could govern themselves. Jefferson, when President of the United States, in a letter to Monroe dated November 24th, 1801, discussed a plan by which the United States should buy somewhere land for the colored people and should let them, for various reasons, live by themselves. He said: "However our present interests may restrain us within our own limits, it is impossible not to look forward to distant times, when our rapid multiplication will extend itself beyond those limits, and cover the whole northern, if not southern continent, with a people speaking the same language, governed in similar forms, and by similar laws; nor can we contemplate with satisfaction either blot or mixture on that surface." Jefferson then spoke of the advantages of the West Indies as a place of retreat for the colored people. In a long letter to Jared Sparks, under date of February 4th, 1824, Jefferson argued that the proceeds of the public lands should be devoted to the abolition of slavery. He claimed that while the measure was "more important to the slave States," yet that it was "highly so to the others also." He said that "a liberal construction of the Constitution, justified by the object," would enable the United States to do much towards abolishing slavery, "and an amendment to the Constitution the whole length necessary" to accomplish the beneficial purpose. It may here be noticed that Madison and Chief-Justice Marshall were desirous of seeing the proceeds of the public lands applied to the emancipation of slavery. In a letter to Robert J. Evans, June 15th, 1819, Madison said:

"It is the peculiar fortune, or, rather, a providential

blessing of the United States, to possess a resource commensurate to this great object, without taxes on the people, or even an increase of the public debt.

"I allude to the vacant territory, the extent of which is so vast, and the vendible value of which is so well ascertained."

Madison made a calculation of the number of acres which would suffice to appropriate for the purpose. He then said : "And to what object so good, so great, and so glorious, could that peculiar fund of wealth be appropriated? Whilst the sale of territory would, on one hand, be planting one desert with a free and civilized people, it would, on the other, be giving freedom to another people, and filling with them another desert. And if in any instances wrong has been done by our forefathers to people of one color, by dispossessing them of their soil, what better atonement is now in our power than that of making what is rightfully acquired a source of justice and of blessings to a people of another color?" As Madison continued he thus argued : "No particular difficulty is foreseen from that portion of the nation which, with a common interest in the vacant territory, has no interest in slave property. They are too just to wish that a partial sacrifice should be made for the general good. * * * That part of the nation has, indeed, shewn a meritorious alacrity in promoting, by pecuniary contributions, the limited scheme for colonizing the blacks, and freeing the nation from the unfortunate stain on it, which justifies the belief that any enlargement of the scheme, if founded on just principles, would find among them its earliest and warmest patrons. It ought to have great weight that the vacant lands in question have, for the most part, been derived from grants of the States holding the slaves, to be redeemed and removed by the sale of them."

10

Madison did not maintain that the national government could purchase the slaves unless the people would
agree to its so doing, but he did not doubt that the nation
had the power, if it had the inclination, to bring about
"the great object in question." Under date of March
20th, 1820, in a letter to Tench Coxe, he said : " I have
long thought that our vacant territory was the resource
which, in some way or other, was most applicable and
adequate as a gradual cure for the portentous evil, without, however, being unaware that even that would encounter serious difficulties of different •sorts." The
words of Jefferson and Madison, which have here been
presented, give some faint idea of the sacrifices—estimated
at hundreds of millions of dollars—which they wished the
Republic to make rather than to permit slavery to continue to exist in the United States.

Lincoln, for years, if not indeed to his death, held the
idea that it would be wise, for various reasons, for the
United States to aid emancipated colored people to colonize some part of the world beyond the limits of the
United States. In the early part of the Civil War Congress
also entertained this opinion, and made an appropriation
with which to buy such a territory. Lincoln selected a
part of New Granada, known as the Chiriqui Lagoon. As
I write I have before me an English volume written by
Commander Bedford Pim of the Royal Navy, during the
United States Civil War. The book is entitled " The
Gate of the Pacific." In this work Commander Pim, who
had spent considerable time on the coast of Central
America, in language which at times may well cause an
American to feel highly indignant, urges the English
government to take advantage of the struggle in which
the United States was engaged, to put to silence the
"Monroe Doctrine " of the "Yankees"—as he stigma-

tizes the people of the United States,—by seizing the magnificent territory for England. He speaks with rapture of the gorgeous territory and of its splendid harbors. Alluding in a characteristic manner to the Anglo-Saxon Republic, he gives, in order to enlighten, and arouse to opposition, his own government, a speech delivered by Abraham Lincoln on August 14th, 1862, to a deputation of colored people who made him a visit. In the course of his speech Lincoln said : " Your race are suffering, in my opinion, the greatest wrong inflicted on any people. * * * See our present condition ;—the country is engaged in war ; our white men cutting one another's throats, none knowing how far it will extend ;—and then consider what we know to be the truth. But for your race among us there could not be a war. Although many men engaged on either side do not care for you one way or the other, nevertheless I repeat, without the institution of slavery and the colored race as a basis, the war could have no existence." Lincoln then argued that if the colored people who were already freed and were in some degree intelligent would found a new colony—a colony which would offer an asylum to the colored people who from time to time would obtain their freedom,—the colonists could feel a nobility of purpose something like unto that which animated Washington when he went through the hardships of the War of Independence. Lincoln then, speaking of the American colony at Liberia, said : " The question is, If the colored people are persuaded to go anywhere, why not there? One reason for an unwillingness to do so is, that some of you would rather remain within reach of the country of your nativity. * * * The place I am thinking about for a colony is Central America. It is nearer us than Liberia—not more than one-fourth as far as Liberia—and within seven days' run by steamers. Unlike Liberia, it is on a great line of travel—it is a highway. The country is a very excellent one for any people, and with great natural resources and advantages. * * * The particular place I have in view is to be a great highway from the Atlantic or Carribean Sea to the Pacific Ocean ; and this particular place has all the advantages of a colony. On both sides there are harbors among the first in the world. Again there are evidences of very rich coal-mines. A certain amount of coal is valuable in any country, and there may be more than enough for the wants of the country. * * * I shall, if I get a sufficient number of you engaged, have provision made that you shall not be wronged. If you will engage in the enterprise, I will spend some of the money entrusted to me. I am sure you will succeed. * * * Besides I would endeavor to have you made equals, and have the best assurance that you would be made equals of the best. The practical thing I want to ascertain is whether I can get a number of able-bodied men, with their wives and children, who are willing to go when I present evidence of encouragement and protection. Could I get a number of tolerably intelligent men with their wives and children, I think I could make a successful commencement." Lincoln, as he concluded his address, said that the scheme was fraught with consequences not confined to the present generation, but extended to distant times, as

> " From age to age descends the lay,
>   To millions yet to be,
>   Till far its echoes roll away
>   Into eternity."

Commander Pim, after giving this speech in full, presents a circular which was issued to colored men upon the proposed colonization enterprise. The following sentence from this circular will give an idea of its purpose: "If this travail and pain of the nation become the birthday of your freedom, let us plant you free and independent beyond the reach of the power that has oppressed you." Events of such a nature occurred that the plan of founding a colony in New Granada was not carried out. Moreover, a certain infamous treaty, which I may be enabled at some future time to show embraced a policy for which slavery was responsible, known as the Clayton-Bulwer treaty, forbade the United States forever and forever from colonizing or annexing the country, even though the people should request the United States to permit them to become a part of the Republic, as Nicaragua once did, when the slave power in Congress defeated the beneficent arrangement, partly, if not indeed solely, because the people had abolished slavery, and the leaders of the slave States feared that the sight of free colored people might injuriously affect "the peculiar institution" of the Southern States. It could be shown that the deadliest enemy which the "Monroe Doctrine"—a policy which was intended to secure liberty to the American continent and to make one brotherhood of the inhabitants of the Western Hemisphere—has ever had to contend with was the slave power in the United States!

This is not the place to dwell upon the storm of civil war which swept over the United States—a war in which the aggregate number of the soldiers engaged amounted to 3,756,053 — men representing myriads of homes shadowed with death;—a war which cost the nation thousands of millions of dollars and rivers of blood and tears. A faint idea of some of the features of civil war can be inferred from the following illustrations. Two forces met each other in battle. A soldier wounded and captured a prisoner—his own brother. Aiming his gun

at a man behind a tree, the wounded prisoner said:
"Don't fire there, Bob, that is father!" Even Edward
Coles, who had saved Illinois from becoming a slave
State, had his heart wrung with anguish by finding that
his son—a mere boy—while fighting on the side of the
Confederate States had been wounded unto death. A
mother one day opened a letter which read as follows:

> "EXECUTIVE MANSION, WASHINGTON,
> "November 21, 1864.

"DEAR MADAM: I have been shown in the files of the War
Department a statement of the Adjutant General of Massachusetts, that you are the mother of five sons who died gloriously
on the field of battle. I feel how weak and fruitless must be
any words of mine which would attempt to beguile you from
the grief of a loss so overwhelming. But I cannot refrain from
tendering to you the consolation that may be found in the thanks
of the Republic they died to save. I pray that our Heavenly
Father may assuage the anguish of your bereavement, and
leave you only the cherished memory of the loved and lost,
and the solemn pride that must be yours to have laid so costly
a sacrifice upon the altar of freedom.

> "Yours, very sincerely and respectfully,
> "ABRAHAM LINCOLN.

"To Mrs. BIXBY, Boston, Massachusetts."

At the dedication of the Soldiers' Cemetery at Gettysburg, Lincoln in a singularly solemn speech urged the
people to resolve "that this Nation, under God, shall
have a new birth of freedom; and that Government of the
people, by the people, and for the people, shall not perish
from the earth."

The history of the Civil War and its effect upon slavery were in a single sentence, in a speech delivered on
June 29th, 1867, thus condensed by John Bright: "The

ground reeled under the nation during four years of agony until at last after the smoke of battle had cleared away, the horrid shape which had cast its shadow over one whole continent had vanished and was gone forever."

At the close of the war about four millions of people who had been slaves became citizens of the Republic. The vote of any colored man has now the same weight in State and national affairs as does the vote of any other citizen of the Republic. These four millions of new citizens were, with scarcely an exception, unacquainted with even the alphabet of the English language. How it happened that people living under the United States flag were thus illiterate will be the better understood after taking a brief view of some of the laws in force at the time of the abolition of slavery. In South Carolina an act which was adopted as early as 1740, and was in force with cruel amendments until slavery was abolished, read thus: "Whereas the having of slaves taught to write, or suffering them to be employed in writing, may be attended with great inconveniences, *Be it enacted*, That all and every person and persons whatsoever who shall hereafter teach or cause any slave or slaves to be taught to write, or shall use or employ any slave as a scribe in any manner of writing hereafter taught to write, every such person or persons shall for every such offence forfeit the sum of one hundred pounds current money." * In 1800, leaving the enactment of 1740 in force, it was decreed that : "Assemblies of slaves, free negroes, mulattoes and mestizoes, whether composed of all or any of such description of persons, or of all or any of the same and of a proportion of white persons, met together for the purpose of *mental instruction* in a confined or secret place, &c. &c., are de-

---

* 2 Brevard's Digest, 243. Quoted by George M. Stroud in his " Sketch of the Laws Relating to Slavery." 1856, p. 60.

clared to be an *unlawful meeting;* and magistrates are hereby required, &c., to enter into such confined places, &c. &c., to break doors, &c. if resisted, and to disperse such slaves, free negroes, &c. &c.; and the officer dispersing such unlawful assemblage *may inflict such corporal punishment, not exceeding twenty lashes upon such slaves, free negroes,* &c., as they may judge necessary for DETERRING THEM FROM THE LIKE UNLAWFUL ASSEMBLAGE IN FUTURE." * Another section of the same act declared " That it shall not be lawful for any number of slaves, free negroes, mulattoes or mestizoes, even in company with white persons, to meet together for the purpose of *mental instruction*, either before the rising of the sun, or after the going down of the same." † On December 17th, 1834, as though the laws already in existence were not sufficiently severe to satisfy the slave-master, it was enacted that, " If any person shall hereafter teach any slave to *read or write*, or shall aid in assisting any slave to *read or write*, or cause or procure any slave to be taught to *read or write*, such person, if a free white person, upon conviction thereof, shall for every such offence against this act be fined not exceeding one hundred dollars, and imprisoned not more than six months; or if *a free person of colour*, shall be whipped not exceeding *fifty* lashes, and fined not exceeding fifty dollars; and if *a slave*, shall be whipped not exceeding *fifty* lashes.; and if *any free person of colour* or *a slave* shall keep any such school or other place of instruction for teaching any slave or free person of colour *to read or write*, such person shall be liable to the same fine,‡ imprisonment, and corporal punishment as are by this act

---

* 7 Statutes of South Carolina, 440. See Stroud's " Sketch of the Laws Relating to Slavery," pp. 60, 61. † Ibid.

‡ If a slave could not pay the fine he was liable to be sold into slavery, and the money of his sale would be appropriated by the State.

imposed and inflicted on *free persons of colour* and *slaves* for teaching slaves to read or write." *

Virginia, the State in which Jefferson and Washington and Madison were born, all of whom hated slavery, by its code of 1849, announced that, " Every assemblage of negroes for the purpose of instruction in *reading* or *writing* shall be an *unlawful assembly.* Any justice may issue his warrant to any officer or other person, requiring him to enter any place where such assemblage may be, and seize any negro therein ; and he or any other justice may order such negro to be punished *with stripes.*

" If a *white* person assemble with negroes for the purpose of instructing them to *read* or *write*, he shall be confined to jail not exceeding six months, and fined not exceeding one hundred dollars." †

In Georgia there was a statute which seems to have been in force from 1770 until about the time of Lincoln's death, which was similar to the one enacted in South Carolina in 1740, only it was even better calculated than was the South Carolina law to keep its colored slaves illiterate.‡ As though the law in Georgia already in force, making it a crime to teach colored people to read and write, was not severe enough to satisfy the owners of slaves, in 1829 it was enacted that, " If any *slave, negro* or *free person of colour*, or *any white person*, shall teach any other slave, negro or free person of colour to *read or write* either written or printed characters, the said free person of colour or slave shall be punished by *fine and whipping*, or *fine* or *whipping, at the discretion of the court ;* and if a white person so offending, he, she or they shall be punished with *fine* not exceeding *five* hun-

---

* 7 Statutes of South Carolina, 468.   Quoted by Stroud, p. 60.
† Code of Virginia, 747, 748.   Given by Stroud, p. 61.
‡ For this law of Georgia, see Cobb's Digest, 981, and Stroud's Work, p. 61.

dred dollars, and imprisonment in the common jail at the discretion of the court." *   Even this additional law did not satisfy the slave-owner. In 1833 it was further enacted that, " If any person shall *teach* any *slave, negro* or *free person of colour* to *read* or *write* either written or printed characters, or shall procure, suffer or permit a slave, negro or person of colour *to transact business for him in writing*, such person so offending shall be guilty of a misdemeanor, and, on conviction, shall be punished by *fine* or *imprisonment* in the common jail, or both, at the discretion of the court." †

In North Carolina, the law forbidding any one to teach a slave to read or write, which was in force when Abraham Lincoln's proclamation abolishing slavery in the insurgent States was issued, read thus : " Any free person who shall hereafter teach, or *attempt* to teach, any slave within this state to *read* or *write*, the use of figures excepted, or shall *give* or sell to such slave or slaves *any books or pamphlets*, shall be liable to indictment, and upon conviction shall, at the discretion of the court, &c., if a *white* man or woman, be fined not less than *one hundred* dollars, nor more than *two* hundred dollars, or *imprisoned ;* and if a free person of colour, shall be *fined, imprisoned* or *whipped*, at the discretion of the court, not exceeding *thirty-nine* lashes, nor less than *twenty* lashes.‡ And for a similar offence *as to instruction*, a slave shall receive thirty-*nine* lashes on his or her *bare* back." §

The law forbidding any one to teach a slave to read or

* Ibid., 1001. Also see Stroud's " Sketch of the Laws Relating to Slavery in the United States," 1856, p. 61.

† Ibid., 828.   Also Stroud's " Sketch of the Laws Relating to Slavery in the United States."

‡ Revised Statutes, ch. 34, § 74, p. 209.

§ Ibid., ch. 3, § 27. See Stroud's " Sketch of the Laws Relating to Slavery," p. 61.

write in Louisiana, a law enacted by its Assembly in March, 1830, read thus: "All persons who shall teach or cause to be taught any slave in this state to *read* or *write* shall, on conviction thereof, &c., be imprisoned not less than *one* nor more than *twelve* months."

The law in force in Alabama at the time that the "peculiar institution of the South," as slavery was politely called, was swept away, provided that, "Any person who shall *attempt* to teach any *free person of colour or slave* to SPELL, *read* or *write*, shall upon conviction, &c., be fined in a sum not less than $250 nor more than $500." *

To present a full view of the laws which had a direct and indirect influence in keeping the colored people in abject ignorance of letters,—laws in force at the time when the leaders of the Southern States undertook to war against the United States,—would require a volume. As I write I have such a volume beside me.† My heart sickens as I contemplate the cruelties inflicted beneath the stars and stripes. In the States which have just been named, a colored person, whether man or woman, was in danger of being flogged if he or she "*attempted*" to learn how to read or write.‡ How far the flogging could be carried may be inferred from the fact that in one or more of the slave States the laws especially provided that if a slave should die while receiving "moderate correction," no one should be punished for murder. Colored people in some of the States were forbidden by law to even worship together. For example, in Virginia, a law, in force at the breaking

---

* Clay's Digest, 543, *act of* 1832, § 10.   See Stroud's "Slavery in the United States," p. 61.

† George M. Stroud's "Collection of Laws respecting Slaves in the United States."

‡ It seems that the laws of Kentucky, Mississippi, Missouri, Arkansas, Florida and Texas were silent in respect to the education of slaves.

out of the Civil War, reads thus : " Every assemblage of
negroes *for the purpose of religious* worship, when such
worship is conducted by *a negro,* shall be an unlawful
assembly ; and a justice may issue his warrant to any officer or other person, requiring him to enter any place
where such assemblage may be, and seize any negro
therein, and he or any other justice may order such negro
to be punished with stripes." *   In Mississippi, under certain circumstances, a colored person was allowed to attend a religious meeting conducted by a white man.†
Practically, in some of the Southern States, a Sabbath-
school or church service could not lawfully be attended
by slaves.   Doubtless, even in such States as South Carolina and Virginia, some kind-hearted slave-owners might
teach slaves to read.   What could the slave power do to
meet such cases ?   Humboldt, when travelling in the
United States, thought it singular that in the Southern
States no colored man could ever be seen driving a mail-
wagon.   In order to keep books and reading-matter from
the hands of slaves, the slave power enacted in the national Capitol, in the year 1810, that none but free white
people should be employed in carrying the mails.   The
national government at an earlier date had been made
to decree that in no part of the United States should
even free colored people be allowed to serve in the militia.   The slave-power jealously kept in mind that with
slaves ignorance of letters is weakness, and that it was
from its point of view wise to keep the colored people
unlettered.   On some of the vessels entering the harbors
of South Carolina and Louisiana there might be a few
free colored people who could read and write.   These
colored men might, in some way, communicate informa-

* Code of Virginia of 1849, p. 747.
† Mississippi Revised Code, p. 390.

tion to the dark mind of the slave—information of a kind which might not be pleasing to the slave power. In defiance of the national Constitution, State laws were made by which colored . sailors were incarcerated in prisons during the period the vessels on which they came remained in port.

Who will ever measure the evil wrought by slavery! Wilberforce, filled with a righteous indignation, when endeavoring to put a stop to the slave-trade, was constrained to exclaim that slavery was " the full measure of pure unsophisticated wickedness, and scorning all competition or comparison, it stands alone without a rival, in the secure, undisputed possession of its detestable preëminence ! "

That at the close of the Civil War slavery left the United States—especially the Southern part of the Republic—a fearful legacy of ignorance, was only what might have been expected. Jefferson's plan of emancipation, as is evident by his letter to Edward Coles, dated August 25th, 1814, embraced a provision for the education of the colored people. In the book which he published and gave to students of the college of William and Mary, entitled " Notes on Virginia," he proposed that the colored people should be taught at the public expense the " arts and sciences, according to their geniuses." In a letter to Mr. Barrow, under date of May 1st, 1815, Jefferson, after stating that the abolition of slavery had been a subject of " early and tender consideration " with him, and after speaking of the change which would have to take place in the mind of the master, added " that of the slave is to be prepared by instruction and habit for self-government, and for the honest pursuits of industry and social duty." Jefferson in his book even wished the United States to give the colored people, as he expressed it, " implements of the household and of the handicrafts, seeds, pairs of the useful domestic animals." To these noble words of Jefferson's it may be interesting to add that when Washington, who hated slavery, and wished to God that it were abolished, freed at his death the slaves that belonged to his estate, he very wisely made an especial provision for their being taught to read and write. In a letter which Jefferson wrote to Mr. Jullien, under date of July 23d, 1818, he said of the celebrated General Kosciuszko : " On his departure from the United States in 1798, he left in my hands an instrument appropriating after his death all the property he had in our public funds,* the price of his military services here, to the education and emancipation of as many of the children of bondage in this country as it would be adequate to."

Jefferson, when contemplating the importance of the United States making provision for the intellectual improvement of the colored people, was actuated principally—if not indeed altogether—by a generous desire that a humane and much-needed act should be performed, which he believed the nation to be under peculiar obligations to perform. One can imagine how he would have been startled had he foreseen clearly that a time would come when all the slaves would suddenly be made American citizens,—the men, although but a very small proportion of them could read and write, be made voters, and in many communities be made practically the masters of the whites, and that the United States government should scarcely, if at all, make any provision for their intellectual culture ! A condition of things not only dangerous to the people of the Southern States, but endangering the well-being of the United States !

---

* Kosciuszko being entitled, by a military certificate, for services rendered to the United States government, by a special act provided that he should receive interest from the 1st of January, 1793, to the 31st of December, 1797.

Many years have passed since the thunders and storm of a great civil war, in which hundreds of thousands of children were made orphans and vast numbers of women were made widows, have been succeeded by the sunshine of peace. A large part of the generation of slaves who, as an outcome of the war received their liberty, have passed from the scenes of earth. The colored people live—save a small percentage of them—in the Southern States. The once slave States have an area of 851,448 square miles, while the States which were called free at the commencement of the Civil War have an area of only 612,597 square miles. The Southern States cover one of the most beautiful and fertile sections of the world. Could these States but be blessed with good public-school systems and with good government, vast numbers of intelligent emigrants would esteem it a happy privilege to make for themselves homes within their attractive borders. These States, blessed with a population in the best sense of the word intelligent, might soon be expected to become wealthy, and to add, to a greater extent than they have ever done, to the well-being of the entire Republic. A few of many facts which might be mentioned, will give at least a faint idea of the intellectual condition of the people in the Southern States. The census of 1880 reveals the fact that in Alabama, Florida, and Georgia, at least 47 per cent. or more of the people are colored. While even in North Carolina 37.9 per cent. of the people are of African descent, and while in Virginia 41.7 per cent. of the people are black, in Louisiana 51.4 per cent. of the people—or more than half—are of African descent. In South Carolina 60.6 per cent., or more than half, of the population are black. In Mississippi 57.5 per cent. of the people are colored. It was predicted in very strong and bitter language, during the excitement of war times, by Jefferson Davis, that the slaves freed by Lincoln's Proclamation of Emancipation would perish off the land. The prediction that the colored people could not live in a state of freedom has been astonishingly, by results, contradicted. These people are—as revealed by statistics,—increasing so fast that in a good many States they are likely soon to be more numerous than the whites; all the more likely to control the destiny of States in which they reside, as white people are emigrating from the Southern States. In a sadly large number of these States the intellectual darkness of the people may truly be characterized as awful. In eight of the Southern States, which have been especially characterized as the black belt,—not to speak of other Southern States,—an army—as shown by the census of 1880— of 2,250,438 colored people ten years of age and upwards could have been marshalled at the taking of the census,—all of whom had confessed that they did not even know enough of letters to escape being classed among "illiterates." One might here speak of the great army of white illiterates which are to be found in this beautiful land, over which has passed the blight of slavery and the whirlwind of civil war; but it is to the colored population that attention is here being drawn. In the sixteen Southern States there were, in the year 1880, 4,695,253 colored people. Of the voters among these people—that is, of the men allowed to vote,— 78.5 per cent. could not read and write. In the State of Georgia 81.2 per cent. of the colored adults admitted— and many colored people decline to make such a confession if they have even a very slight acquaintance with the alphabet—that they were unable to read and write. In Virginia, whose territory adjoins the national capital, and where Washington and Madison and Jefferson lived,—

a State which has been proudly called the "Mother of Statesmen,"—78.01 per cent. of the colored voters could not, in the year 1880, so much as write their names. In Alabama 81.4 per cent. of the colored adult males, and in Louisiana 80.2 per cent. of these American citizens were, in 1880, illiterate. To understand these figures, let one think of the 128,257 colored voters in Virginia. Out of these American citizens who are called upon to vote on State and national affairs 100,210 do not know how to write their names. There are four other States in which the illiteracy among colored voters is larger than it is in Virginia. One might here speak of the 23.4 per cent. of the white voters of North Carolina, who cannot so much as write their names, but suffice it here to confine attention to the 6,518,372 colored people who are in the United States, and to remark that in South Carolina the majority of the voters in 1880,—including white and colored,—according to the census, were unable to read and write.

The ignorance of letters in some of the Southern States is not as general as it is in others, but in all it is wofully great. Mr. Albion W. Tourgée, in his valuable book entitled "An Appeal to Cæsar"—by which he means an appeal to the American people,—a book which is highly worthy of the earnest attention of every intelligent friend of the Republic, has pointed out that the figures of the census present much too mildly the awful intellectual darkness which reigns in the late slave States. This fascinating and judicious writer presents reasons for believing that the desire of the colored people, when they know ever so little of letters, to be classed among those who are not illiterate is accountable for only 70 per cent. of their number ten years of age and upwards being enumerated by the census-taker as devoid of a knowledge of reading and writing. He presents facts which he discovered when living in a Southern State, which he believes justifies one in inferring that the figures of the census—as startling as they are—would be much nearer the truth if 90 per cent. of the vast colored population were regarded as illiterates.*   What must be the social condition of the once slave States when 3,042,444 of the people of color and 1,672,951 of American-born whites are incapable of reading and writing?   Taking together eight of the Southern States in which the colored population is largest, and averaging the number of white and black people, it is found that 48.5 per cent. of the population of these States, ten years of age and upwards, are illiterate. In this region—not to speak of the awful illiteracy of a large percentage of the white voters—78.5 per cent. of the vast number of colored men who are entitled to vote—who are American citizens!—could not, in the year 1880, so much as write a single word.   In the sixteen Southern States—including Missouri, West Virginia, Delaware, and Kentucky,—on an average, 36 per cent. of the people—including the white population—cannot read and write.   In these States 4,715,395 of people are as little able to communicate with their fellow-citizens by means of writing as are the savages of Africa.   Practically, at least one half of these people are unable to read the ballots which they use at elections, in which the honor and well-being of not only the States in which they live, but interests of priceless value to the United States,

---

*See Mr. Albion W. Tourgée's interesting and valuable work entitled, "An Appeal to Cæsar." He has also published an instructive novel entitled "Bricks without Straw," in which—as in various other writings— he forcibly draws attention to the educational needs of the Southern States, and to a practicable plan by which the national government could help the Southern States to secure to themselves the great blessing of good school systems.

are at stake. Well may posterity regard it as a heavy re-proach to the people of the United States that in 1880—many years after the close of the Civil War—67.7 per cent. of the colored voters in the United States should be utterly illiterate, and that 1,125,749 colored women, who are to no inconsiderable extent to influence the destiny of the coming generation of American citizens, should not so much as know how to write their names. Surely such a republic as that of the United States should aim at protecting at national elections the ballot from the degradation which necessarily must characterize a condition of affairs such as has been entailed upon the United States by its former system of slavery. There are moments when, upon the wisdom, energy, and decision of character of its statesmen—as truly as there are hours when, upon the valor and awful sacrifices of its soldiers—the destiny of a nation is decided. As the wounds of a stricken deer upon the mountains or lonely plains invites the attack of the vulture and of the wolf, so does illiteracy in a nation invite the enslavement of a people by temporal and ecclesiastical despots. As low as unlettered nations of all ages have sunk, as high as are the possibilities of future grandeur before the Republic, even so vastly important it is that adequate provision should be made for the intellectual elevation of the millions of neglected youth of the United States. In the year 1870 the number of people, white and colored, ten years of age and upwards, who could not read and write, according to the census, which, there is reason to fear, gave too low a figure, was 5,658,144. In the year 1880 the number had risen to 6,239,958, or to 581,814 more than in the year 1870. Make whatever excuse which any one can suggest for these sad and awfully vast figures, they deserve to receive consideration by American statesmen. When the question, "What can be done to secure to American youth the blessing of intellectual culture?" shall be considered in State Capitols and in the National Legislature, one could wish that the spirit of Thomas Jefferson would enter the council-chambers, and, with the earnestness which ever characterized him when considering the inseparable connection which should exist between civil liberty and a good school system, would urge upon the statesmen of the present generation the importance of rendering their country what he considered "the greatest of all services" by making a good educational law—what he called "the keystone of the arch of our government." As of old with burning earnestness Jefferson would say : "The people should be rendered "the safe as they are the ultimate guardians of their own liberty." * "It is better" that the illiterate "should be sought for and educated at the common expense of all, than that the happiness of all should be confided to the weak and wicked." † "No other sure foundation [can be laid than that of public education] for the preservation of freedom and happiness." ‡ "The tax which will be paid for this purpose," "if tax can be called that which we give to our children in the most valuable of all forms, that of instruction," § "is not more than the thousandth part of what will be paid * * * if we leave the people in ignorance." ‖ "Experience * * * teaches the awful lesson that no nation is permitted to live in ignorance with

---

* Jefferson in his "Notes on Virginia," chapter on Education.

† Wording of the educational bill which Jefferson introduced into the Legislature of Virginia in 1779.

‡ Letter to George Wythe, August 13th, 1786.

§ Educational bill draughted by Jefferson in 1817.

‖ Letter to George Wythe, August 13th, 1786. See also letter dated January 14th, 1818, to J. C. Cabell.

impunity." * " In all enlightened countries a national education has been considered one of the first concerns of the legislature and intimately connected with the prosperity of the State * * * It would be a melancholy reflection, if a single youth of our country should from poverty be deprived of every ray of knowledge. And yet how many of the first geniuses of our land are condemned to grope out their days in a state of darkness." † Would that the spirit of Washington would take up the exhortations of Jefferson, and speak as he spoke of old when he, with the noblest eloquence bade farewell to his countrymen—adding to what he had already with peculiar impressiveness twice spoken in annual messages, on the importance of the National Legislature's aiding the cause of learning throughout the republic—the counsel: " Promote * * * as an object of primary importance institutions for the general diffusion of knowledge. In proportion as the structure of a government gives force to public opinion, it is essential that public opinion should be enlightened." Would that to this visitation of departed statesmen the spirit of Abraham Lincoln were joined ; and that once more he would speak as he often spoke, saying: " Universal education should go along with and accompany the universal ballot in America. The best, the firmest and most enduring basis of our Republic is the thorough, universal, education of the great American people. The intelligence of the mass of our people is the light and the life of the Republic." Lincoln's voice, however often raised with eloquence in behalf of free schools in Illinois, may never more be heard by mortals. One who was

---

* Report of Thomas Jefferson as Rector of the State University to the President and Directors of the Literary Fund of Virginia.

† Report of the Directors of the Literary Fund—of whom Jefferson was one—to the Legislature of Virginia.

twenty-five years his law partner has stated to me in writing that he has again and again heard Lincoln speak in substance the words of his which have just been quoted. He has also kindly sent me an extract from an address which Lincoln wrote and published in the year 1832—but seven years after the opening of the University of Virginia,—and distributed throughout one of the counties of Illinois, explaining it himself on the stump, and pledging himself to champion the causes which it represented, if elected a member of the Legislature of Illinois.   In this address Lincoln said : " Upon the subject of education, not presuming to dictate any plan or system regarding it, I can only say that I view it as the most important subject which we as a people can be engaged in.   That every man may receive at least a moderate education and thereby be enabled to read the histories of his own and other countries, by which he may duly appreciate the value of our free institutions, appears to be an object of vital importance, even on this account alone, to say nothing of the advantages and satisfaction to be derived from all being able to read the scriptures and other works, both of a religious and moral nature, for themselves."

Abraham Lincoln, as President of the United States, signed what was known as the Freedman's Bureau Bill. He thus had the honor of helping in some degree to elevate, in the truest sense, to American citizenship a large number of colored people.   By this Bureau about three millions of dollars was spent in providing school instruction for the colored people.   Lincoln, however, was not permitted to live to see the grand policy which he had a part in inaugurating consummated.   The noble work of securing to American youth of every color an education which will help to fit them to become worthy American citizens is laid upon other statesmen !

Once as I thoughtfully stood within the tomb in which Abraham Lincoln's remains await the resurrection call, I felt that by a mysterious providence Lincoln's career had been affected by Jefferson. I thought of Lincoln's labors in behalf of the colored race. Scenes of the past as a great panorama passed before me. I wondered whether Edward Coles would have acted the wise and heroic part he did had he not been encouraged by Jefferson to hate slavery; whether if Coles had not in Illinois fought one of the most momentous battles for freedom that was ever fought on the American continent Lincoln's heart would have been fired to espouse the cause of the oppressed; whether Jefferson's labors in helping to secure to the great Northwest Territory liberty and education, and his efforts, in a quiet way, to arouse in the hearts of certain youth in Virginia right feelings respecting man's enslaving his fellow-beings,—had not been links in the chain of great events which have redeemed a race from a cruel bondage. I thought how earnestly Jefferson and Lincoln would labor, could they return to this world, to induce the national government to do whatever wise statesmanship can do to aid in the great work of securing the blessing of intellectual culture to all the future citizens of the Republic of the United States.

V.

A JEFFERSONIAN AMENDMENT TO THE CONSTITUTION OF THE UNITED STATES.

JEFFERSON in a letter to Washington dated January 4th, 1786, thus wrote: "It is an axiom in my mind, that our liberty can never be safe but in the hands of the people themselves, and that, too, of the people with a certain degree of instruction. This it is the business of the state to effect, and on a general plan." These words of Jefferson's may well raise the question whether statesmanship can elaborate a practicable plan by which the blessing of school instruction will be secured to the youth of every part of a vast republic.

The United States of America had, in the year 1880, an area of about 3,603,000 square miles. Should the United States flag—which is but the emblem of a great republic or democracy in which the people are sovereign, and the mechanism of whose government is contrived to give effect to the wishes and to promote the happiness, and well-being, of its citizens—be raised over all of North America, it would wave over an area of 8,000,000 square miles; should it be unfurled over Central and South America, and over the islands off the coast of the American continent, it would wave over an area of about 15,099,480 square miles. "How would it be possible," some one may ask, "to provide for the establishment and for the maintenance in adequate numbers of public schools and institutions of learning of various kinds, in all parts of an empire which may become continental in its extent?" Such a question may well have a philosophic, a momentous, interest to American students of the science of government.

One who will turn his attention to the forms of government of civilized, and even of what may be called half-civilized, nations, may well be interested as he observes that, as a rule, it is expedient, for administrative purposes, to divide and to subdivide the domains over which these governments have jurisdiction. As an army is divided into brigades, and into regiments, and into companies, each division having a certain degree of autonomy of its own, so statesmen have found it useful, for administrative purposes, to subdivide realms for which they legislate. One might point out with much interest the internal governmental arrangements of one nation after another when illustrating this truth. Even the Chinese Empire, which embraces an area of 3,937,000 square miles, an area larger than that covered by the United States at the present time, has her provinces and various subdivisions, which, to an important extent, govern themselves. How highly important it is to the best interests of nations that communities should, in an intelligent manner, within quite a wide sphere govern themselves, would be sadly illustrated by a panoramic view of certain dark periods in the histories of Italy, Spain, France, and of Austria and Germany,—of periods when the communities and subdivisions into which these lands were subdivided had but very little or no control of the management of their own local affairs.

It would be interesting to observe the mighty influence on the prosperity and the glory of Great Britain, an empire which covers an area of at least 9,050,032 square miles, or an area more than twice that covered by the

United States in the year 1880, and to notice how latent powers of nations have at times been evoked by even a very imperfect system of self-government. One of the secrets of Russia's strength is what may, in a good sense, be called her communal system. Russia already possesses more than one half of the continent of Europe, and has in Asia a territory vaster than the entire continent of Europe. Russia has an area of 8,500,000 square miles, or more than twice the area of the United States. Silently, ever and anon, her borders are extended. Again and again people living near the borders of this mighty empire have seen Russian institutions established on new territory. The Russians, owing in part to a peculiar training to which attention is presently to be called, have a disposition, in which they in some respects resemble Anglo-Saxons, to establish self-governing communities. As pioneers in the western part of the American continent often fall in love with the natural scenery upon which they look, and with various charms of a new country, and establish communities of their own which they govern after the pattern of the liberal institutions amid which they have been reared, so bold Russian hunters, and even exiles of Siberia, and such monks of the Greek Church as visit the frontiers of the Empire of Russia, unite in founding the singular Russian community known as the *mir*—a word meaning in the Russian language "little world."

The *mir* may be regarded as a village, or commune, in which the people in many respects govern themselves. The people elect chiefs, and establish customs, of their own. The land claimed by the community is at stated times divided and re-divided among the people according to the size of each individual family. Early marriages are encouraged by their laws. Each family is expected to cultivate its own share of land and to do its own work. The only social unit that is recognized is a man and his wife, and is styled " a house." " A house " is entitled to a kitchen-garden, and to a proportion of woodland to supply fuel for domestic purposes. The community sets apart a certain proportion of land to be held in common by its members for the pasturage of cattle. The land is divided among " the houses "—to be re-divided again at the expiration of three years. When the land is divided, a sort of village Parliament is held in the open air. The land is divided among " the houses " exclusively—the bachelor receiving nothing. If the bachelor wishes land he must marry, and thus with his wife become a " house." In the division of the land the richness of the soil and its location are considered. At the communal councils the men are all peers. In many cases, women— except heiresses and wives whose husbands are away from the *mir*—are not allowed to take part in the discussions. A so-called Elder is elected to act as a sort of chief in the community. He is clothed with, in some respects, despotic power. His powers are somewhat un-classified and are sometimes great. He is the only man who can lawfully strike any one. He has been, however, forbidden by a decree of the imperial government to flog a woman. The people, on their part, can, when they are displeased with an Elder, remove him and appoint another man in his place. The Elder is held responsible by the imperial government for the good behavior of every one living in the *mir*. He it is who must carry out imperial mandates. The citizens of these Russian village-democracies have inherited from quite ancient times various local rights which it would be unwise for the imperial government to abridge. Evil-doers in these peasant republics are tried before their own councils, where punishments, not being regulated by law, are sometimes very cruel. The people have the right to call meetings, to propose measures, and to provide in a general way for the welfare of their commune. If a peasant wishes to take a journey, he must get permission to do so from the Elder. Although in the Russian *mir* forms of liberty are sometimes sadly blended with forms of despotism, the *mir* is a feature of Russian civilization which is one of the secrets of Russia's greatness. A large majority of the people of Russia are peasants and members of *mirs*. The people who live in cities of course live under a form of government of a different kind. A number of *mirs* lying contiguous to each other form a *volost*, which in English means a " canton." The canton is similar in some respects to a county in an American State. In recent years another division, also designed to be in a measure self-governing, has been introduced into Russia.

If a Russian Minister of War wishes to raise money by taxation, or to summon men to the Russian standard, he can send word to the *mir* or to the canton to raise and to send him its proportion of men and money. The councils held in the little communes scattered over Russia, notwithstanding criticisms which an American might well make respecting them, save the imperial government much trouble. A nation with even such an imperfect system of local government as have a large proportion of the people of Russia, could be, there is reason to believe, highly raised in the scale of civilization, should its central government enact wise laws encouraging the people to establish and to maintain, in their communes and towns, good schools for their youth and libraries for themselves.

A form of local government which captivated Jefferson is what is known as the township system of New England.

A visitor to the New England States, driving through their beautiful rural districts, sometimes passes a neat, although perhaps an humble, building, which, he may be told, is called the Town Meeting Hall. At a certain season of the year he may have the pleasure—and it will be no ordinary pleasure—of witnessing the proceedings which take place at a township meeting. He can see the citizens of a neighborhood—many of whom are farmers—assemble in a neighborly and intelligent manner to promote the welfare of the little section of the State in which they reside.

A New England township may have three or four hundred, or several thousand, inhabitants. It may have only some farm-houses, or it may have a town within its borders. The township is, in the eye of the law, a corporation. Where representation in the State Legislature is by districts, the township is entitled to a representative in the lower house of the State Legislature. When the government of a New England State imposes a tax for the public welfare, each township is assessed, and duly raises, its proportion of the tax. It has been estimated that a New England township pays voluntarily in promoting its own welfare at least eight times as much as it pays for State purposes. Each township is expected to elect officers to perform various duties. Some of these officers are charged with attending to school matters, others give their attention to roads and bridges, others have imposed upon them the duty of assessing and collecting taxes, or are entrusted with such other responsibilities as the town meeting may lay upon them. A town-clerk is charged with the care of the records of the proceeding of the town meeting—records which in time may become especially interesting to the historian. As the largest of nations are in danger of having controversies with each other respecting the exact boundaries of the territories over which they respectively have dominion,—controversies which at times have given rise to wars,—so might vexatious questions respecting the exact limits of townships give rise to difficulties of various kinds, did not the New England township carefully guard against such a danger to its peace. A certain class of officers are charged with the duty of seeing that each post which marks the boundaries of their little democracy is in its proper place. These officers must, within certain periods, make the circuit of the entire township. At a New England town meeting any citizen can speak upon questions of local interest. For example, he can point out to the meeting that it would be well to have a bridge built over a certain stream, or that a school-house should be built. Of course, a constable to bear the sword of justice is elected at a town meeting. Should extraordinary circumstances arise which make it necessary that men should defend their homes, or their State, or the great Republic of which their State is a subdivision, against an enemy, by a decree from the town meeting men could be assembled and equipped with arms in a well-nigh incredibly short time. Every township is an organization by itself, so complete that anarchy in a New England State is difficult to even imagine. If all the members of a New England State Legislature were captured by an enemy, township government would still continue. If an invader captured twenty townships, yet every twenty or thirty miles of a New England State would have a government of its own and would be prepared to offer organized resistance to its foe.

Should any one in a New England township happen to be injured when crossing a bridge or riding on a road, owing to the neglect of a public officer, he can sue the township in a court of law for damages. Although, as a rule, only the officers, who are called selectmen, are expected to call a town meeting, yet should any ten citizens think it desirable that such a meeting should be held, they can, by uniting in making a formal request of a selectman, have such a meeting assembled. As a rule, at a meeting a selectman presides. The people are notified in advance of the character of the business which is to be transacted. Dignity and wisdom often characterize to a truly remarkable extent the debates which take place in these small, and at times very humble, parliamentary gatherings.

It has been found in New England—and, indeed, to a certain extent in all parts of the United States—that local government, when wisely established, often awakens the genius and energies of a people. The citizen is apt to become interested in a happy manner in public affairs. Every citizen is sensible of a degree of political importance, and feels that he is in a measure responsible for the well-being of the community in which he lives. Men gathering together at the township meeting, and having common interests, become acquainted with each other and ties of friendship are often formed. The people of New England can appeal to an experience dating from the days when New England was first visited by the Puritans, in support of the belief that communities are capable of themselves managing a certain class of affairs.

Jefferson greatly admired New England's system of local government. In a letter dated May 26th, 1810, to Governor Tyler, Jefferson wrote: "You wish to see me again in the Legislature, but this is impossible. * * * I have indeed two great measures at heart, without which no republic can maintain itself in strength. 1. That of general education, to enable every man to judge for himself what will secure or endanger his freedom. 2. To divide every county into hundreds, of such size that all the children of each will be within a central school in it. But this division looks to many other fundamental provisions." Jefferson then sketched a system of local government similar to the township system of New England. Continuing, he said : " These little republics would be the main strength of the great one. We owe to them the vigor given to our revolution in its commencement in the Eastern States." He then pointed out the practical working of such a system. " General orders," he wrote, " are given out from a centre to the foreman of every hundred, as to the sergeants of an army, and the whole nation is thrown into energetic action, in the same direction in one instant and as one man, and becomes absolutely irresistible."

Jefferson wished a State and national school system to have ever in view the importance of setting in motion, and keeping in motion, what is known as local self-government. In a letter dated April 2d, 1816, which he wrote to Governor Nicholas, he alluded to the subdivisions into which he had proposed, in the bill which he introduced in the Legislature of Virginia in the year 1779, to divide his native State. Alluding to the school district he said : " My partiality for that division is not founded in views of education solely, but infinitely more as the means of a better administration of our government, and the eternal preservation of its republican principles. The example of this most admirable of all human contrivances in government, is to be seen in our Eastern States ; and its powerful effect in the order and economy of their internal affairs, and the momentum it gives them as a nation, is the single circumstance which distinguishes them so remarkably from every other national association."

Jefferson believed that a good school system and local government would react in a happy manner upon each other. To his cherished friend, Joseph C. Cabell, he wrote on January 31st, 1814: " There are two subjects, indeed, which I claim a right to further as long as I breathe, the public education, and the subdivision of counties into wards. I consider the continuance of republican government as absolutely hanging on these two hooks." In another letter which Jefferson wrote to Cabell on February 2d, 1816, he drew attention to a system of public schools for Virginia, and then continued: " If it is believed that these elementary schools will be better managed by the Governor and Council, the Commissioners of the Literary Fund, or any other general authority of the Government, than by the parents within each ward, it is a belief against all experience. * * * My friend, the way to have good and safe government, is not to trust it all to one, but to divide it among the many, distributing to every one exactly the functions he is competent to. Let the National Government be entrusted with the defence of the nation, and its foreign and federal relations; the State Governments with the civil rights, laws, police, and administration of what concerns the State generally; the counties with the local concerns of the counties; and each ward direct the interests within itself. It is by dividing and subdividing these republics from the great national one down through all its subordinations, until it ends in the administration of every man's farm and affairs by himself; by placing under every one what his own eye may superintend, that all will be done for the best. What has destroyed liberty and the rights of man in every Government which has ever existed under the sun? The generalizing and concentrating all cares and powers into one body, no matter whether of the autocrats of Russia or France, or of the aristocrats of a Venetian Senate. And I do believe, that if the Almighty has not decreed that man

11

shall never be free (and it is blasphemy to believe it), that the secret will be found in making himself the depository of the powers respecting himself, so far as he is competent to them, and delegating only what is beyond his competence by a synthetical process, to higher and higher orders of functionaries, so as to trust fewer and fewer powers, in proportion as the trustees become more and more oligarchical. The elementary republics of the wards, the county republics, the State republics, and the republic of the Union, would form a gradation of authorities, standing each on the basis of law, holding every one its delegated share of powers, and constituting truly a system of fundamental balances and checks for the Government. Where every man is a sharer in the direction of his ward republic, or of some of the higher ones, and feels that he is a participator in the government of affairs, not merely at an election, one day in the year, but every day; when there shall not be a man in the State who will not be a member of some one of its councils, great or small, he will let the heart be torn out of his body, sooner than his power be wrested from him by a Cæsar or a Bonaparte. How powerfully did we feel the energy of this organization in the case of the Embargo? I felt the foundations of the Government shaken under my feet by the New England township. There was not an individual in these States whose body was not thrown, with all its momentum, into action; and, although the whole of the other States were known to be in favor of the measure, yet, the organization of this little selfish minority enabled it to override the Union. What could the unwieldly counties of the Middle, the South, and the West do? Call a county meeting, and the drunken loungers at and about the court-houses would have collected, the distances being too great for the good people and the industrious generally to attend. The character of those who really met would have been the measure of the weight they would have had in the scale of public opinion. As Cato then concluded every speech with the words ' *Carthago delenda est,*' so do I every opinion with the injunction 'divide the counties into wards.' Begin them only for a single purpose, they will soon show for what others they are the best instruments."

To the extracts from Jefferson's letters which have just been presented, one additional extract may well be here given so as to illustrate how highly important he considered a system of local government. Writing to Samuel Kerchival on July 12th, 1816, alluding to his favorite idea of dividing counties into wards or townships, he said: " These wards, called townships in New England, are the vital principle of their government, and have proved themselves the wisest invention ever devised by the wit of man for the perfect exercise of self-government and for its preservation."

The form of township government which Jefferson esteemed as highly as he did still characterizes New England. Some of the States, it may here be noticed, have forms of local government different from, and perhaps even better than, those of New England. In the year 1870 the average size of a New England township was about thirty-four square miles. In that year there were not less than fourteen hundred and twenty-four townships in New England. To maintain a prison and a court-house in each of these townships would be extravagant. It has been found expedient that groups of these townships should unite and form a county. The county easily maintains a court-house and a prison. By wise State laws every township, however small, must maintain a school. When its population reaches a certain size it must also

have a grammar school. In some cases two small townships may unite in maintaining one high school. Should
a township neglect to obey these State laws any parent
can appeal to the courts. Whenever a New England community becomes sufficiently populous to do so, it can, by
complying with certain forms of law, become a city and
have a municipal form of government. In some of the New
England States no one can vote who cannot at least read.

One may be permitted to indulge the hope that by a
wise system of polity—a system making provision for
what may be called local government—the wants of every
section of vast empires can be cared for and the people
be infused with enterprise, and be enabled to enjoy a freedom that will have a happy influence upon them, while
the national government and its various divisions remain
free from the odium of any unnecessary interference in
local concerns. By wise State laws in New England the
sphere in which township government revolves is so
arranged that it fits into the sphere in which the State
government moves, somewhat, one might almost say, as
the cogwheels of one piece of machinery fit into the
wheels of another piece of well-devised machinery,—the
State in its turn having its own relation to the national
government. People may indeed make mistakes when
governing themselves, but their self-interest is enlisted on
the side of good government, while the interests of a
ruler who from a position outside the community governs
its people may be, at times, different from the best interests of those for whom he legislates. A people who
govern themselves are ever urged by their own interests
to endeavor to act wisely for the common good.

The establishment of an effective system of local government in all parts of the United States is, by many
statesmen, an end much to be desired. By the history of

every State it is found that a good school system aids in establishing what may be called local self-government. The State of New York, in 1812, enacted some school laws which gave it almost at once, at least as far as its schools were concerned, a system of local government. State laws provided a State school fund for which money was to be paid to each county which itself raised by taxation an amount of money equal to the sum to which it was entitled, provided it complied with certain laws, to receive from the State. A Mr. Gideon Hawley, a highly gifted man, was appointed State School Superintendent, to help to give efficiency to the State school system. The people of every neighborhood were thus given an incentive to take action respecting the education of their children. The fact that each district was entitled to receive money from the State fund, and to hold meetings to levy a tax for school purposes, was well calculated to excite the interest of the people. It was not long before some of the districts began to enter into a generous rivalry with each other to have the best schools in their section of country. Although the amount of money which each district received from the State was small,—perhaps on an average not more than twenty dollars a year,—it was enough to set in motion, in a very happy manner, the machinery of local government. In many instances handsome school-houses were cheerfully raised by the people. The people were enabled to feel that the schools belonged to them as truly as would a public library, a bridge, or a public road, and that the school was a place which their children could attend without the slightest loss of self-respect. Not only were the public schools much cheaper to parents than ordinary private schools would have been, but they were also much better. Wise arrangements were made for the supervision of these popular schools,

which insured to youth the advantage of having able
instructors. In districts in which, owing to conflicting
interests, or to a lack of united action among the people,
no one would have ventured to hope to see a school,
youth who had been in danger of growing up illiterate
received instruction. The school law of 1812, to which
attention has been drawn, being supplemented from time
to time by other wise laws, bore astonishingly good fruit.
DeWitt Clinton, Governor of New York, in his annual
message in the year 1822, spoke with eloquence of the
stand which the State of New York had taken respecting
public schools. While dwelling on the subject he said:
"The excellent direction which has been given to the
public bounty, in appropriations for common schools,
academies, and colleges, is very perceptible in the multiplication of our seminaries of education, in the increase of the number of students, and in the acquisition
of able and skilful teachers." Clinton then, having
in view some of Jefferson's labors in Virginia, added,
as he continued to speak of what was being done
in New York: "I am happy to have it in my power to
say that this State has always evinced a liberal spirit in
the promotion of education, and I am persuaded that no
considerations short of that of total inability will ever
prevent similar demonstrations. The first duty of a State
is to render its citizens virtuous by intellectual instruction and moral discipline, by enlightening their minds,
purifying their hearts, and teaching them their rights and
their obligations. Those solid and enduring honors
which arise from the cultivation of science and the acquisition and diffusion of knowledge will outlive the renown
of the statesman and the glory of the warrior; and if any
stimulus were wanting in a case so worthy of all our
attention and patronage, we may find it in the example

before our eyes of the author of the Declaration of Independence, who has devoted the evening of his illustrious life to the establishment of an university in his native State." As Clinton proceeded he spoke of New York's interest in the public lands of the United States, and of the wisdom of her exerting her influence to induce the national government to help, by consecrating public lands to the cause of education, to secure to the youth of the Republic of the United States the blessing of school instruction.

To-day some of the States have systems of local government to which they are indebted, in large part, to national laws. The State of Kansas illustrates this fact. When Kansas became a State she came into possession of a vast amount of land which the national government had appropriated for educational purposes. In the year 1886 she had a school fund of not less than $3,500,000. By selling a million acres of land which she had received from the Government of the United States, she could have swelled her school fund to $15,000,000 or to $20,000,000. By her Constitution the interest of her school fund is devoted to common schools. One can perhaps truly say of this fund that its chief value is the influence which it is made, by wise statesmanship, to exert in promoting local government. The revenue obtained from it, divided among the many school districts, gives to each district but a small sum, but that small sum is disbursed in a way which causes it to multiply in amount and to greatly encourage the establishment of a system of local government in every part of the State. In the year 1880, in Kansas, notwithstanding the number of foreigners within her borders and her colored population, there were but 25,000 persons, ten years of age and upwards, who could not read. In the year 1886 Kansas had 8,219 school teachers, to whom she paid in a single year nearly $2,000,000. She had not less than about 6,673 school-houses and a State university, a State normal school, and a State agricultural college. The people in many communities cheerfully taxed themselves for school purposes to a degree that the Legislature of Kansas would not have dared to have taxed them. During the five years from 1880 to 1885 Kansas spent $12,630,480 in providing the means of instruction for her youth.

Kansas, whose early history has left a deep impress on the history of the United States, became a State in the year 1861. In the year 1860 she had but a population of 107,206 people. According to an interesting paper on "The Progress of Kansas," in the April number of the *North American Review* of the year 1886, by her Governor, John A. Martin, a paper to which I am indebted for these statistics, Kansas had, in the year 1886, a population of 1,350,000. This young State has great natural resources, but its prosperity may be considered as, at least in part, a natural consequence of its system of local government.

Hand-in-hand with the establishment of any school fund for a State should go wise laws. This fact Jefferson discovered while laboring to establish a public-school system in Virginia. He was one of the managers of what was known as the Literary Fund of Virginia. This fund amounted in the year 1818 to about $1,500,000. It was established by the State of Virginia at the instance of the distinguished statesman Mr. James Barbour. Barbour had been Governor of Virginia, a member of the Cabinet of John Quincy Adams, and had represented the United States as Minister to England. When, however, he was about to die he requested that, if any monument should be reared to his memory, it should bear on it only

the inscription, " The Originator of the Literary Fund of
Virginia." The establishment of a good school system
in Virginia was a work beset with difficulties. Slavery
made it especially difficult to establish a wise system of
local government. What schools were established Jefferson found, were in some respects too independent of the
State.* The money from the Literary Fund was disbursed
in a way which was wasteful, and in a way which very
imperfectly advanced the educational interests of the
State. It should be remembered, however, that the school
system of Virginia was at the time in its infancy.

When a form of local government is established by a
State, or by a township, or by a city, a means is provided
by which many useful laws respecting educational affairs
can at least be considered by the people or by their
representatives, and be, perhaps, happily enacted.

One of the ways in which Jefferson wished to see governments advancing the interests of learning was by making wise provisions in aid of the establishment of public
libraries. A free library may justly be called a home of
science, of poetry, of history,—indeed, one may almost say
of every branch of learning,—a home to which the lover
of truth, of knowledge, of the human race, may repair to
fit himself, or herself, by means of valuable learning for
usefulness to human kind. Could one imagine a commonwealth blessed with a mystic building in which abide
learned authors of all lands, even the shades of the
accomplished dead, ever holding themselves compla-
cently ready to freely advise any visitor who needs light
on subjects to which they have given laborious and especial attention, if not even life-long study ; such a commonwealth would scarcely be more favored than is at

---

* See Letter of Jefferson's, dated Feb. 15th, 1821, to Gen. Breckenridge.
" Jefferson's Works," vol. vii., p. 205.

present many a town and village in the United States in which a free library is wisely supported by the people. Many men and women who have access to libraries are enabled to act a better part in the history of their times than they could did they not have access to books which are often as necessary to learning as is sustenance to the body. At the present time many men and women fail to be the half of what they might be if the town, or district, in which they live had established a public library. Such an institution has often been the means of awaking some noble spirit to a useful and even to a glorious life. It is told of a farmer, who lived in a frontier town in New Hampshire, that he helped to establish a circulating library in his neighborhood. One of the frequenters of this small garner-house of knowledge was the son of that farmer. The father, who was pleased at seeing his son endeavoring to acquire useful knowledge, one day, as he was riding with him in a sleigh, told him that he proposed to endeavor to send him to college. The youth, whose name was Daniel Webster, being filled with emotion, could not for a time speak, knowing that his father was poor. In time he went to a town in which to pursue some studies before presenting himself at Dartmouth College. In this town he found another library. In this silent university his mind broadened. At college he had an opportunity to still further store his mind with the wisdom of the learned. When, in after years, he held the Senate of the United States entranced by his eloquence, little did his admirers know of the silent hours which he had spent in company with books.

That a town in which there is a public library is a more desirable place to live in than it would be without such an institution, will be probably granted by every one who appreciates at their true worth such places of culture. It

has sometimes been whispered by men of letters in the
old world, that the education of many American men
and women is surprisingly shallow. If there was a free
library in every district and town, from the Atlantic Ocean
to the Pacific main, certainly the standard of true learning
would be higher in the United States than it is. The
personal resources of even the wealthiest citizen cannot
always acquire books which might be found in such silent
schools.

Many authors are " workers for posterity." The words
of the orator, unless committed to the custody of the
press, soon die upon the air. Many an author is encouraged in self-sacrificing work,—amounting to heroism,—
amidst hopes and fears and innumerable obstacles, by
feeling that the result of his labors may be reaped by,
and be a blessing to, humanity, when he shall be sleeping
with the dead, and that thus, when dead, he shall exert for
a time an influence in behalf of truth, or of civil liberty,
or of some noble cause in which he has hoped to benefit
his fellow-beings. Surely those statesmen, or citizens,
who labor to found free libraries enter into the labors of
such men, and thus sometimes become benefactors to the
human race.

On May 19th, 1809, about six weeks after retiring from
the presidency of the United States, Jefferson wrote thus
to a Mr. John Wyche : " Your favor of March 19th came
to hand but a few days ago, and informs me of the establishment of the Westward Mill Library Society, of its general
views and progress. I always hear with pleasure of institutions for the promotion of knowledge among my countrymen. The people of every country are the only safe
guardians of their own rights, and are the only instruments
which can be used for their destruction. And certainly
they would never consent to be so used, were they not

deceived. To avoid this, they should be instructed to a
certain degree. I have often thought that nothing would
do more extensive good at small expense than the establishment of a small circulating library in every county, to
consist of a few well-chosen books, to be lent to the people of the county, under such regulations as would secure
their safe return in due time. These should be such as
would give them a general view of other history, and a
particular view of that of their own country, a tolerable
knowledge of geography, the elements of natural philosophy, of agriculture, and mechanics. Should your example lead to this it would do great good. Having had
more favorable opportunities than fall to every man's lot
of becoming acquainted with the best books on such
subjects as might be selected, I do not know that I can
be otherwise useful to your society than by offering them
any information respecting these which they might wish.
My services in this way are freely at their command."

However much Jefferson would have liked to have seen
a public library in every county of Virginia, he died without the sight. In the New England States of the present
day every city and township is encouraged by wise provisions, enacted by their respective State governments, to
tax itself, within prescribed limits, for the maintenance of
public libraries. The State law authorizing any township
or city to itself provide for a library has been found by
experience to be eminently wise. One could wish that
in every State there was such a law.

It is pleasant to be able to state that in many, if not
indeed in all, the cities on the Pacific coast one finds valuable free circulating libraries. The traveller is sometimes
surprised and charmed even when visiting towns among
the Rocky Mountains, to find valuable collections of
books. Not to speak of the public library of Minneapolis,

or of Cincinnati, or of one town after another in rapidly growing States, a visit to the city library of Chicago is on some accounts especially interesting. When in the year 1871 the telegraph spread the news that Chicago was in flames, and that many thousands of houses were in ashes, and that a vast multitude of citizens were shelterless, some thoughtful English friends undertook to show their sympathy for the impoverished people by, among other acts of kindness, at once helping in making provision for the intellectual culture for the new city, which they foresaw was to arise from the one which had been partially destroyed by fire. Mr. Thomas Hughes, who was at the time a member of Parliament, issued a circular to booksellers and to friends of literature in England, suggesting that Chicago should be helped to have a public library. In this circular it was stated that " the library to be established would be regarded as a token of that sentiment of kinship which, independently of circumstances, and independent of every other consideration, must ever powerfully affect the different branches of the English race. * * * While the home literature of the present day and the last hundred years will form an important portion of the New Library, the characteristic feature of the gift will consist in sending to the Americans works of the thirteen preceding centuries, which are the common inheritance of both peoples." This circular was signed by Queen Victoria, John Bright, William E. Gladstone, and by many others. Soon packages of books commenced to reach Chicago directed to the Mayor, with such messages as these : " To renew lost library, with sympathy and best wishes." "With kindest remembrances," etc. One of the largest of the packages came from Queen Victoria. A number of citizens of Chicago requested the Mayor to call a public meeting in behalf of a free library. The meeting met in the Plymouth Congregational Church, which had happily been spared by the great fire. The result of the meeting was that Mayor Medill, who appreciated the value to Chicago of a free library, framed an enactment which was at once passed by the Legislature of Illinois. This enactment, which was perhaps overcareful in limiting the amount of money to be raised by taxation, was copied in part from a law which has been the means of doing much good in England, and which, with improvements, has been adopted in Massachusetts.* This law read thus: " Be it enacted by the People of the State of Illinois represented in General Assembly, That the City Council of each incorporated city shall have power to establish and maintain a Public Library and Reading Room for the use and benefit of the inhabitants of each city, and may levy a tax of not exceeding one mill on the dollar annually, and in cities of over 100,000 inhabitants, not to exceed one fifth of one mill annually, on all the taxable property in the city—such tax to be levied and collected in like manner with other general taxes of said city, and to be known as the Library Fund."

The Common Council of Chicago without a dissenting voice approved this act and soon, with the aid of a large sum of money given by Mr. Thomas Hughes and his associates in England, Chicago had a public library, destined

---

* Some of the laws governing public libraries in Massachusetts may here be noticed : "Any City or Town of this Commonwealth is hereby authorized to establish and maintain a public library, within the same, with or without Branches, for the use of the inhabitants, and to provide suitable rooms therefor under such regulations for the government of said library as may from time to time be proscribed by the City Council of such city or the inhabitants of such town. * * * Any Town or City may receive in its corporate capacity and hold and manage any devise, bequest, or donation, for the establishment, increase, or maintenance of a Public library within the same."

to be yearly visited by many thousands of her citizens. Now that the city of the great lakes has become one of the wealthiest cities of America, it can hardly be doubted that her patriotic citizens will do as much for the cause of learning as St. Louis is doing. St. Louis has a beautiful building for its public library,—not, however, as large and beautiful a one as is that of Cincinnati.

Jefferson felt that it was very important that wisdom should be shown in the selection of books for public libraries. As a rule each community which founds a public library determines for itself what class of books shall be admitted to its shelves. To say that the value of books depends more upon their character than upon their quantity is to make a trite remark. Some people place a greater value upon works of fiction than do others. Jefferson looked upon the novels of his day, with some exceptions, as a "mass of trash." Perhaps some people have gone too far in excluding all works of fiction from public libraries, while others have erred in the opposite and probably worse extreme, and have provided almost exclusively romances for readers. It was found in one library that when people who had been accustomed to reading the novels of the day visited it a few times and learned that it did not, as a rule, have novels, they were led to make the acquaintance—an acquaintance which became very pleasant—of useful and well-written books, and thus many readers were weaned from merely reading romances. A desire for self-culture was engendered. Literary recreation became profitable to such readers as well as pleasant. Books taken to the domestic fireside elevated the conversation, made homes more attractive, and in a very happy manner advanced the cause of learning.

Citizens who propose to establish a public library would do well to bear in mind the importance of cataloguing books in a judicious manner. Too often, it is to be feared, many books in a library might as well be locked up in a vault for any use they are to the public, owing to the imperfect manner in which they are classified in a catalogue. In the great library of the British Museum a gentleman is specially engaged in helping visitors to select books that may be useful to them, so that they may be enabled to use to greatest advantage the resources of the institution.   Some libraries are divided, to a greater or less extent, into alcoves on whose shelves books are placed according to the subjects upon which they treat.   The history of each nation is by itself. The books on each science are found together. It is in some respects peculiarly pleasant to visit such a granary of knowledge.

To the statesman who has upon his mind the high concerns of a republic, a public library may at times be invaluable. In the work which he has to do, it may be well indeed for his country if he successfully seeks to consult the wisdom and the lore of ages. Often would statesmen have avoided errors highly injurious to their country had they had access to, and had they profited by the results of human experience to be found in, books. Jefferson, at an early period in his career, and at a time when no other State except New Hampshire had a State library, endeavored to induce Virginia to lay out a sum of money, large for that period, in providing a library for the Capitol of Virginia. When the Congressional Library at Washington was burned by the British in the year 1814, he offered his own large and valuable library to the national government at whatever price it should place upon it. In the course of a letter, dated September 21st, 1814, authorizing a friend to offer his library to the national government, he said: "You know my collection, [of books,] its condition and extent. I have been fifty years making it, and have spared no pains, opportunity, or expense, to make it what it is. While residing in Paris, I devoted every afternoon I was disengaged, for a summer or two, in examining all the principal bookstores, turning every book with my own hand, and putting by everything which related to America, and indeed whatever was rare and valuable in every science. Besides this I had standing orders during the whole time I was in Europe, on its principal book-marts, particularly Amsterdam, Frankfort, Madrid, and London, for such works relating to America as could not be found in Paris. So that in that department particularly, such a collection was made as probably can never again be effected. * * * During the same period, and after my return to America, I was led to procure, also, whatever related to the duties of those in the high concerns of the nation. So that the collection, which I suppose is of between nine and ten thousand volumes, while it includes what is chiefly valuable in science and literature generally, extends more particularly to whatever belongs to the American statesman."

Jefferson's offer to the national government was accepted, and about six thousand seven hundred of his books were bought and became a nucleus for a new Congressional Library. The national government, having been taught by experience that a fire-proof building should be provided for the Congressional Library,—and the number of books for which provision should be made rapidly increasing,—has made provision for a national library which is in a measure to be worthy of the Republic. This library is, to a certain extent, destined to be a national university such as Washington, Jefferson, and Madison wished to see established at the capital of the United States. Many students, historians, statisticians, and men of letters from all parts of America, as well as statesmen, will, at times, visit this national library.

There are many ways in which governments can indirectly encourage the cause of learning. In probably few ways have governments done more in recent years to give an incentive to people to acquire a certain degree of useful knowledge than by establishing certain regulations respecting their forms of civil service. Every nation may be said to have what is known as a civil service and a military service. As a rule, men who command in the army or the navy of the United States have to be possessed of a certain degree of education. In short, the military service is conducted on a wise system established by law. In the United States, one branch of the civil service is what is called elective. It is made up of the representatives of the people. This branch of the civil service is in a measure supervised by the people themselves, and to it attention is not here to be called. But there is an immense branch of the civil service of the United States composed of men and women who are not elected by the people,—such as employés engaged by the government to do various kinds of work. It would be an easy matter to here make some startling statements respecting the manner in which the civil service of the national and State governments have been in the past conducted, and how evils foreseen by Jefferson followed a law which made unreasonable changes among the government's employés, occur on every new election for President of the United States. Suffice it to say that a movement has at last been successfully inaugurated by which applicants for a large class of public offices are examined respecting their ability to read, to write from dictation, to write an original letter, and are expected to pass an examination in the history and geography of the

United States. They are expected to have also an acquaintance with the national Constitution, and with the Constitution of the State in which they reside, and with such learning as may be especially important in the positions which they seek. A person seeking a high position of course is expected to know more than one who is a suitor for but a lowly place. The examinations are designed to be only such as any youth who has passed through the public schools should be easily able to pass. The tenure of office is during good behavior and efficiency. Great care is taken not to make the examination unfairly difficult. Youth of rich and of poor parents have an equal opportunity to enter the civil service of the United States. By this system many shocking abuses known as bribery, favoritism, jobbery, and patronage, and many forms of corruption, are removed, and the youth of the land are given an additional incentive to acquire a certain degree of education. Employment in the civil service of the United States has been made more honorable than it could be when, as was once too often the case, it meant a dishonorable servility to chiefs rather than faithful service to the public. It is found that a good administrative system exerts a silent but important influence in aid of popular education.

That nations can aid the cause of letters indirectly by means of a civil-service system has been illustrated for many centuries, or for thousands of years, in the great Chinese Empire, whose population has been estimated in recent years by S. Wells Williams, who spent forty years in China, to be probably four hundred and fifty millions of people. For perhaps more than forty-five centuries the Chinese have had an educational system which has had a tendency to make them a homogeneous people. Many nations have been born and have passed away, while the people of this vastest of Oriental empires have maintained their nationality. Their educational and civil-service systems have been interwoven with each other, and may be regarded as being the secret of the greatness of the stability of their empire. In China there can scarcely be said to be a nobility, except the descendants of Confucius. No one, however rich he may be, is allowed to enjoy public station unless he can pass a governmental examination. It is claimed that the poorest boy, from the moment he enters a town or village school, knows that if he can acquire the education demanded by any position of state, save that occupied by the Emperor himself, who claims to be Infallible, and is styled the Son of Heaven, he can hope to obtain the position. The examination which he may have to pass may be hard, indeed, but it is said that the words, " The general and the prime-minister are not born in office," are in every school-boy's mouth. The works which the youth studies are the writings of Confucius, who lived about five hundred years before the Christian era. These works are believed to be studied by about fifty millions of people in addition to the vast population of the " Flowery Kingdom." The boy has to study in great measure by heart words whose meaning he no more understands than does an ordinary European youth the Latin service of the Roman Catholic Church. As, however, the young Oriental proceeds in his studies, more useful learning—at least to a limited extent—engages his attention. To master the very difficult Chinese written language takes ten to thirty years. There are at least three grades in the Chinese schools—the primary, the middle, and the so-called classical. An immense number of examining officials are engaged by cities and by the imperial government to confer honors upon scholars who pass satisfactory examinations, and to install them into public office. The government supports an academy from which examiners are despatched to all parts of the vast empire to pass judgment on the merits of aspirants to high national positions. From this academy, which is only open to men who have already shown themselves learned, some of the highest State officials—even the men esteemed worthy of a place in the imperial Cabinet—are often taken. When the news is brought to a village that some one of the innumerable honors of the empire has been conferred upon one of its citizens, the joy at times is at once exciting and affecting. One of the privileges enjoyed by a Chinaman who has successfully passed certain examinations is that he cannot be whipped or bastinadoed with a bamboo stick. In a land in which prisoners are examined often "by torture," and in which prisoners are shockingly illtreated—although, perhaps, not more so than they are in some prisons in other countries,—to enjoy immunity from castigation with a bamboo stick is an honor not to be lightly esteemed by the Oriental scholar.

When a Chinaman, having passed successfully public examinations, is invested with official station, his position is, during good behavior, secured to him. For, however, any one of eight causes he may be removed from office: for a grasping disposition; for cruelty; for indolence; for inattention to duty; for being too aged for a position; for indecorous behavior; and for inactivity.

Unhappily the Chinese have but a narrow range of studies in their schools. Much that goes with them by the name of learning is unworthy, in a true sense, of the name. That, however, the civil service system of these Asiatics has been an incentive to many millions of their number to learn the very difficult Chinese letters, can be recognized by any student of the history of the far East.

It will be noticed that these pagan people make but little, if indeed the least, provision for the illumination of the mind of the gentler sex. For women there is not the same incentive for men. No hope of acquiring honor and public station is held out by the imperial government for them. It is even a superstition in China, which found its way with other false ideas of true religion into Spain, that it is immoral for women to be acquainted with letters. Difficult it is indeed to estimate how injurious to an immense division of the human race is this neglect to provide for the mental cultivation of the gentler half of human kind.

The civil service of China is at most suited but to aid the cause of intellectual culture. It fails sadly to accomplish what a good school system would do for the so-called Celestial Empire. The learned W. A. P. Martin, whose essays on "The Chinese, their Education, etc.," are especially valuable, as he is the president of Tungwen College, Peking, and may be considered a high authority, has thus written: "Of those who can read understandingly, the proportion is greater in towns than in rural districts. But striking an average, it does not, according to my observation, exceed 1 in 20 for the male sex and one in 10,000 for the female—rather a humiliating exhibit for a country which has maintained for centuries such a magnificent institution as the Hanlin Academy." Mr. Martin, however, points out various ways in which the Chinese civil-service system enlarges the liberties of the people, strengthens the state, gives occupation to certain restless and aspiring characters, and secures not only tranquillity to the public, but the very existence of the government. He argues that without such a system there would be strife and bloody revolution in the great Oriental Empire.

The Chinese civil service wisely provides, in some instances, that a greater or less number of men who pass a good examination shall be classed as "ready for office," and as vacancies occur lots are impartially drawn, to settle which one shall take a position which needs to be filled. In any civil service much care should be exercised not to tempt youth to endeavor to pass examinations which are so difficult as to be likely to injure their health. In recent years England and some other nations have adopted civil-service systems, which, it is believed, have been instrumental in helping to a highly important degree the interests of education.

Jefferson for many years was deeply interested in the work of establishing a public-school system for Virginia. Some of his views respecting the course which it would be wise for the State to pursue will presently be here presented. He was, as has already been stated, a member of the State's "Literary Fund." In the year 1816, the Legislature of Virginia requested the president and directors of the Literary Fund to favor it with a carefully prepared report on a system of public instruction calculated to give effect to the appropriations of money which the State had already provided for public schools. The Legislature also desired recommendations respecting the establishment of colleges and a university. In the report which the president and directors sent to the Legislature it was stated that, "in all enlightened countries a national education has been considered one of the first concerns of the Legislature, and intimately connected with the prosperity of the State." As the report proceeded it alluded especially to primary schools: "The object of primary schools," it said, "is to have a school so convenient to each citizen that his children may be taught the rudiments of learning. It would be a melancholy reflection," it added, " if a single youth of our country should, from poverty, he deprived of every ray of knowledge. And yet," it continued, "how many hundreds, of perhaps the first geniuses of our land, are condemned to grope out their lives in a state of intellectual darkness. To obviate this calamitous state of things must be the object of the primary schools." With this report the gentleman managing the Literary Fund presented the Legislature of Virginia with a very expensive school system for the State. Before acting on the school bill the Legislature published Jefferson's school bill of the year 1779 and a long letter which he had written respecting education to Mr. Peter Carr. In the year 1817 Jefferson draughted another educational bill. In a foot-note to one of the sections of the bill he alluded to the tax that would be required to support such a system of public instruction,—adding, "if a tax can be called that which we give to our children in the most valuable of all forms, that of instruction."* Alluding to a certain provision of the bill in a foot-note, he made a remark for which his friends feared that the people of Virginia were not prepared. In this foot-note, he said: "What is proposed here is to remove the objection of expense, by offering education gratis, and to strengthen parental excitement by the disfranchisement of his child while uneducated. Society has certainly a right to disavow him whom it offers and is not permitted to qualify for the duties of a citizen. If we do not force instruction, let us at least strengthen the motive to receive it when offered." In this educational bill Jefferson provided that women who could not read should not be recognized as citizens of Virginia. The closing words of section 5 * of this bill read thus : " And it is declared and enacted, that

---

* " Jefferson's Works," vol. ix., p. 493.

no person unborn or under the age of twelve years at the passing of this act, and who is *compos mentis,* shall, after the age of fifteen years, be a citizen of this Commonwealth until he or she can read readily in some tongue, native or acquired."

Jefferson by providing that no one, whether man or woman, should possess certain privileges of citizenship in Virginia, would touch a subtle spring of action in the feelings of a people. The mental horizon of many illiterate parents is so sadly circumscribed that they do not even know of the intellectual realms which would be thrown open to their children were they possessed of a knowledge of letters. The distinguished writers on political economy, Adam Smith and John Stuart Mill, have recognized this ignorance on the part of many parents, and have given it as one of the reasons why governments should support public schools. Jefferson's plan would create such a motive for sending youth to school, or otherwise providing to a certain degree for their instruction, that even the lowest grade of human intelligence would be apt to feel to some extent its force. Should there be found, however, parents so dead to the interests of their offspring, their boys would in time have brought home to them the fact that an inability to read and write had been branded with disgrace, and that they had a strong motive for acquiring useful knowledge. Even the timid girl who realized that she was debarred from certain important privileges, among which would sometimes, perhaps, be the owning, in her own right, of property, would be encouraged to herself seek the instruction which it might be necessary for her to have to acquire the rights of citizenship in a commonwealth.

Some distinguished statesmen, while keenly realizing the importance to a republic of public schools, have not in an unqualified manner given their assent to the belief that no one should be allowed to vote who could not read.   The learned Dr. Benjamin Rush, a patriot of whom any nation might be proud, having written to John Adams thus, " Suffrage, in my opinion, should never be permitted to a man that could not write or read," the cautious John Adams replied to him under date of August 28th, 1811 : " Free schools, and all schools, colleges, academies and seminaries of learning, I can recommend from my heart ; but I dare not say that a suffrage should never be permitted to a man who cannot read and write.   What would become of France if the lives, fortunes, character, of twenty-four millions of people who can neither read nor write, should be at the absolute disposal of five hundred thousand who can ? "

Undoubtedly, Adams was right in withholding his assent to the belief that no one should be allowed to vote who could not read and write in a land such, as in his day, was France.   In a country in which only one out of two or three hundred of the inhabitants can read,—as according to some authorities was the case in some parts of Europe when the Romish hierarchy was enabled to keep the education of youth in its own hands,—it might be very dangerous to entrust the very few who could read and write with absolute power.   It might happen that entire communities would be destitute of a single person acquainted with letters or who possessed any knowledge of the science of government. Despots might endeavor to keep the people illiterate in order to retain power in their own hands. When a people, however illiterate, have to vote upon questions, they naturally discuss them among themselves. Such discussions, at least in some instances, excite curiosity and implant a desire among some of them to improve their minds.   The most unlettered of men if injured too boldly would, under certain circumstances, quickly learn enough to use their ballots in their own defence. It might even happen that reformers would arise among them who would counteract, to some extent, the influence of dema- gogues and exert a good influence in the communities in which they reside. Where every one is allowed to vote, intelligent citizens have a special interest, as a matter of self-defence, in providing instruction for the untaught,— indeed they have weighty reasons for establishing schools which they would not have if they knew that they were free from the danger flowing from people's voting who were even unacquainted with the alphabet. Jefferson's idea, however, was that schools should be established in every neighborhood and that youth should be made to feel that it was a duty which they owed to their country to attend them, and that if they neglected to attend the schools and thus, to some extent, qualify themselves for citizenship, they were, as long as they remained illiterate, not to be entrusted with the control of public affairs.

As a rule, in a State such as Massachusetts, youth ought not to grow up illiterate. The fact that a youth of Massachusetts is illiterate is a proof that he has not obeyed the school laws of the State. For the same reason that children are not allowed to hold office and to legislate for the State, men who are unable to read the Constitution of Massachusetts—are, in short, as illiterate as babies— are not allowed to vote. A paragraph of the Constitution of Massachusetts reads thus: "No person shall have the right to vote or be eligible to office under the Constitution of this Commonwealth, who shall not be able to read the Constitution in the English language, and write his name; *provided however*, that the provisions of this amendment shall not apply to any person prevented by a physical dis- ability from complying with its requirements, nor to any person who now has the right to vote, nor to any persons who shall be sixty years of age or upwards at the time that this amendment shall take effect."

Jefferson, in the educational bill which he draughted in the year 1817, incidentally alluded to the question whether the rights of parents were infringed upon by obligatory school laws. In a quite lengthy foot-note to section 5 of his bill, he said : " A question of some doubt might be raised on the latter part of this section, as to the rights and duties of society towards its members, infant and adult. Is it a right or a duty in society to take care of their infant members in opposition to the will of the parent ? How far does this right and duty extend ?— to guard the life of the infant, his property, his instruction, his morals ? The Roman father was supreme in all these : we draw a line, but where ?—public sentiment does not seem to have traced it precisely." * Upon these questions Jefferson did not dwell at length in his bill, but contented himself with intimating, that if no one should be allowed to enjoy citizenship who was illiterate, the cases in which youth would not learn to read would be rare.

Quite a large number of States, and England and many European countries, and even the people of Japan, have now obligatory school laws. There are many arguments which can be justly urged in their favor. People who are compelled to pay taxes for the support of free schools, on the ground that it is of vital importance to the well-being of society that youth should receive instruction, naturally expect that the State will see to it that the money is expended for the purpose for which it is collected. If the English people should find that their royal family was growing up utterly illiterate, and that the one who was to be their sovereign was not even able

---

* See " Jefferson's Works," vol. ix., p. 493.

to read and write, Americans would applaud their wisdom, as far as it went, if they should insist that the future ruler of Great Britain should receive a certain degree of instruction. In the United States the people are themselves possessed of sovereign power, and, if incapable of wisely acting on certain occasions, may do irreparable injury to their Republic. The jury system in the United States makes it peculiarly important to all classes of people that their neighbors should be possessed of intelligence, as might easily be feelingly illustrated. Compulsory school laws have been found to do a vast amount of good in cities, as has been illustrated in a very interesting manner by the records of crime in police courts. How quickly youth who are neglected in cities become criminals, and frequent recruiting dens of crime, where they learn as much evil as they would have acquired good in well-ordered schools, is a subject that would be found to be the more interesting the better it was understood. Schools would be, to a great degree, useless if they were not attended by youth. It has been found by experience —and indeed a thoughtful person can readily understand that such must be the case—that if scholars are frequently absent, they often receive but comparatively little benefit from the best of schools. They cannot keep up with their classes, and it is not right that their classes should be kept back for them. Something needs to be done to prevent young people from acquiring habits of irregularity in their attendance at their lessons. In the United States there are many people—some of them poor foreigners— who are disposed to be negligent in attending to the educational needs of their children. Some of them, it is to be feared, have no sensible idea of the value to their offspring of an acquaintance with letters. They live in neighborhoods where it is made the birthright of youth to have certain educational advantages. But these people—many of whom are well-meaning, and have lovable children in whose welfare they are tenderly interested—often remain ignorant of the beneficent school provision which has been made by law in behalf of youth. Where there are no wise truancy laws it is not the business of any one to even tell them where a school-house is to be found. Wise truancy laws give a certain degree of vigor to a school system, and thus, as well as in various other ways, exert a healthful influence upon society. Without them it is perhaps often impossible for a State to properly guard the interests of youth and its own safety. However well disposed American parents are, as a rule, towards their children, it is necessary that the statesman should bear in mind that the children of the drunkard and of the reprobate have a hard enough lot without being compelled to grow up destitute of school instruction, and that to stake the school instruction of a republic's future rulers and mothers upon the consideration of such parents would be to endanger the public welfare. To maintain that a State has not the right to insist upon its youth acquiring a certain amount of useful knowledge, would be to maintain a doctrine respecting the freedom of the individual will which might lead to lawlessness and anarchy. Society has rights and responsibilities as truly as have individuals. As has been said, however, Jefferson believed that if a State made adequate provision for public instruction, and then allowed no one born after a certain period to enjoy certain rights of citizenship, that even without laws requiring youth to attend schools, the number of illiterate men and women would be small.

In modern times many of the States provide in their Constitutions for the cherishment of the interests of public education. Jefferson in his "Notes on Virginia," which, although published when he was in France, were mostly written during the war for independence, pointed out that Virginia should provide in her Constitution for a public-school system. In this book he pointed out how necessary it was to a people who wished to enjoy the blessing of civil liberty to provide for the public instruction of their youth, and gave an outline of a school system which it was proposed that Virginia should adopt. This outline was in reality in part the school bill which he had himself, amid much applause, introduced into the Assembly of Virginia in the year 1778. When he was in France at the period when the French Revolution was about being inaugurated,—a revolution which was to give birth to wars in which perhaps not less than ten millions of human lives were to be lost,—he was visited by Lafayette and by a number of statesmen who were deeply interested in securing to the French people a republican form of government. It is interesting to observe that the memorable Constitution which Lafayette and his colleagues helped to give France contained provisions for public education which so much resembled Jefferson's bill for the diffusion of knowledge in Virginia, that one may naturally infer that that part of the Constitution for the French Republic was suggested by the Virginian statesman. When Jefferson became President of the United States he wished to see the federal government doing more for the cause of education throughout the length and breadth of the United States than it was doing. In two annual messages he made suggestions to Congress respecting amending the national Constitution so as to secure to the youth of the Republic certain educational advantages. In his last annual message to Congress he thus spoke: " The probable accumulation of the surpluses of revenue beyond what can be applied to the payment of the public debt, whenever the freedom and safety of our commerce shall be restored, merits the consideration of Congress. Shall it lie unproductive in the public vaults? Shall the revenue be reduced? Or shall it not rather be appropriated to the improvement of roads, canals, rivers and education, and other great foundations of prosperity and union under the powers which Congress may already possess, or such amendment of the Constitution as may be approved by the States." From these words of Jefferson's one might not be able to form a decided opinion as to whether he had in view simply the founding of a great national university at Washington,—a favorite project with him,—or the aiding of all the States in the work of supplying educational advantages for their youth. In private letters, however, he spoke with a freedom that was highly interesting to friends of national education. To Monsieur Dupont de Nemours, who it will be remembered had written a book at the instance of Jefferson, on national education for the United States, he thus, under date of April 15th, 1811, wrote: "I keep up my hopes that if war [with Great Britain] be avoided, Mr. Madison will be able to complete the payment of the national debt within his term, after which one third of the present revenue would support the government. * * * Our revenues once liberated by the discharge of the public debt, and its surplus applied to canals, roads, schools, &c., and the farmer will see his government supported, his children educated, and the face of his country made a paradise by the contributions of the rich alone, without his being called upon to spare a cent from his earnings. The path that we are now pursuing leads directly to this end, which we cannot fail to attain unless our administration should

fall into unwise hands." *   Jefferson in his desire to see the
national government devoting a part of its resources to
the support of public schools, it is to be feared went too
far, when he pictured the public schools supported entirely by means derived from the national government.
He would, one may readily infer, have wished the United
States government, by wise legislation, to do for all the
States what some State governments, by a wise use of
State school funds, have done for their counties and
townships,—help set in motion the wheels of local
government.

Before considering, for a few moments, the question
whether Jefferson's suggestion that the Constitution of
the United States should be amended so as to make it
the specific duty of the national government to aid the
States in securing to all American citizens the blessing of
at least a certain degree of intellectual culture, it may be
interesting to notice what Jefferson, as President of the
United States, did do towards rendering national aid
to the cause of public education.   On March 3d, 1803,
he signed a bill by which public land was set apart for a
university to be established in Ohio.   On the same date
he signed a bill by which it was provided that in the
public domain south of the State of Tennessee, there
should be land appropriated for a college, and every section
of land numbered 16 in every township was consecrated
to the support of common schools.   For the use of the
college—which as a compliment to Jefferson Congress
named "Jefferson College"—thirty-six sections of land

---

* About the same time that this letter to Dupont de Nemours was written,
Jefferson wrote a letter to Kosciuszko,—a letter which has already been
quoted in the first chapter of this volume,—in which he used almost the same
words respecting the national governments aiding the cause of public education, as those which he addressed to Dupont de Nemours.

12

were appropriated,—an appropriation which was increased under President Monroe's administration. On March 26th, 1804, Jefferson signed a bill which provided that not only in every township in what was then Indiana Territory section 16 should be devoted to school purposes, but that three entire townships should be reserved " for the use of a seminary of learning." On April 16th he signed a bill by which one hundred thousand acres of land in Tennessee were set apart for the use of two colleges. Another one hundred thousand acres of land, with certain wise conditions attached to the appropriation, were set apart, as the bill read, "for the use of academies, one in each county in said State, to be established by the Legislature thereof." At the same time an appropriation of land was made, to which wise conditions were, by the national government, attached, for common schools. Jefferson also had the honor of signing the bill by which the military academy of West Point was founded. Without pausing to point out all the ways in which Jefferson when President of the United States may be considered to have helped in inaugurating a policy by which the national government has aided States to establish and maintain school systems, it may here be noticed that on February 27th, 1806, a report was presented to the House of Representatives by one of its committees, an extract from which read thus: "Your committee are of the opinion [that] it ought to be a primary object with the General Government to encourage and promote education in every part of the Union, so far as the same can be consistent with the general policy of the nation, and so as not to infringe the municipal regulations that are, or may be, adopted by the respective State authorities on the subject. * * * The national legislature has, by several of its acts on former occasions, evinced in the strongest manner its disposition to afford the means of establishing and fostering with a liberal hand such public institutions." Soon after this report was made in Congress, Jefferson, as will presently be seen, signed a bill making an immense appropriation of land for school purposes. It will be remembered that under Jefferson's administration — largely if not altogether through his personal influence — the United States obtained from France a territory embracing 1,124,682 square miles. At the time of this purchase the area of the United States was but about 820,000 square miles; thus by one act the area of the United States was more than doubled. On April 21st, 1806, when a part of this new and vast territory was being opened for settlement, Jefferson affixed the executive signature to a bill which not only reserved section 16 of every township for the support of common schools in each township, but also devoted an entire township for, in the words of the bill, " a seminary of learning." This appropriation for a seminary of learning was increased under Madison's administration.

And now to return to Jefferson's suggestion, that an amendment be made to the Constitution of the United States by which the national government shall be specifically authorized to co-operate with the States in the great work of securing to American youth the privilege of acquiring a certain degree of culture. The independence in certain respects of States, and of townships, and the nationality of them all united under one government, are features of the polity of the people of the United States which should be viewed in a comprehensive manner by the student of the science of government. The securing of a knowledge of letters to any section of the United States may justly be deemed to be a matter worthy of national concern, no less truly than of local interest.

American citizens, it is to be feared, are in danger of confining their attention too much to only what transpires within the boundaries of the county, or of the State, in which they reside, and of not giving to a proper degree attention to the affairs of a great Republic,—a Republic destined, it may be, to become continental in its extent. The thoughtful statesman should be reminded that it is highly important at times that his vision should sweep over the entire United States, and that he should recognize that in some respects the national Republic should be considered in its entirety. However simple to an American citizen may appear the form of government of the United States, a European might well think it strange to be told that every State is an aggregation of lesser republics, every county a group of self-governing units, and that all the States united form a great national Republic, and that each of these republics has a sphere of action of its own, and yet is designed to work in perfect harmony with every other unit of the national Republic.

There are various elementary principles upon which republics are founded. For example, all men are supposed to stand upon an equal footing. Very much as men unite to carry on a business, or to accomplish some undertaking which singly they could not execute, so people unite to accomplish certain ends conducive to their convenience, —or, in other words, establish a commonwealth. They unite, although wisely reserving to themselves certain specified rights, with the same freedom that a Pagan, a Mohammedan, and a Christian might unite to move out of a common pathway a stone which was too heavy for any one of them to alone move. As business men, when forming themselves into a company to carry on a business, have partnership papers in which they carefully guard certain rights and specify the purposes for which they join themselves together, so do the people of an American State and of the United States have partnership papers, or, in more common phrase, a "Constitution." The Constitution of Massachusetts thus speaks of a State : "The body politic is formed by a voluntary association of individuals. It is a social compact, by which the whole people covenants with each citizen and each citizen with the whole people, that all shall be governed by certain laws for the common good." The Constitution of Maryland declares: " That all government of right originate from the people, is founded in compact only, and instituted solely for the good of the whole. * * *" It may be remembered that the American citizen has a citizenship common to a State, and to a national, government.

In the United States it is realized that, as a company of business men might provide that the sons of the members of the company should have provided for them certain educational advantages, and should be admitted as partners into the firm provided that they acquired a certain degree of knowledge to enable them to do a worthy part in carrying on the business, so the people of a republic can incorporate in their constitution a provision that no one shall be invested with the responsibilities of citizenship until he has acquired, to at least a certain degree, a knowledge of reading and writing.

It is one of the happy characteristics of the form of government established in the United States, that the national government itself can profit by experiments made by States in the art of government. At the present day a large number of States provide in their constitutions for public schools. During the war for Independence—at about the same time that Jefferson brought forward his first educational bill for Virginia—

John Adams draughted a provision for the Constitution of Massachusetts, by which it has been made the duty of all who subscribed to that Constitution to cherish the interests of learning in that State. Perhaps to no other one cause has Massachusetts been more indebted for its success in maintaining its system of local self-government than to its constitutional requirements respecting the interests of education. If provisions in a State Constitution for the interests of learning do much good, one might hope that American statesmanship would be equal to framing a wise provision for the national Constitution which would help to secure a certain degree of learning to all American citizens.

At the time that Jefferson published in his " Notes on Virginia " the opinion that Virginia should provide in her Constitution for a public-school system, her counties were practically as far apart as are States and Territories at the present day. There were then no railroads, no steamboats, no telegraphs, and, comparatively speaking, there were few roads of any kind. Far more easily could the government of the United States encourage, and aid in various ways, States and Territories to cherish the interests of learning, than could the government of Virginia, in Jefferson's day, aid counties to secure to their youth school instruction. Yet Jefferson argued ably even during the war for Independence for an educational provision in the Constitution of his State. And when President of the United States it was but natural that he should suggest to Congress the wisdom of providing in the national Constitution for a yearly, special fund to be raised by duties on luxuries, with which to enable the national government to duly aid in the great work of securing school instruction to the youth of all parts of the Republic of the United States.

It is to be feared that nothing less than an amendment to the Constitution of the United States can be relied upon to secure to all sections of the national Republic a certain degree of intelligence. The federal government has indeed done much—though seldom, if ever, as much as it did under Jefferson's administration—in aiding States to establish and to maintain school systems. It has done enough to give some faint idea of how much good, there is reason to hope, would result if, by the Constitution of the United States, it was made the duty of the national government to wisely aid and encourage in a systematic manner the States and Territories in maintaining effective school systems.

When it has been proposed that the government of the United States should aid the States in maintaining public-school systems, there have been at least some statesmen who have honestly questioned whether the national government, notwithstanding the many precedents which have been established for its so doing, has authority to render such aid. Some critic of American history may even whisper that Jefferson was so deeply imbued with a sense of the importance to civil liberty of public schools, that he did not apply to the question, Has the United States government authority to cherish in an effective manner the interests of public education? some of his own principles respecting the proper interpretation of the Constitution of the United States. Some of these statesmen, while agreeing with Jefferson that at least a certain degree of intellectual culture is of vital importance to the citizens of a republic, have doubted whether they were at liberty to vote for even measures which were well designed to scatter light over States, some of which, as divulged by the United States census, were intellectually in such darkness that a majority of the voters could not write their names. Some of these statesmen, if there had been such a specific provision for education in the Constitution of the United States, as Jefferson believed that the best interests of the United States demanded that there should be, would have ranged themselves in the national Capitol among the warmest friends of public education.

One may well wonder that any statesman should have objected to the national government's helping by an appropriation of money the Southern States to establish school systems at the close of the Civil War, when four millions of colored people were suddenly freed from the shackles of slavery and invested with the honors and duties, and the high responsibilities, of American citizenship. It was as though the Southern States had, at a time when they were greatly impoverished by the devastations of war, been suddenly inundated by a flood of African barbarism. The most precious interests of society, and of American civilization, were to a large extent in the power of a people who had been degraded by generations of bondage and of an enforced ignorance of even the alphabet. Local self-government in some of the Southern States was to a large extent impossible. Its forms, if observed at all, were in many cases converted into instruments of danger to the people. A provision of the Constitution of the United States reads thus: "The United States shall guarantee to every State in this Union a republican form of government." Another provision, which should be read in connection with the one which has just been quoted, provides that the government of the United States shall be authorized, "To make all laws which shall be necessary and proper for carrying into execution the foregoing powers and * * * all * * * powers vested in the Constitution in the government of the United States, or in any department or office thereof." By these provisions of the Constitution of the United States, it is to be seen that no measures necessary or proper to secure to the States a republican form of government is unconstitutional. States, when in the power of hordes of people as unlettered as barbarians, ought hardly to be expected to possess a proper degree of civil liberty. States such as these might naturally expect the national government to guarantee to them a republican form of government by aiding them to establish educational institutions for their youth. The national government cannot secure to States in such a situation a republican form of government by overrunning them with armies at a cost of many millions of dollars, nor by establishing a military government over them. If Jefferson's most cherished convictions respecting the intimate relationship which must exist between intellectual culture and civil liberty were well grounded, the national government can in no way known to political science guarantee to such States a republican form of government, without seeing to it that suitable provision is made for certain educational needs of their youth.

By the United States census of 1880 the startling fact was brought to light that in eight of the Southern States the average of the white and colored voters united who confessed that they could not write their names was 45 per cent.! As some of the people were too proud to acknowledge their illiteracy if they could do a very little writing, the number of unlettered voters was probably larger than the figures of the census indicated. In sixteen of the Southern States entitled to as many Senators in the national Capitol as any sixteen Northern States, at least 40 per cent. of the men were illiterates. These sixteen States represented 76 per cent. of a majority of the Electoral College, which gives a President to the Republic of the United States. The people living in these States are citizens of the national Republic as well as of the States in which they live. These sixteen States can do much to direct the policy of the national government.

In the year 1880 many millions of dollars were spent in some of the Northern States and in Western States in supporting common schools, high schools, colleges, and public libraries. In some of the States no one was allowed to vote who could not read and write. But the influence of any Northern State—no matter how many millions of dollars was spent in providing instruction for her youth—could be nullified in the United States Senate by even the votes of South Carolina, a State in which the majority of the voters were unable to write their names. In Mississippi and Louisiana, as well as in South Carolina, the majority of the people were colored. These colored people, it was found by the census, were indeed poor! It hardly needs to be pointed out that it is not strange that they were poor. Their fathers and mothers had watered the fruitful earth with their sweat, and at times with tears, while the lash might at any time fall heavily upon them, but by accursed laws they received no pay for their toil. The national government, by laws, known as "fugitive-slave laws," and by other cruel laws, helped to rivet upon them the shackles of a shameful bondage. These people, or their descendants, are to be numbered by millions. Although they are not armed with muskets yet they are armed with ballots, and thus in many localities are in a certain sense masters of the white population —indeed they are a mighty power, if not the masters of the whites, in the politics of the United States. Unless they are helped to become intelligent American citizens they are sadly likely to help in various ways to drag down American citizenship to their own lowly level.

Impoverished by a devastating civil war, it has been difficult if not indeed impossible for some of the Southern States, to adequately provide school instruction for the floods of illiterate people which were suddenly made not only citizens of their own States but also citizens of the United States. A simple calculation of the cost of the many thousands of school-houses needed for the illiterate youth in the Southern States would show that to secure to these States good school systems is a work calling for the best talents of the highest statesmanship. The American citizen may well ponder over the fact that the vast host of unlettered people in the Southern States are not a mere local affliction. It is an evil which is only too likely to again and again in various ways affect sadly the fortunes and the civil-liberties of the people of the United States collectively considered. It is manifestly of vast importance to the people of the United States, considered as a whole, that all American youth should have secured to them a certain amount of intellectual culture. A wisely framed provision in the Constitution of the United States, by which the national government would specifically be charged to duly cherish the interests of learning, would be perhaps the greatest safeguard which civil liberty and a republican form of government can ever have in the western hemisphere.

One of the difficulties, perhaps the greatest difficulty, in the way of the Republic of the United States becoming continental in extent, is that the people of Mexico and of Central and of South America, and the people of most of the West India Islands, do not speak the English language. Indeed, large numbers of them cannot read in any language. Although in a republic blessed with a mechanism which secures to all its parts local self-government, the people of States whose languages differ may well be imagined enjoying very many great advantages by living in union with each other, yet statesmen, when taking into view not only the present time, but the years and ages which a well-ordered republic may endure, may well wish to secure to the hundreds of millions of people which are, let it be hoped, to people the United States, the inestimably great blessing of a common language—especially one as rich in a noble and learned literature as is the English tongue.

Jefferson, when President of the United States, writing to Monroe under date of November 24th, 1801, remarked: "However our present interests may restrain us within our own limits, it is impossible not to look forward to distant times, when our rapid multiplication will expand itself beyond those limits, and cover the whole northern, if not the southern continent, with a people speaking the same language, governed in similar forms, and by similar laws." Jefferson's vision of the English language covering a continent may, by wise statesmanship, be made a reality.

There was a period in a remote age when the human family spoke a common language. To-day, a traveller who takes a survey of the world, finds that a thousand and more languages—not to speak of dialects of these languages—are spoken on the earth. The man who writes a book in Europe, on even subjects of the greatest interest to his fellow-man, can communicate his thoughts to only the people occupying a small division of that continent. A traveller in Europe at the close, one may almost say, of every day's ride on the railroad finds himself surrounded by a people to whom he cannot speak intelligibly, and whose mode of speech he cannot understand. He is thus a stranger among a strange people.

In the Empire of Austro-Hungary about twenty different languages and dialects were in use in the year 1880. In Russia, whose population in the year 1880 was about 106,000,000 people, not less than forty different languages were spoken. The number of languages in Turkey may well very greatly amaze an American traveller. On the continent of Europe there are some sixty or more languages spoken.

One may well consider how great would be the blessing to the people of Europe could they all speak a common language. Many of the prejudices, and estrangements, and emnities, which separate the nations of Europe would be removed. The people of all Europe would find themselves cherishing a feeling of sympathy and of brotherhood for each other.

In the states of India which are united under the name of the British Empire, forty or more languages and about one hundred and seventy dialects are spoken. One of these languages, however, the Hindi, is used by about 60,000,000 of people, and thus, although it is spoken by but a small fraction of the people of India, it may be called one of the principal languages of the world. In different parts of China the dialects in use differ so greatly that a Chinese merchant travelling in different parts of his native land is very much in the same position as is an American travelling on the continent of Europe. He may learn how to speak several dialects, but to learn to speak them all he would find to be very difficult, or impossible. As, however, the written language in use among the learned in China—who are but a small fraction of the population—is the same, the Chinese traveller can at times make himself understood by writing what he wishes to speak. A story is told of a devoted missionary who left America, or England, to bear to the people of China the elevating truths of the Christian religion. His heart being in his noble work, he spent years in endeavoring to qualify himself to speak to the great Mongolian race. In preaching to the people of certain parts of China he found difficulty in conveying to them some of the great truths respecting the Almighty. After years spent in his great work, he made the sad discovery that the word which he had been employing to designate God was a word which the people in their language had given to one of their idols, and that thus, while faithfully endeavoring to act the noble part of spreading the elevating truths of Christianity, he had unwittingly been doing the opposite to what he had wished to do. Grand, indeed, would it be for the vast Chinese Empire if the statesmen of China could secure to the hundreds of millions of people in China a public-school system better than the present educational system of China,—could, indeed, by means of public schools secure to China a common language spoken in its purity.

If a traveller surveys the continent of Africa he is soon made aware of the strange fact that the languages and dialects spoken within the bounds of the " Dark Continent " are to be counted by scores,—indeed, one may say, by the hundred.

When the American continent was discovered by Columbus, and long afterwards, almost every Indian tribe had a language of its own. The learned Bancroft has already catalogued six hundred different languages spoken by the Indians living between the points which are now known as Northern Alaska and Panama. While it may be true that some of these Indian languages might be characterized as dialects, yet the learned historian of the Pacific coast has probably come far short of giving a full catalogue of the Indian tribes of the American continent. To-day one of the greatest difficulties in the way of the moral elevation, and of the advancement in civilization, of many of the Indian tribes living within the borders of the Republic of the United States is that they speak what may be called a gibberish of their own and are unable to speak English. Naturally among the various tribal languages there is a very limited literature. The missionary who goes among Indians who cannot speak English finds it often difficult or impossible to find any suitable words in a rude tribal language in which to speak to them of great truths which would awaken in their breasts the best of emotions. As the Indian population have not been represented in the government of the United States, sadly few statesmen have duly considered how hard it is for their Indian brethren to rise above the degradation, and the cruel surroundings, which environ them as long as they are obliged to live practically prisoners upon reservations guarded, at great cost to the United States, by soldiers.

Far too many of the Indians, owing to their not being able to speak the English language, are unable to acquire much knowledge that even American children acquire insensibly by hearing people conversing about them in English. Should the children of white parents be treated as the government of the United States, under a mistaken policy, has too often treated Indian tribes, such children would remain savages through life. One may well think how great would be the blessing to a large class of American Indians who are growing up on reservations if they were compelled to go to public schools and to learn the English language. Happily, in recent times, at least some wise and highly praiseworthy efforts are being made by the United States government to found schools among these children of the plains and forests. Wise obligatory school laws may indeed be made a great blessing to them.

Strange it is that, within the borders of the United States, there should be youth under the special care of the government of the United States who are growing to manhood and to womanhood unable to speak the English language. This strange anomaly may be accounted for in various ways. The government of the United States has not felt, to the extent that it would have felt, if there had been a direct—a specific—provision in the federal Constitution such as Jefferson would have had it have, making it the duty of legislators duly to cherish the interests of public education throughout the length and breadth of the Republic. The Indians have had no representative of their number in Congress to remind the government of their condition. Although the policy by which Indians are kept upon reservations by force was supposed by Jefferson to be but a temporary policy, it has been continued for many years, working cruel injury to great numbers of Indians and costing the United States hundreds of millions of dollars. In some instances Indian youth, who have, under exceptional circumstances, received a far better education in some State institution of learning than is at present possessed by millions of citizens of the United States, they have been compelled to return to the wretched reservation on which they were born, there to drag out a miserable existence. By an unwise, and deeply lamentable, policy towards the Indians, the United States government has been obliged to employ, at an enormous cost, a part of its army in keeping the Indians in barbarism on reservations, thus weakening the army of the United States in a manner which might be doubly costly to the Republic should it become engaged in a foreign war. It would not be strange if Indians should wish to ally themselves to almost any power which would help them to be delivered from the thraldom in which they are forced to live. Sometimes when Jefferson thought upon the Indians of the United States, a grand vision passed before him—a vision which he nobly sought to make a reality. As President of the United States, he wrote under date of February 18th, 1803, to Col. Hawkins, who was charged by his administration with the care of the Indians, as follows: " Although you will receive through the official channel of the War Office every communication necessary to develop to you our views respecting the Indians, and to direct your conduct, yet, supposing it will be satisfactory to you, and to those with whom you are placed, to understand my personal dispositions and opinions in this particular, I shall avail myself of this private letter to state them generally. * * * In truth, the ultimate point of rest and happiness for them is to let our settlements and theirs meet and blend together, to intermix, and become one people. Incorporating themselves with us as citizens of the United States, this is what the natural progress of things will of course bring you, and it will be better to promote than to retard it. Surely it will be better for them to be identified with us, and preserved in the occupation of their lands, than þe exposed to the many casualties which may endanger them while a separate people. I have but little doubt but that your reflections have led you to view the various ways in which their history may terminate, and to see that this is the one most for their happiness." Jefferson's policy respecting the Indians as unfolded to Col. Hawkins was again repeated in an address which he made on May 4th, 1808, to some chiefs of the Cherokees. He said: " My children, I shall rejoice to see the day when the red-men, our neighbors, become truly one people with us, enjoying all the rights and privileges we do, and living in peace and plenty as we do." In another address which Jefferson made, as far back as the year 1781, to an Indian, he said: "You ask us to send you schoolmasters to educate your sons and the sons of your people. We desire above all things, brother, to instruct you in whatever we know ourselves. * * * As soon as there is peace we shall be able to send you the best of schoolmasters."

Passing from Jefferson's time to the present day, it may here be noticed that there were in the United States in the year 1889 about 12,000 Indian children attending schools. It is pleasant to be enabled to state that Cleveland, when President of the United States, had the high honor of inaugurating a beneficent policy, by which at least all Indian youth attending schools must be taught in English.

Scarcely, if indeed ever, in the history of the world has there been a language spoken over as wide an area of the world as is the English tongue. It is spoken by a larger number of people professing the Christian religion than is any other language in the world. It has a vast and an inestimably valuable literature. It may be called one of the greatest of all the blessings which the people of the United States have received from the old world and from the by-gone ages. On the American continent— to say nothing of old England and of Australia, and of various colonies of Great Britain—English is already spoken over an area about twice the size of the entire continent of Europe. Innumerable, and inestimable, are the advantages which the people of the United States reap from having such a common language. On the American continent one can travel from the far north to the Gulf of Mexico, and from the Atlantic Ocean to the Pacific main, and, except on some of the Indian reservations, everywhere hold intelligent converse with his fellow-man. Valuable information given to the printed page can be read within this vast area by all men. The English language in the United States is spoken, as a rule, with remarkable purity, a fact which may well cause one to ponder over the grandeur of the work accomplished by public schools, especially when it is duly borne in mind how many millions of American citizens were born in foreign lands, or are descended from people who have spoken a foreign language, and have emigrated to America. Youth of parents who have come from the old world have become assimilated with the people of the United States.

If the English language is not spoken in the Southern States with all the purity that many a patriotic states- man could wish, it is largely because public education has not been looked after in these States, and by the national government, with that provident legislation which the best interests of the American continent demands that they should receive. Jefferson believed that republics should incorporate in their Constitutions provisions for securing to all their youth the blessing of school instruction. He wished to see the United States government supplied with a permanent fund—a fund which he suggested could be raised by a duty imposed upon luxuries—with which to aid, and to encourage, the interests of public education throughout the length and breadth of the Republic of the United States.

Such an educational fund as Jefferson wished to have secured to the United States government could be used in a manner which would not in the least interfere with the proper sphere of State governments, but would in a very wise and happy manner set in motion, and continually keep in motion, in all parts of the Republic, the wonderful mechanism of local self-government. He believed that as a State government should aim at wisely aiding, and encouraging, the establishment of institutions of learning throughout its length and breadth, and should see to it that every county within its borders provided for certain educational needs of its youth, so should the government of a vast Republic duly cherish and wisely aid the interests of learning throughout the wide domain over which its power extends. He believed that as a State should endeavor to so legislate that every county within its borders should be made to realize that it had grave duties respecting the education of its youth to its fellow-counties, and to the State, so should the United States government endeavor to see to it that States realized that they had duties, in respect to the education of youth, to their fellow States. He believed that as a State should even provide that no one growing up illiterate in a county within its borders, where provision was made for his instruction, should be allowed to vote, so the government of the United States should insist that no man born after a suitable date, who refused to qualify himself for American citizenship, to at least the extent of learning how to read, should be allowed to influence national affairs by means of a ballot.

The English language, even with all the aid that the highest statesmanship can secure it, will have a long and a severe struggle with various languages before it becomes universal on the American continent. The contest of the English with the languages spoken south of the Republic of the United States will probably, however, be less severe than one might at first imagine. In the year 1880 there were, it is supposed, in Mexico about 9,389,461 people. Although among those who may be called the educated classes of Mexico Spanish is spoken, yet, it is interesting, as well as startling, to an American to notice that within the borders of Mexico thirty or more languages, and about ninety or more dialects, are spoken. The English language is thus enabled to meet in its advance a divided foe. If, in all parts of the United States public schools should flourish, while in Mexico the education of youth should be neglected, the peaceful triumph of the English tongue over the numerous languages and dialects of Mexico would be apt to be quite rapid. It might, indeed, be expected to become so should the people of Mexico and of the United States join hands in becoming one republic. South of Mexico lies the beautiful land of Guatemala, whose form of government is claimed to be, to a large extent, a copy of that of the Republic of the United States. In Guatemala there was, in the year 1880, probably a population of about 1,500,000 people. Of this population it has been estimated only 20,000 of the people were of pure Spanish origin. More than 900,000 of the people were what are called Indians, but of a much higher type of humanity than are the Indian tribes of North America. These Indians speak at least nineteen languages, which a European author * divides into four distinct linguistic stocks greatly differing one from the other. In Central America, including Guatemala, in the year 1880 there were about 2,534,586 people, among whom quite a number of languages were spoken. South of the American isthmus stretches the great and magnificent land of South America, where a number of languages are spoken—by many of the people in a very imperfect manner. One may well think of the many advantages the people of South America would enjoy if English were spoken throughout its length and breadth!

---

* Dr. Otto Stoll's work on the " Ethnography of Guatemala," Zurich, 1884.

—or at least if that splendid land were a part of the Republic of the United States, and enjoyed the life-giving energy, and the unnumbered blessings, which might flow, under certain circumstances, from such a union!

To word, in the best manner, a provision for the Constitution of the United States,—a provision suited to securing to all parts of a vast Republic national encouragement to duly provide for the education of youth who are to become American citizens,—much wisdom will be greatly needed. Grant, as President of the United States, presented to his country his views of what provisions respecting public schools should be added to the Constitution of the United States. In his annual message to Congress in the year 1875, he said:

"I suggest for your earnest consideration, and most respectfully recommend it, that a constitutional amendment be submitted to the Legislatures of the several States, for ratification, making it the duty of each of the States to establish and forever maintain free public schools, adequate to the education of all the children in the rudimentary branches within their respective limits, irrespective of sex, color, birth-place, or religion, forbidding the teaching in said schools of religious, atheistic, or pagan tenets, and prohibiting the granting of any school funds or school taxes, or any part thereof, either by legislative, municipal, or other authority, for the benefit or in aid, directly or indirectly, of any religious sect or denomination, or in aid or for the benefit of any other object, of any nature or kind whatever." At the close of his message, Grant named among his recapitulation of questions which he deemed, as he expressed it, of "vital importance,"—questions with which Congress was expected to deal:

1. "That the States shall be required to afford the opportunity of a good common-school education to every child within their limits."

2. "No sectarian tenets shall ever be taught in any school supported in whole or in part by the State, nation, or by the proceeds of any tax, levied upon any community. Make education compulsory so far as to deprive all persons who cannot read and write from becoming voters after the year 1890 [that is fifteen years after the adoption of the amendment], disfranchising none, however, on grounds of illiteracy who may be voters at the time this amendment takes effect." This recommendation of Grant's, which has just been presented, did not, in some respects, include as much as Jefferson wished to see secured to his country. Jefferson wished the Republic of the United States to have secured to it, by a provision in its Constitution, a fund, to be obtained from the surplus in its treasury which he foresaw that it would have,—or from a revenue to be derived from a duty imposed upon luxuries imported into the United States,—with which to aid and to encourage, in a systematic manner, the establishment of public schools throughout the length and breadth of the Republic, and to also maintain a great national university. He believed that the national government had a very important part to act in the great work of securing to the youth of all parts of the Republic of the United States a measure of education, as truly as have States and counties and school districts, in securing to youth living in all parts of their respective boundaries, a certain degree of school instruction indispensable to good citizenship in a republic.

Jefferson, at times, indulged in bright hopes for the future of his country. Writing to Madison, under date of April 27th, 1809, he pictured the United States annexing Cuba and all the territory north of the United States. He then said: "We should have such an empire for liberty as she has never surveyed since the creation; and I am persuaded that no constitution was ever before so well calculated as ours for extensive empire and self-government." In another letter, written to his French friend, M. de Marbois, under date of June 14th, 1817, Jefferson wrote: "I have much confidence that we shall proceed successfully for ages to come, and that, contrary to the principle of Montesquieu, it will be seen that the larger the extent of country, the more firm its republican structure, if founded, not on conquest, but in principle of compact and equality. My hope of its duration is built much on the enlargement of the resources of life going hand in hand with the enlargement of territory, and the belief that men are disposed to live honestly, if the means of doing so is open to them."

Madison and Monroe, as well as Jefferson,—although they could have had but a faint idea of the wonders wrought by telegraphs and railroads,—were deeply impressed with the adaptability of a republican form of government to a very large area of territory. The learned Madison, writing when far advanced in years,—in the year 1833,—after making a very able argument illustrating how well a representative government such as that of the United States was suited to be applied to a large territory, thoughtfully added: "It will not be denied, that the improvements already made in internal navigation by canals and steamboats, and in turnpikes and railroads have virtually brought the most distant parts of the Union, in its present extent, much closer together than they were at the date of the Federal Constitution. It is not too much to say, that the facility and quickness of intercommunication throughout the Union is greater

now than it formerly was between the remote parts of the
State of Virginia." * If Madison, one of the most gifted
statesmen of the age in which he lived, could, when the
invention of railroads was but in its infancy, thus write,
it is not perhaps too much to say that when the railroad
systems of North and South America are united by means
of a railroad running longitudinally across the great
American isthmus which, as a vast natural bridge, unites
them, the American continent will be practically not as
large, in various respects, as was the Republic of the
United States before the days of railroads and of telegraphs. And yet the area of the American continent,
including the area of the West India Islands, is, as has
been seen, about 15,099,480 square miles.

The Republic of the United States may already be
considered one of the wealthiest, if not indeed the
wealthiest, power in the world. In the year 1884 its
fortune, so to speak,—that is, the aggregate wealth of
its citizens,—was estimated † to be two and one-fifth
times as great as that of the German Empire's, and to
be ten thousand million dollars larger even than the
wealth of Great Britain. The United States, however,
is a power which, happily for the peace of the world,
confines its sphere of action to the political affairs of the
western hemisphere.

On the entire American continent in the year 1880,—
including about 4,412,703 people in the vast area of
Canada, and over 50,000,000 of people in the United
States, and including about 4,412,703 people in the
West India Islands,—there was a population of about
99,417,524 people,—a number which is but a very small
fraction of the hundreds of millions of people who may

---

* Madison's Works, vol. iv., p. 329.

† See the *Scientific American*, number dated the 21st of September, 1889.

be expected to live on the American continent within the next few hundred years. In the year 1880 the population of America was less than was probably the population of Russia. It was many millions less than half of the number of people in the British Empire in India. It was but a small fraction of the population of the empire of China,— and yet the American continent is destined to become the home of a much vaster number of people, there is reason to believe, than the soil of Asia and Europe united can support.

The day is fast hastening onward when all the West India islands—islands which aside from their commercial value are greatly needed by the United States for strategic purposes—may, with Central and South America, be led, by natural laws of self-interest, to join the United States in forming a republic which will embrace the western hemisphere.

A continental republic involves the idea of a great union of American States under a constitution devised with wonderful wisdom to give effect to the just wishes, and to promote the happiness and the well-being, of American citizens. To picture such a republic in a worthy manner would require the noblest eloquence. One could wish to speak of how the almost boundless natural resources of the American continent would be evoked as if by magic ; how such a republic would become the home of friends of civil and religious liberty from all parts of the world ; how near to each other would be brought its most distant parts by means of railroads ; how when one State had any grievance against another it could, instead of maintaining a standing army which might be used against the liberties of the people, submit its cause before the Supreme Court of the United States—the most just and learned tribunal of arbitration that can be imagined. One could wish to speak of some of the innumerable advantages which the people of a hemisphere would realize by using a common coinage and enjoying with each other the freest trade imaginable, and how rich might be the constitutional provision made for the public instruction of youth destined to be citizens of America—indeed, for instruction which would greatly help to make the people of a continent homogeneous, and to imbue youth, in the best sense of the word, with American principles. One could wish to especially picture the happy working in all parts of a continent of a wonderfully well contrived—a sublimely beneficent—mechanism of self-government;—but suffice it to say, that the world will, when such a republic is established, see with admiration one of the grandest achievements of American statesmanship.

It may again be asked, Is it possible for American citizens to elaborate a practicable plan by which the blessing of school instruction will be secured to the youth of every part of a vast empire? This is a question upon the solution of which, it is highly probable, depends the destiny of the dearest interests of civil liberty in the new world. Happily, it is believed that this question can be answered in the affirmative. Yes, the present generation of Americans can, as far as it is possible for mortals to ensure blessings to their posterity, secure the happiness and well-being of the unnumbered millions of people who are to live on the western hemisphere. Let a wisely worded provision be incorporated into the Constitution of the United States, making it the specific duty of the national government to duly cherish the interests of learning in all the States and Territories beneath the American flag. Let the people in all parts of America take an intelligent and patriotic interest in seeing to it that the national and State governments and the humblest school districts shall, in the years to come, co-operate in happy harmony in cherishing,—each in its respective sphere,—the cause of true learning in the western hemisphere. In short, let all well-wishers of their country take something of the same praiseworthy interest in the education of youth as did Thomas Jefferson, and republican institutions may be expected to realize, even more than they do at the present day, a grand ideal of a noble destiny.

THE END.

INDEX.